MURDER IN THE NORTH COUNTRY

MURDER IN THE NORTH COUNTRY
AN ADIRONDACK MOUNTAIN MYSTERY

BY A.M. ROWLANDS

NORTH COUNTRY BOOKS, INC.

UTICA, NEW YORK

ISBN-10: 1-59531-048-7
ISBN-13: 978-1-59531-048-4

Design by Zach Steffen & Rob Igoe, Jr.

Library of Congress Cataloging-In-Publication Data in progress

North Country Books, Inc.
220 Lafayette Street
Utica, New York 13502
www.northcountrybooks.com

To my husband and family

PROLOGUE

The Adirondack State Park of northeastern New York State covers more than six million acres. The mountains are sprawled across an expanse of forest and lakes, all of which make it a treasure trove of year-round tourism. It is late autumn, the trailing end of a brief and transient interval in time during which the towering peaks and valleys, no longer deep displays of lush, verdant green, variant shades of gold, burnished copper, and passionate reds, have faded to an ashen gray, leaving behind only a pale reminder that the interlude of autumn's flight into glory is over. With winter's onset, only the evergreens will stand regally defiant, arms outstretched across the sad and dying mountains, protecting their fallen brothers now outlined against a steely Adirondack sky. Until, come spring, there will be a rebirth, and the cycle of life and death will begin anew.

TUESDAY, NOVEMBER 3
The first rays of the morning sun crept silently through the trees and across the forest floor, a shimmering glow dancing into the darkened shadows, daybreak in its wake. Nature's creative prelude to another day was begun.

On one of the higher Adirondack peaks, two men in hunting garb, rifles slung over their shoulders, were moving along the furrowed path of an old deer trail long rutted and trodden down by generations of hunters before them. Progress over the frost-encrusted path was slow, the warm breath of the men streaming wisps of white into the brisk morning air. Except for the crunch of booted feet over a carpet of dead, rimy leaves, the only sounds to be heard were the raucous shrieks of crows and the flap, flap, flap of their wings as the hungry scavengers searched voraciously for prey.

The trail the men were following snaked down the mountainside, their passage made more cumbersome by a web of shallow streams and moss-encrusted gullies which served to impede their progress into the lower reaches of the rugged terrain. Two impatient hours had elapsed with no sign of game. Seasoned hunters, the men plodded doggedly forward, the sun rising higher above the shadows cast by the overhead canopy of trees. Eventually, the surrounding woodlands began to thin out and the trail widened, now twisting erratically from one direction to another until it came to and crossed another thin, trickling stream. Now thick brush and heavy undergrowth stretched out into a darkening distance on either side of the footpath. The mud and slime had been left behind. Relief in their steps, uncertain of where they had ended up, they hurried forward to eventually emerge into a lightly wooded clearing where, to their surprise, they were able to make out the obscure contours of a highway off in the distance. It was here, only a few feet away from where they had entered the clearing, that they stumbled upon the body of a young woman. Her clothing was soaked in blood; her decomposing body lay half-shrouded in a blanket of dead, decaying leaves. She had been brutally stabbed to death, then abandoned for the weather and the scavenging wildlife to have their way.

The dead woman's name was Rose Clifford. Single, attractive, thirty-four years of age, the victim was a grade school teacher in the Adirondack town of Weston where she had grown up. On the Friday previous, Rose had spoken of a dinner engagement for that same evening. College friends, she had cheerfully told a colleague, were driving north for a ski weekend. It was not until the following Monday morning, when she failed to appear to teach her third grade class, that anyone realized Rose was missing.

John Logan, a heavy-set, dignified man in his late fifties, had served as principal of Weston Elementary for more than twenty years. During the last several of those years, he had come to know and appreciate Rose Clifford as a dedicated, dependable teacher who loved her job as well as the children she taught. Certain on that Monday morning that something was very wrong, Mr. Logan telephoned Rose at her home. When there was no reply, he opened Rose's file and called the first person listed there, her mother, in hopes of an explanation. Unfortunately, he was to find none.

After returning the phone to its cradle, Sally Clifford sank back into her chair, her thoughts still echoing John Logan's message and words of concern, while cold threads of fear resisted any attempt at calm and logic. Rose had not shown up to teach her class? Impossible. There had to be a valid reason, she told herself. But what could it be?

A skiing accident? Had this been the case, surely they would have been notified. Could Rose have returned to her apartment on Sunday evening so exhausted that she overslept? Eager to grasp at any straw of hope, she found the number for Samuel Barker, the manager of the High Ridge Apartment complex where Rose lived, and called him. Minutes later, after explaining the situation in a nervous stream of words, she was given the assurance that Barker would personally check Rose's apartment and call Mrs. Clifford back at once.

True to his word, ten minutes later Barker phoned Mrs. Clifford directly from Rose's apartment to report that no, her daughter was not there, but everything seemed to be in order. Nor, he added, was her Honda Civic in the parking lot. He had checked there first.

After thanking the gentleman for his kindness, Sally struggled to regain her composure before telephoning her husband, Lewis Clifford, at his real estate office in downtown Weston. They must see the sheriff at once, she told him, her voice tight and controlled. Something had happened to their daughter. She was missing.

CHAPTER ONE
THE SHERIFF

In the county sheriff's office in downtown Weston, Alex Banks carried a mug of fresh coffee from the back room, past the desks and files which comprised the outer office of departmental headquarters and into his own private space where he sat down behind the wide, scarred desk he had inherited from his predecessor. Thirty-seven years of age, Alex stood an inch over six feet tall. He had a full head of sandy-brown hair, blue eyes, and an easy grin. He had grown up in Weston, attended school there. When his parents retired to Florida after Alex graduated from high school, he chose to remain in New York State. He proceeded to enroll at the State University at Albany, and four years later, degree in hand, was admitted into the New York State Police Academy.

The two years following graduation from the academy Alex spent on the streets with the NYPD, finally concluding, with some regret, that life in the Big Apple was not for him. Upon his return to Weston, he was fortunate to be hired to fill an opening as deputy to the sheriff of Collier County, Leo Connelly. A few years later, when Connelly's health began to fail and it was time for him to retire, he took Alex aside with the proposal that Alex consider himself a candidate for the office. Thus, with Connelly's staunch support when election time rolled around, Alex joined the race. To his surprise, when the ballots were counted Alex found himself the newly elected sheriff of Collier County. He had won by a landslide.

By this time, he had met and begun dating Lisa Owens, a pretty young woman employed by a local savings bank. Within a year of their introduction, the two were married. The following year they were joined by a son, Carl. Anyone curious enough to glance through the window of their life together at that time would have found the couple busy and content, Alex at his job and Lisa at home with their son. They had purchased a house and were thinking about having another child. And then everything changed. Sudden tragedy struck, and their world ended.

A gentle knock on the open door to his office broke Alex's concentration on the papers he had been shuffling through. When he looked up, Marge Grant, office receptionist, was standing in the doorway. A small, slim woman in her late forties with short, gray-blonde hair, Marge was peering at him over the rim of the eyeglasses perched on the bridge of her nose, a frown replacing the usual, affable smile.

"You have visitors, Alex," she murmured, her voice a half whisper. "It's Mr. and Mrs. Clifford and they seem upset. Okay to bring them in?"

Alex had just set his coffee cup and stack of papers to one side when Marge ushered the couple into the room. He greeted them with a handshake, directed them to a pair of comfortable visitor chairs, closed his office door, and went back behind his desk.

Throughout Collier County, Lewis Clifford, as owner-broker of Clifford Realty, was a familiar figure to most residents. Alex's own memory of the family went back to the days when he was a senior and Rose Clifford a sophomore at Weston High. A square-built man now in his early sixties, Lewis' graying hair fringed a shiny pate; gold-rimmed glasses circled intelligent, brown eyes. Impeccably dressed, as always, he removed his tweed overcoat and laid it carefully over the back of a chair. Then he frowned slightly and glanced toward his wife.

Sally Clifford was a petite woman, a small ghost next to the imposing figure of her husband. She wore her short, light-brown hair brushed away from the high cheekbones of her angular face. Wide, hazel eyes exchanged a quick, meaningful glance with her husband as she pulled her coat closer around her shoulders, gave him a faint nod, and settled into a chair.

Lewis, still standing, cupped a fist over his mouth, cleared his throat, and turned to face Alex, a fixed, determined set to his gaze. "We're here because Rose is missing," he said, his voice rumbling into the intense quiet of the room. "We haven't heard from her since last Thursday, and this morning my wife was informed that she didn't show up at school to teach her class." His face reddened. "It doesn't make sense!" he blurted out. "If something was wrong, she would have called."

"When she phoned last Thursday," Sally Clifford broke in, "she was happy and excited because two of her college classmates were coming north for the weekend." She blinked back a sudden glistening of tears. "They planned to ski and party, I guess. She wanted to let us know she wouldn't be around for a few days. She knows we worry."

"Naturally, we didn't expect her to call until today, most likely after school when she was home and settled in," Louis added huskily.

Louis then brought Alex up to date on the chain of events that had taken place from the time of Rose's absence from her class that morning to John Logan's call. "By the time Sal phoned me," he finished, frowning down at his wife, "she was frantic. Now we both are."

Pausing a moment to regain control, Lewis slipped off his eyeglasses, pulled out a neatly folded handkerchief, and tapped away the sweat that had broken out on his brow. Then he replaced the glasses, braced his palms on Alex's desk, and leaned forward to face him.

"Something is wrong here, Alex," he said wearily. "This isn't like Rosie. You know her. You know we're right. You've got to help find her."

During the course of the few minutes during which the Cliffords poured out their story, Alex took in their words, a cold sense of foreboding taking root as they spoke. Lewis was on the money. He did know Rose. And there was no doubt in his mind that the girl he knew would never simply up and disappear on her own.

"You don't have to convince me, sir," Alex said. He pushed back his chair and stood up. "Of course I'll help, but I'll need help from you, too. First, I'll need the names of Rose's friends and where they planned to stay over the weekend."

Sally snapped open her purse and pulled out a folded slip of paper. "I've already written down all I know," she said quickly. "Here are the girls' first names, which is all I can remember, plus the motel Rose mentioned.

Lewis took the slip of paper from her hand, gave it a quick glance, and passed it to Alex.

"This is a start," Alex replied with what he hoped held some note of confidence. "So let me get to work. On your part, I'm going to ask you to go home and stay by the phone. It's important you be there in case Rose calls. Meanwhile, I'll be in touch with the state police. They'll put out an immediate search for Rose's car which, I believe, is still the Honda Civic?"

"Yes, it is," Lewis replied, relief in his voice. "You'll call us when you hear something, right?"

"Believe me, if I hear anything, anything at all, you'll be the first to know," Alex promised, turning from one anxious face to the other. "You have my word."

When the Cliffords were gone, Alex wasted no time putting in a call to Lt. Harry Donahue at the state troopers barracks. After the usual social exchange between two old friends, Alex gave him Lewis Clifford's story, concluding with the request that the plate number of Rose's Honda be pulled and an alert for the vehicle be put out ASAP. Donahue, as dependable as Alex knew him to be, promised to get right on it and signed off.

Alex scanned the slip of paper Sally Clifford had given him. The motel was one of the better ones used by those who drove north to play in the snow on winter weekends. The manager would be able to identify the two female guests who registered with Rose on Friday. As he told the Cliffords, it was a start. He called in his deputy, Will Burke, and gave him the note, along with a quick briefing on Clifford's story, instructing him to learn what he could and report back.

When he was alone again, Alex sat at his desk staring into space. He thought of Rose, her parents, and the depth of pain that went along with their fear. He could only hope that he would have an answer for them soon.

The next day, Rose's body was found. Her car was not. As news of the murder came through from the state police, Alex listened to the sordid details in a state of suppressed outrage. Then he slammed the phone back into its cradle, swiveled out of his chair, and after grabbing his jacket from its hook, headed toward the front door. He stopped only long enough to tell Marge where he was bound; in the next minute, he was behind the wheel of the county's Ford Crown Victoria, headed out to the Clifford home. He was determined to get there before some impersonal voice on the other end of a telephone line gave them the grisly news of their daughter's death. It was bad enough that within the next few hours they would have the grim task of identifying their only child's body as it lay on a cold and impersonal slab in the morgue. The thought made him sick.

When finally seated in the Clifford living room a short time later, Alex took in the agonized faces of Rose's parents as he broke the news of her death as gently as he knew how. As the tragic truth struck home, Sally Clifford wept convulsively in her husband's arms. Lewis Clifford's face was a stony mask; only his eyes burned with the grief and rage he was feeling. "Who, Alex, who?" Sally Clifford sobbed, tears streaming down the soft creases of her face as she gazed at Alex imploringly. "Who would want to do this to her, Alex? Who?"

That question was one which Alex wanted answered, as well. On a professional basis, certainly, but on a personal basis, too. Emotions awhirl as he drove the highway route back to town, his thoughts turned to focus on another day, a sweeter moment among the thorns of grief he had become too familiar with the last few years. He was suddenly and pleasantly in a part of the past when the world, for the moment at least, lay peaceful and still.

He was back on Main Street one sunny, July afternoon. Rose was window shopping, strolling casually along the sidewalk, pausing here and there to look into the store windows lining the street, all decorated to catch the eye of the seasonal tourist. It was lunchtime. On this particular afternoon, Alex had opted to catch a midday breath of fresh air and was ambling back to his office after a quick burger and fries at McDonald's, traveling the same route as Rose but in the opposite direction. He had taken no notice of Rose's approach, nor she of his. Their glances collided, however, for the briefest passing instant. It was long enough. They both stopped short, reversed a few steps, then stopped again to stare at one another before breaking into laughter.

"Alex!" Rose yelped. "I almost didn't recognize you! Your cop suit gave you away."

Then she glowered at him and frowned. "Were you by any chance going to pass me by?"

"Not on your life," Alex said, laughing. "No gorgeous brunettes get by me these days. That's why I carry a gun."

It was a real treat seeing Rose again. Over the next several minutes, standing together on the sidewalk like the excited kids they once were, they had turned back time to their school days, rousing up the ghosts of people who had shared them and laughing at the antics that were part of it all. When finally they pulled themselves back to reality and to the present, they hugged and said so long. But not before plans were made to get together again. And soon.

That unexpected reunion was the onset of a pleasant, if brief, relationship, Alex recalled with a smile, reminiscing back to a Saturday afternoon spent with picnic lunch and camera, climbing a mountain trail to the crest overlooking the deep green sweep of a valley below. There was the Sunday they had driven to Lake Placid and shared dinner at Mirror Lake Inn while sun-drenched waters sparkled playfully at their feet. For Alex, those weeks had been the first happy departure from the darkest era of his life, one which had begun with the sudden death of his son, then the following year, the separation and subsequent divorce from Lisa, his wife.

Fate had struck with deadly force one ordinary, summer afternoon. It was a day that had begun like so many others: a hasty breakfast, kisses from Lisa and sendoff hugs from Carl, his boy. Later that day, as Lisa went about her housework, Carl had wandered from the backyard on the small bicycle his parents had given him for his seventh birthday. He had barreled out of the driveway of their home and into the street, directly into the path of an oncoming car. He was killed instantly.

After more than a year of carrying the blame along with the grief and of Lisa's cold rejection of his efforts to console and be consoled, Alex accepted the inevitable truth. Their marriage was over. His wife hated him and she hated herself. Finally, disheartened and painfully aware that a finalized separation was the only sane way out for both of them, he took it.

Rose knew the story and understood that Alex's interest in her was not a romantic one. Theirs was a brief encounter, the essence of which came along like a sweet, summer breeze, and then wafted gently on its way. By the time school reopened in September, Alex knew Rose was seeing someone steadily. For her sake he was glad. She was a lovely woman, too full of life to waste her time with a man like himself who was dragging the weight of his past behind him.

It was later that Alex found himself wondering where their relationship might have gone had he been less wrapped up in himself and more receptive to Rose as a woman. The chilling reality now reached him: Rose was dead, and his question would never be answered.

CHAPTER TWO
DOWN MEMORY LANE

WEDNESDAY, NOVEMBER 4

Jenny Wyland sat in the corner of her living room sofa, her legs tucked beneath her. She was wearing a blue pullover sweater with slacks, her short, dark hair just dusting the soft ridge-line of her face. Her eyes were pale and sad, glistening with tears as she gazed at the newspaper, the front page emblazoned with the lurid details of her neighbor's tragic death.

An operating room nurse at Mercy Hospital in Grover, a few miles from Weston via the Northway, Jenny had arrived home from the hospital that Wednesday afternoon, picked up her mail and copy of the Weston *Gazette*, changed out of uniform, then poured herself a long, chilled Chardonnay before settling down on the sofa to read the same horrifying news of the murder which had swept through the hospital some hours before. Despite her initial shock at all she had heard, she had nonetheless been ill-prepared for the sight which greeted her as she turned the hall corner leading to her sixth floor, High Ridge apartment. Garish, yellow crime-scene tape lay stretched across the entrance door to apartment 608, an ugly reminder of the tragedy which had befallen Rose Clifford, her neighbor, but also an old school friend.

Even now, as she lifted the wine glass to her lips, she felt her fingers tremble with the horrific depiction of death, her rage mounting with the realization that the Rose she knew was now nothing more than a memory. She recalled her friend's smile, her energy, her love of life and the pleasures she had woven into it. There was the depth of affection she showed for the kids she taught, their chats over tea mingled with so much shared laughter. Jenny reflected on them all, deep sadness intermixing with anger and grief. And now, Rose was gone. Her life's breath snuffed out as effortlessly as blowing out the flame on a candle. Who could have committed such a vile act? Who would have wanted to? It made no sense. No sense at all.

Suddenly, her thoughts were drawn back to a dramatic and disturbing incident that had occurred a few weeks earlier. Summer vacation was over, Rose's schedule full, and their tea time together was relegated to whenever they could both find a few scattered minutes to chat and share. So Jenny had been quite surprised one evening when Rose appeared on her doorstep, not her usual smiling self but with red-rimmed eyes filled with silent pleading for a friend to talk to.

Confused by the added awareness of Rose's embarrassment, as apparent as it was unusual, Jenny quickly set the tea kettle to boiling with Rose plunked down across from her at the breakfast bar. After a few minutes of gentle nudging and a few sips of tea, Rose took a long breath, let out a deep sigh, and told Jenny her story.

"It's Chuck," she began in a small, angry voice. "He turned out to be a creep."

"What happened?" Jenny asked gently, expecting the worst.

She had run into Rose and her date one evening when they were leaving High Ridge just as she was returning home. Rose had made the introductions. Beyond taking in the muscled pecs straining against the cotton polo he wore, straw-yellow hair pulled back into a ponytail, and some rough, good looks, she had also caught the hint of a snicker behind a salacious smile under a pair of smoke-gray eyes that missed little of the female form.

An independent trucker who made his living hauling freight up and down New York's Canada-New Jersey corridor, Fowler had done well for himself, Rose told her later. But Jenny saw the gap between them as a gulch. A well-educated and warmly empathetic woman, Rose was heads above his ilk. Unfortunately, Jenny had admitted to herself with a resigned sigh, who could predict or analyze a woman's taste in a man?

A few days after that meeting, over a cup of tea and girl talk, Rose had laughed at Jenny's not-too-subtle attempt to pry out details on the status of the relationship. "Hey, loosen up," she had scolded Jenny good-naturedly. "Chuck's a date, period. He may not be Mr. Charming, but I happen to like him. Besides, I'm not looking for a full-timer, Jen. No way, honest!"

But on that tear-filled evening in her apartment, Rose was describing anything but "just a date." Lips quivering, she had struggled ahead with her tale.

"When Chuck got back from his last trip downstate," she began, "he called and asked me out to dinner. Then he asked if there was any place special I'd like to go. I suggested Shepherd's Cove, which was fine with him. He picked me up the next evening and was in high spirits. We both were, in fact." Her expression darkened. "That is, until the Cove."

She took a sip of tea and thought a moment. "When we were being seated at our table, the waiter gave me a big smile of recognition, and I admit," she added with a sigh, "he did give Chuck a funny look. Like maybe he should recognize him but couldn't? Whatever..." She waved a hand dismissively and continued. "That was when everything changed. One minute Chuck was smiling, the next minute his face turned to stone and he wouldn't say a word. It was eerie, Jen. Worse yet, I had no idea why! When dinner was finally finished – what we ate of it – he could hardly wait to get out of the restaurant. By that time, neither could I. Anyway," Rose hurried on, "we walked across the parking lot and were about to get into his car when out of the blue he grabbed me by the arm and spun me around. Ripping mad, he shoved his face into mine, told me he was no fool, and then demanded to know who I was seeing while he was on the road!"

Jenny was astonished. "He did what?" she spouted. "Why, for Pete's sake?"

Rose shook her head. "I don't know," she declared emphatically. "There was nothing to give him the crazy idea that he had a claim on me in the first place. In fact, I liked the way he treated me up until that night. Not pushy or all hands, ya know? But not that night. When I tried to pull away from him, wham! He gave me such a backhand across the face that I saw stars."

Jenny was stunned speechless. Her mouth dropped open and the teacup in her hand began to rattle against the saucer.

"Yeah, he hit me, Jen. Knocked me dizzy, in fact. The next thing I knew he had me backed up against the car. I was scared to death. Then he was in my face again, his eyes wild and his mouth all twisted, spitting at me that he doesn't share. When he ordered me into the car I was too scared to argue, so I got in and hugged the door. He drove me home, thank goodness, without so much as a word on the way. Even that was scary. In fact, the silence was worse. When we finally got here, I scooted out of the car and inside as fast as I could."

"Well, thank goodness you did get home!" Jenny exclaimed, appalled at the story. "He's a psycho, Rose. And I mean that seriously. A psycho! Whatever did you see in the man? It's all so incredible."

Rose's shoulders slumped. "I know I was stupid, Jen. And I know why." A breath caught in her throat and her eyes watered. "It was Alex Banks. I never told you the whole story, but the truth is, even though I saw Alex for such a short time, I fell for him, Jen. Really fell. Unfortunately, I also realized that I didn't stand a chance with him and it hurt. Not his fault, though. It can be a long climb back from one tragedy in your life, much less two." She gave a small, wry smile and shrugged. "I met Chuck at the lake over the summer. When he asked me out, I guess I snatched at the first lifeline that presented itself. Believe me, Jen, I thought he'd be someone I'd enjoy dating, period! Anyway, Alex and I went to the Cove a couple of times and maybe that's why the waiter looked at Chuck funny. People know Alex and he wasn't Alex. Chuck must have picked up on it, and that's why he exploded."

Rose gave a long sigh and shuddered. "Now he's calling me night after night. When I answer the phone, he'll say, 'So you're home waiting for me, babe?' Then he just laughs and hangs up." She slapped a hand down hard on the counter. "I hate myself for being so stupid."

With Rose's words still echoing in her memory, Jenny tried to recall the last time Chuck Fowler's name had come up. As far as she could remember, the calls had come nightly for awhile, even when Fowler was on the road. But then he had faded out of their conversation and presumably, out of Rose's life, as well. Or so she had believed at the time. But had he?

Reaching for the newspaper, Jenny turned back to the write-up of the murder until the sudden, demanding ring of the telephone broke into her thoughts. Uncurling from the sofa, she tossed the newspaper aside and answered the phone. A few minutes later she was in the kitchen attempting to put together a meal she felt too ill at heart to eat. It had dawned on her that Rose's death would launch an investigation into every facet of her friend's private life, beginning on that very evening. It was Alex Banks, another pivotal person out of Rose's past, who had telephoned. The sheriff would be at her place at six o'clock.

Just before six, Jenny buzzed Alex through the main entrance. Other than their old high school days, they had never met on a personal basis. Personal? She amended the thought. His visit that evening was anything but personal.

When Alex announced his arrival at her apartment with a gentle knock and Jenny opened the door to let him in, any shadow of uneasiness she expected to feel faded. Alex stood on the threshold in full uniform, a warm, well-remembered grin lighting his face as he commented on the cold weather and how great it was to see her again. After returning his smile and agreeing that indeed, it had been a long time, and yes, it was nice to see him, too, Jenny hung his parka in the foyer closet and nodded toward the kitchen.

"There's a fresh pot of coffee brewing," she said easily, "with gingersnaps on the side, if you're so inclined to dunk."

"Sounds great," Alex returned. "Sure, I'm inclined. Anyone who knows me can tell you gingersnaps are one of my many vices."

"Then follow me to the kitchen," she replied, sending Alex a warm smile over her shoulder, grateful for a moment's respite before facing the discussion to come. She motioned toward the coffee pot waiting on the breakfast bar. "Fix your coffee the way you like it and dunk away."

A few minutes later they were sitting in the living room in front of a crackling fire. Alex was leaning back in an armchair, one long leg crooked over the other while he sipped from a coffee mug, several gingersnaps lining the saucer's rim.

Sticking to common ground for awhile, they slipped into talk of their school days and the reminiscences that went along with them, both carefully avoiding the mention of Rose's name. When finally the conversation arrived at a silent and thoughtful pause, Jenny felt herself stiffen.

They had moved out of the past, and it was now time to face the present and all the unpleasantness that went with it.

"I know this business is tough on you, Jenny," Alex said gently. "But it's my job and I've gotta do it."

"Yes, I know," Jenny agreed, sighing softly. "Of course you do."

"But first," Alex set down his coffee mug on an end table and uncrossed his legs, "I want to clear up something. As Rose's neighbor and also her friend, you are aware that I was seeing her for awhile this past summer." Leaning forward in the chair, he began rubbing the palms of his hands together, allowing Jenny a moment to wonder where he was headed.

"It was a rotten time for me," he said slowly. "First my son's accident and then a divorce I never dreamed would happen." He put up a palm to restrain comment. His intention was to clarify his personal relationship with Rose, and he told her so. Once his position was made clear, he could move on to the business of their interview. When Jenny agreed to hear him out, Alex recounted his brief acquaintance with Rose.

"Suffice to say that Rose was a special person and my friend as well as yours," he finished up, "I won't forget her."

Then he pulled out a small pad and a pen from his shirt pocket and with his arms braced on his knees, he began. It was time for the questions he had come to ask. Jenny replied to them all, confirming Alex's prior knowledge that she and Rose, old high school chums, had renewed their acquaintance when they found themselves neighbors at High

Ridge. Then, as Alex listened intently, she went on to relate the story of Rose's trouble with Chuck Fowler, covering all the remembered details of his attack as Rose had described it.

"It was awhile after the incident happened that I learned about it," Jenny said in conclusion. "It's possible Rose might have done a good job covering up her bruised face with makeup because I didn't notice it that day. But I can tell you, by the time she came to see me, she was truly frightened. The telephone calls really got to her, I think. I wish she had gone to you about the creep right from the start of the trouble, but..." her voice faltered.

Alex raised an eyebrow. "But?"

"You didn't know, did you?" Jenny asked hesitantly.

"Didn't know what?"

"That Rose was in love with you."

Alex stared into Jenny's eyes. "No," he whispered. He could feel himself begin to choke up inside, a fresh wave of grief pouring into half-healed wounds. "It can't be."

"Look," Jenny said in a firm voice, realizing the impact of what she had told him, "this is no picnic for either of us, okay? Whatever your personal feelings are right now, or mine, let's put them aside so we can get down to what you need to know from me and what I can tell you. We can cover the personal ground another time."

"Yeah, you're right," Alex managed, letting the truth of Jenny's words sink in. There would be time to think about all that later. First came the job of finding Rose's killer. "Go on," he said finally, "finish whatever you were telling me, Jenny."

Jenny settled back into the sofa and took a deep breath. "I was about to say that it seemed Fowler apparently faded out of the picture, and I think Rose felt it simpler to just let the matter slide. She couldn't go to you, Alex. Her pride wouldn't let her."

"I see," Alex said quietly. "And that was the end of it?"

"As far as I know. I have to doubt Rose saw him again." Jenny thought a moment, then frowned. "Of course, she knew other men. But since we were both busy people, it wasn't unusual for a week or more to fly by before we'd get together for a cup of tea and a chat. For one, there was an older man, a teacher by the name of Ben Sayers, whom she saw socially now and then. I met him a few times. He seemed a strange kind of bloke, as they say. But he was okay, I suppose." Jenny lifted her shoulders. "That's it. I think you have whatever I know, Alex. To the best of my knowledge, that is. I wish it were more."

But Alex had another question. "Do you know anything of Rose's plans for the weekend she was killed? Parties, for instance? Other people she planned to see?"

"All I can tell you is that she was meeting a couple of college pals from downstate. They had plans for dinner and skiing at Gore over the weekend. I don't recall the girls' names, but Rose's mom might know them and the name of the motel they were staying at."

Alex snapped his notebook closed and stood up. "You've been more than helpful, Jenny," he said, tucking notebook and pen into his shirt pocket. "But there is one more thing you can do. Would you walk through Rose's place with me and see if everything looks normal to you? It would help to get your perspective, if you have no objection."

Despite her reluctance, Jenny agreed, and a few minutes later, teeth clenched, she stood waiting until Alex broke the seal on Rose's apartment door. Once in the apartment, Jenny was instantly assailed by a sense of Rose's presence wherever she turned. There were pictures of a bright-cheeked Rose clad in parka and knitted hat standing next to her skis. There were pictures of her parents. Rose's favorite pillows were scattered in front of the fireplace where she liked to sit with her tea before turning in for the night. Her kitchen was as she left it, a child's crayoned drawing for the teacher taped to the refrigerator door, cups and saucers on the counter, a kettle and a coffee pot on the stove.

"This is strange," Jenny commented, after lifting up the coffee pot lid. She turned to Alex with a puzzled frown. "There are coffee grounds in here," she said. "Rose was a tea drinker. She never made coffee unless it was for company."

Lifting the lid carefully out of Jenny's hand, Alex laid it on the stove. Then he began to open and close cabinet drawers, rummaging through them until he found what he was looking for. Jenny watched as he picked up both cups with a paper towel, then dropped first one and then the other into separate plastic bags he had removed from a box found in one of the cabinets.

"We missed this, Jenny," he told her. "Thanks for your help. Maybe the lab will send us back something to work with. The cups have only been rinsed, so we can hope."

Later, as Alex drove away from High Ridge into the darkened evening streets, his mind traveled back to the last hour and the stunning impact of Jenny's revelation. Rose in love with him? He hadn't known or even guessed. But would it have changed anything if he had? He doubted it. His life had been a kaleidoscopic mess, just regaining a semblance of balance when they met.

Wow, he thought, what a night! What an hour! Those first few minutes when Jenny opened the door to him were tough enough. He had forgotten what it was like to feel a sudden, unexpected rush of attraction toward a woman. It happened the moment Jenny looked at him and returned his smile. In that flash of a second, he was a senior back in high school and Jenny the remembered, soft, feminine sophomore whose dark, lash-fringed eyes were something you were not about to forget in a hurry.

Then wham! Another bolt of lightning into his guts. Rose. It was no time for weak knees. Someone had murdered a person they both cared about and it was his job to find out who it was. There was no room for personal feelings. First thing in the morning, before he headed out for Grover to meet with the medical examiner, he would get the cups off to the New York State forensic lab for possible prints and DNA. Next he would check out this Fowler character and arrange for a little chat. And there was Rose's missing Honda. It was vital that it be found before any evidence it contained degraded and became useless. The state police were still combing the entire Grover area and Weston highways, and the

Gazette had published the vehicle's description and plate number. Sooner or later, the Honda was sure to turn up. It had better, he added with a grim postscript. They would need more than they had now if there was a hope to catch, much less convict, Rose's killer.

Arriving at his highway turnoff, Alex drove until he reached the street where he lived. A line of houses had been built on neat patches of lawn with a backdrop of thickly wooded acreage behind them. When he came to 70 Woodview Road, he pushed the remote to open the garage door, pulled straight in, and let the door close behind him. Tired and more than a little heart weary, he cut the motor, closed his eyes, and rested his head back against the seat, relieved that the day had finally come to an end. Rose's death had come as a resounding shock to many people, and he was one of them. He had witnessed a lot of degradation and depravity in New York City, more than he ever wanted to see again. Only now, the ugly side of man had arrived in Weston and cost a vital and lovely young woman her life.

Alex finally got out of the car and stretched, willing the tiredness from his muscles and bones. Then, as the reflection of Jenny Wyland's smile came back to him, he straightened and went inside.

CHAPTER THREE
The Investigation Begins

THURSDAY, NOVEMBER 5

Alex arrived at headquarters early, anxious to get the bagged cups from Rose's apartment off to the lab. Once they were on their way, he got in touch with Harry Donahue and ran through the story Jenny had told him, detailing Chuck Fowler's attack on Rose, the nightly phone calls, and her resultant fear of the man, adding other pertinent particulars including the reference of a social connection to another teacher, Ben Sayers.

Before hanging up, Donahue promised Alex a quick background check on both men. As promised, twenty minutes later the trooper was back on the line with the information.

"Got what I could for ya, Banks," Donahue clipped in his deep tenor. "Your boy Fowler got into a skirmish a few years back. Nothing more than a tavern brawl over a woman. Ended up spending the night in county jail. Was released the next day; no charges made. A tough guy, or tries to be, but that's it. No outstanding warrants, no history of arrests for violent behavior. At least," he added, "not in New York State. We're checking national databases; the guy was originally from Oregon."

"Almost whistle clean," Alex commented dryly. "Just another bully boy who can't keep his fists to himself. Anything else?"

"I'll fax you the info on Fowler's vehicles, a blue, late-model Chevy and a green Ford Ranger pickup. Plus he's got a license to haul freight. Owns his own rig. You'll have all the dope: registration data and plate numbers, blah, blah. As for Ben Sayers, he got his BA from SUNY Albany and his master's from another New York college. Not married. Took a teaching job here in Weston about four years ago. Anything else you need?"

Alex told him no, with thanks, and hung up. He could already hear the humming of the fax machine. He picked up the sheaf of papers from the tray and fingered through them. Donahue never missed much. Fowler's phone number was included, plus his address on Old Mill Road in Weston and the other information Donahue had promised. The same with Ben Sayers.

Back at his desk, Alex called Fowler at the number on the sheet. He was in luck. Two rings and Fowler answered. After identifying himself and the reason for the call, Alex politely asked if Fowler would come by his office the next day to discuss the Clifford case.

"Sure," Fowler replied with exaggerated politeness. "I'll be glad to oblige, Sheriff. Your office tomorrow about ten, if that's okay?"

It was. Alex hung up.

The Clifford inquest was scheduled for two o'clock in the afternoon, but by ten-thirty, Alex was standing in the bleak dankness of the morgue's postmortem chamber while Dr. Jake Morris, the county medical examiner, adjusted the light above the autopsy table where Rose's body now lay face-up under a green lab sheet. As Dr. Morris pulled back the sheet and began to recite the litany of death that was an ongoing part of his vocation in life, Alex felt his stomach lurch at what he saw and heard and smelled. Struggling to keep his facial expression one of practiced, professional detachment, his jaw worked with fresh outrage.

"She was struck on the side of the head, initially," Dr. Morris related somberly as he pointed to the gaping wound on Rose's scalp amid a surrounding area of blood-matted hair.

"Probably with the forked end of a hammer. If the blow had been more direct, she would have died then and there. But she must have turned or shifted her position just enough to cause the hammer thrust to glance off here on the side of the head where the scalp is torn open. Probably knocked her unconscious but didn't kill her. Scalp wounds bleed like the devil. Make quite a mess."

He looked at Alex a moment, then continued. "She was stabbed directly into the left ventricle of the heart while either stunned from the blow or unconscious. Killer probably used a buck knife or something very much like it." He pointed to several bruised areas about the neck and shoulders. "These marks were made postmortem. She was killed in one location, ostensibly some time early Friday evening before dinnertime, because her stomach was fairly empty, but then she was transported elsewhere and eventually dragged into the woods and dumped there. Nothing sexual here. She wasn't touched. Nasty business, nonetheless."

Dr. Morris drew the sheet back over the grisly remains of what had so recently been a vital young woman, pulled off the plastic gloves he was wearing, picked up a report folder from a work table behind him, and handed it to Alex. "It's all in there," he said. "Corresponding to the stage of the body's decomposition and other relative factors, I call the time of death early evening, most likely sometime between five and seven o'clock on Friday, October thirtieth."

Alex opened the report and skimmed over it, asked a few questions, then shook the doctor's hand and left the building. As he drove back to Weston over the winding mountain roads, with autumn's faded exodus evident in every direction, Alex felt too sick and numb to notice. Once back in his office, he fixed himself a cup of coffee and proceeded to review the autopsy report Jake Morris had given him. It covered most of what he already knew but he would read it again, anyway. Although the photographs included made his stomach knot, he scrutinized everything.

As always, the forensic team had done a thorough job at both Rose's apartment and the entire well-trodden section of forest where her body was found. Whatever trace evidence they came up with was already on its way to the forensics lab and would be included in the follow-up report which would eventually reach him. Alex then ran through the preliminary report that his deputy, Will Burke, had left on his desk. Reading it over, Alex saw that the forensic team had completed a thorough luminal search of Rose's apartment looking for blood stains. There were none, which ruled out the apartment as the crime scene.

As soon as the formal examination by the state forensic team had been finalized, Alex and his deputy made their own tour of the apartment. It was just as the High Ridge manager had reported to Mrs. Clifford. The apartment was neat and clean. There were no messages on her answering machine they didn't expect to find there. Where Rose had been killed remained an unknown, and they were still searching for the blue Honda Civic and, of course, the murder weapon.

After draining the last of his coffee, Alex snapped the file closed and got to his feet. He felt tired and edgy and more than a little frustrated. He hated having to wait for information to be channeled back to him and had no intention of letting precious minutes waste away. Not while there were still people to interview and more questions that needed answers.

But first, there was an inquest he had to attend.

FRIDAY, NOVEMBER 6

It was close to ten fifteen on Friday morning when Chuck Fowler sauntered through the front door of the sheriff's office. Marge Grant was in her usual place behind the reception desk and Deputy Burke was downloading reports onto a computer when Fowler approached Marge's desk, bent over slightly, and in a slow, almost seductive tone of voice, identified himself. Gazing up at him indifferently over the rim of her glasses, Marge buzzed Alex's office.

"Go right in," she said to Fowler, indicating the open doorway toward the rear of the room. "You're expected."

Alex was behind his desk when Fowler entered. Without rising or offering the courtesy of a handshake, he motioned toward a chair next to his desk and told Fowler to take a seat. Fowler did so, hunching over far enough to rest his lower arms on his thighs, the brim of his high-crowned hat dangling idly from the tips of his fingers. Alex began by letting Fowler know the reason he was being interviewed, namely to explain his relationship with Rose Clifford and to detail where he was at the time of her death.

"So okay, I knew Rose," Fowler admitted with a bemused smile. "Saw a lot of her there for awhile, as a matter of fact. So what?"

Alex asked the last time he had seen or talked with her, not attempting to disguise the underlying contempt in his voice.

Fowler sent him a sharp, angry look, his temper rising to the surface. "What's going on?" he snarled belligerently. "You're sayin' I'm a suspect? Well, for your information, Sheriff, Rose was killed on a Friday night, right? Well, it happens that it was the same Friday night I was shootin' darts and watchin' a football game with some buddies of mine in a bar in Glens Falls." He made a snide, chuckling sound and sat up straight in his chair. "So you really think I mighta killed her, do ya?"

"You roughed her up, and that I don't think, I know," Alex replied coldly, ignoring Fowler's questions and wondering just how far the pseudo cowboy would allow his temper to fly when he had a man to contend with, not a woman.

"Yeah, sure," Fowler admitted, his voice toning down a pitch. "Rose and I had some words. But it wasn't so bad. A lovers' quarrel, ya might say." He lifted his shoulders in a gesture of mock innocence and grinned. "An argument. I got a little jealous and she got a little mad." His grin slackened. "Doesn't mean I killed her."

"I know you backhanded her in the face while in the Shepherd's Cove parking lot. I know you harassed her with phone calls every night after that, right?"

"Hey, I wanted to tell her I was sorry for losin' my temper, but she just kept hangin' up on me," Fowler snapped back. "So I just kept callin'. I liked the girl. She had class. But I finally got the message and kissed her off. That was the last until I heard she was dead."

Alex let out an audibly disgusted breath. "All right, that's it for now, Mr. Fowler," he snapped, ending the interview. "On your way out, stop by the reception desk and leave the name of that bar in Glens Falls, along with the name or names of anyone who can confirm you were there. And incidentally," he added, as he pushed himself away from the desk and stood up, "make yourself available in case we need to have another little talk."

Fowler grinned. "Bet I will, Sheriff. Bet I will. I'll be sure to leave word where you can reach me. I'll be sure to do just that."

Then, with a last cocky glance in Alex's direction, Fowler scraped back his chair, lumbered to his feet, and headed out the office door. Alex watched from the doorway as Fowler took the pad Marge handed him and started scribbling on it. After he tossed it back on the desk, he looked down at Marge with a grin, gave her a wide, suggestive wink, arranged his hat at a jaunty angle on his head, and went out the door.

"Slimy cuss," the deputy commented half under his breath as he watched Fowler conclude his performance and leave. Will Burke was a tall, lanky lad in his mid-twenties. He had a low, lazy voice and straight, brown hair that refused to stay in place. He was clean and steady and dependable, qualities which gave Alex reason to both like and trust him.

"Yeah, that he is," Alex commented dryly. "A real slimy cuss, is right."

"I can't figure out why a gal like Rose'd give somebody like him more than a minute of her time," Will drawled. "And he sure don't seem any too broken up by her murder, either."

"Oh, we aren't through with Mr. Fowler yet," Alex assured him. "He's a coiled rattler that needs to be put someplace where he can't hurt another woman. As to the murder, the fact is that we can't do anything without evidence, and all we've got so far is a cold trail. Let's hope forensics comes up with something solid, and pretty quick."

But Alex was not going to wait for forensics. He had to keep moving. After a few words to Marge and Will, he grabbed his parka and headed out for Weston Elementary. An interview with Ben Sayers was overdue.

On his drive through the quiet, midmorning streets of Weston, Alex did a mental review of Donahue's background report on Sayers. He was from Poughkeepsie, a college graduate, and he was single. He'd lived for about four years here in Weston. Not much more than bare bones. He would soon see what he could do to fill in the gaps.

A few minutes later, Alex turned into the school parking lot. Weston Elementary was a relatively new, three-story brick building on a generous spread of acreage which accommodated the school, a playground, a baseball field, and an ample parking area. Alex recalled the small grade school he had attended another lifetime ago, and the recollection wrought a quick smile. The last time he had driven by the place, it had evolved into a busy daycare center. Time had a way of changing many things, Alex thought wryly, the smile fading. More than he had ever thought possible.

With several empty parking spots to choose from, Alex swung the Ford into an opening close to the school's side door entrance marked "faculty only" and killed the motor. Moments later, he was listening to the sound his footsteps made echoing off the tile floor of the school's main hall as he passed a large, empty auditorium and a few nondescript, closed doors. He finally came to the office of John Logan, the school's principal. Standing at the door of the outer reception area, he took in the row of folding chairs lined against one wall, two of which were occupied by a pair of very unhappy-looking boys wearing sweatshirts and baggy pants. He smiled inwardly as their eyes grew wide and wary watching him enter the room.

Directly inside the door, a young woman sat behind a reception desk, her gaze transfixed on a computer screen while long, agile fingers flew over a keyboard. The nameplate on the corner of the desk read: Lorna Kelly, Receptionist. Alex cleared his throat, then smiled as green eyes suddenly released their hold on the computer screen and flashed upward.

"Oh, Sheriff," she said, flushing with embarrassment. She pushed back her chair from the desk and stood up. "I didn't hear you come in. I'm sorry."

"No problem, Miss Kelly," Alex assured her. "I'm here to see Mr. Logan. That possible?" he asked, noting the closed inner-office door.

"Of course." She rose from her desk and held up a finger. "One minute, please, Sheriff. I'll just let Mr. Logan know you're here."

She had barely opened the door and disappeared into the principal's office when John Logan came striding out of the room, his hand extended in welcome. "Come right in, Sheriff," he invited in a deep, relaxed tone of voice. Once inside his office, Logan indicated a comfortable chair next to a wide, neatly organized desk. "Please, sit down. And I would also very much appreciate it if you would call me John. I already know your first name." He chuckled. "I should know it, Alex. I voted for you."

"Everyone here at the school is very shaken by Rose's death," Logan began after they were both seated and the amenities dispensed with. He took a long breath and leaned forward, fingers locked together, his brow furrowed into a deep frown. "Rose was a special person," he said sadly. "I knew something had to be very wrong when she wasn't in her class on Monday. Since then I've tried to think of the questions you might ask, but found the task of searching for the answers a difficult one. But please, understand me, I do want to help. So tell me, Alex, what can I do?"

"To begin with," Alex replied slowly, meeting the earnest appeal in the man's eyes, "we have little to go on at the moment. Right now I'm interested in the name of any close faculty friend of Rose's you might be aware of, or any personal knowledge of her you can pass on. I need a foothold, John." He made a helpless gesture. "Rose had no enemies. She was liked by everyone. Her life seems to have been wrapped up in her work. So here I sit."

The older man pursed his lips for a long, thoughtful moment. "Frankly," he replied slowly, "the only person who might possibly be of help to you is our sixth-grade teacher, Ben Sayers. Rose and Ben worked on many of the children's special programs here at the school. They may even have seen one another on the outside. I believe so, but can't say for certain."

"What can you tell me about Mr. Sayers," Alex asked. "Just briefly, if you will."

Logan pursed his lips, again. "Hmmm," he murmured. "Well, Ben is," he paused, searching for words, "How shall I put it? A loner might be an apt description for lack of a better one." He shrugged. "He and Rose seemed to get on well, however."

"I understand Mr. Sayers has been teaching here for about four years?" Alex pursued.

"Correct," Logan replied, nodding. "We were fortunate to find him, as a matter of fact. He taught downstate for quite a few years prior to coming here. His references were excellent."

He gave Alex a wry grin. "A good teacher in this neck of the woods can be hard to find. And he is a good teacher. A little strict, but nothing that crosses the line. Very dependable, as well."

"That's quite a positive resume, I dare say," Alex commented. "Anything else?"

Logan shook his head. "Frankly, I believe Ben can probably tell you more of what you want to know, Alex. Perhaps you should talk to him." "He might be able to shed a brighter light on what's behind this tragedy than I'm able to do."

"That interview was next on my list," Alex said. "I'll also need statements from all of your other teachers." He rose and extended his hand. "I appreciate your time, sir. I'll be in touch."

Logan reciprocated, then stepped from behind his desk. "You might as well meet Ben now," he said, heading for the office door. "I'll have Lorna show you the way. She can monitor his class while you talk." He put a hand on Alex's shoulder. "I wish you luck."

A few minutes later, Lorna Kelly was leading Alex up a wide staircase to Ben Sayers' sixth-grade classroom. When they reached his door, she stopped, turned to Alex, and smiled. "I'll send him right out," she told him, then slipped inside.

Not at all certain what type of man he expected to meet, Alex was somewhat disconcerted when Ben Sayers stepped into the hall and introduced himself. Appearing to be at least in his mid-forties, Sayers was of medium height with sharply angular features. He wore his thinning brown hair combed carefully to one side; round, rimless eyeglasses accented deep-set, probing brown eyes. While his manner of speech was rapid and clipped, Alex caught the slightest hint of an occasional lisp. He recalled Jenny Wyland's description of him as an "odd bloke" and smiled to himself. Whatever perception of him others might have, Alex found Sayers to be quite the dapper character, very much in command of himself.

"I've given out an assignment to keep the kiddies at bay," Sayers was saying. "If you'll stroll along with me down the hall, Sheriff, we'll be out of earshot." He glanced at his watch. "Classrooms will be emptying out in about ten minutes and then pandemonium, as you can well imagine, will ensue. Lorna told me why you are here, so I'll get right down to business and tell you whatever I can."

Allowing Sayers the floor, Alex nodded in agreement, and the two fell into step past a succession of closed classroom doors, the only sounds other than their footsteps being the drift of muffled voices and an occasional creak of movement emanating from behind them.

"When I came here to teach about four years ago," Sayers began, "Rose went out of her way to make me feel welcome and comfortable. I don't make friends easily so I appreciated both her empathy and her help. Eventually, we put our ideas together and worked with the kids, merging the younger children into programs with the upper grades. They were fun, creative projects and the kids loved them." He shook his head, noting the question in Alex's sidelong glance. "Nothing romantic between us, Sheriff, I assure you. But believe me, I'll miss her a lot." He stopped and turned to face Alex directly. "What else do you want to know? Rose and I were coworkers. I can't think of anything more to tell you."

Alex turned the subject to Rose's private life and asked if she had ever mentioned anyone she was seeing on more than a casual basis.

"No," Sayers replied with a shake of his head as they continued their stroll. "I don't know of anyone she was seriously dating." He slipped a glance at Alex out of the corner of his eye. "Except you, of course."

Momentarily caught off guard by the sudden reference to himself, Alex stopped short, holding Sayers with a long, deliberate scowl that left no doubt that the subtle barb had found its mark.

"Yes," Alex replied carefully, "I was seeing Rose last summer. But for a very brief time, and that was it. Just for the record, Rose and I went back to our teenage years. We were friends. Only that. And also for the record, that relationship has nothing whatsoever to do with this investigation. I hope I'm making myself clear?"

Sayers waved a dismissive hand and uttered a scoffing sound. "Of course! I happen to know she thought a great deal of you, Sheriff," he said placatingly. "Rose could be a rather reticent person, as you must already be aware. She didn't talk much about her private life, so I couldn't say who she saw or didn't see, romantically or otherwise. Understandably, you were the exception. Be realistic – you're a high profile figure in the community. And, though I confess to having harbored a degree of curiosity about you, I never felt it was my place to pry."

Before Alex could make a retort, Sayers suddenly snapped his fingers. "Wait!" he exclaimed, his voice high and excited. "I just remembered the mystery woman. Or, I should say, Rose's mystery woman. Hold on, Sheriff," he said, breathlessly. "You have to hear this."

"I'm not going anywhere," Alex said, still bristling. "I'm listening."

With hands clasped together as if in prayer, Sayers slowed his step. "We have to go back to a school day in early September," he began. "It was lunch break and I had darted off to pick up a package from the post office. I had just returned and was locking the parcel in the trunk of my car when I caught sight of Rose with another woman. They were standing next to Rose's car parked in the end section of the lot. Which, I may add, was unusual since we have our own faculty parking area closer to the side entrance." His brow furrowed in thought for a moment.

"The woman acted like she was ready to detonate. Unfortunately, I couldn't hear what was being said; they were too far away. But the woman was definitely distraught. Luckily, Rose's back was to me, a fact which saved both of us the embarrassment of explanations later on had she turned and caught me watching. I didn't wait for that to happen; I cut out of there on the double. If the other woman noticed me, I couldn't say one way or the other. Later that afternoon I dropped by Rose's classroom to say hello, relieved that she didn't mention the incident. Needless to say, neither did I."

"This woman, can you describe her?"

Sayers put a finger to his lips. "Well, let's see now. She was about Rose's age, or younger; thin, with short, very light hair. She was wearing slacks and a jacket. The two of them were standing between Rose's blue

Honda and another car, perhaps the woman's."

"And the other car, can you describe it?"

"It was an older model. Dark blue, maybe? A Ford, I believe, but I'm not sure."

"Anything else you can think of?" Alex pressed. "Why the woman may have been in the parking lot in the first place. An angry parent, perhaps?"

"The way I figured it at the time," Sayers replied without hesitation, "was if the woman's visit concerned a student, she would have scheduled a meeting with Rose after school hours. Ergo, I doubt the woman was a parent. And Rose had lunch in the faculty room just about every day, so I'm left to wonder why she was in the parking lot in the first place instead of inside the building." He rubbed his chin. "You know, I had almost forgotten about that incident until today."

Alex was about to ask another question when the loud clamor of a schoolbell shredded the silence. "That's it," Sayers said with an apologetic shrug. "Nice meeting you. For now, anyway. If I can be of further help, let me know." Then he turned and hurried away.

At the sudden sound of raised voices and the scuffle of young feet, Alex proceeded to make his own hasty retreat. He would arrange for one-to-one interviews with the faculty on Monday. When he reached the exit door, he stepped outside and looked across the parking lot, trying to imagine the scene as Sayers had described it. The thought suddenly came to him that on some occasion, perhaps over one of their tea get-togethers, Rose might have mentioned the incident to Jenny. He would talk to Jenny tonight after Rose's wake. She was sure to be there. And so would he.

CHAPTER FOUR
HAUNTING VISIONS

FRIDAY, NOVEMBER 6

As Alex had planned, he did see Jenny Wyland that night, but under far different circumstances than he could have imagined.

Rose's wake was being held at Howell's Funeral Home, a white-shingled, converted Victorian on the corner of Lennox Avenue and Hart Street in the center of town. An ancient elm dominated the corner on which it stood. In summer, the tree's foliage cast a broad shadow over the spacious, old-fashioned veranda and the wide, shallow steps leading up to Howell's front door. Tonight, however, its long, leafless, skeletal limbs extended haphazardly above the sidewalk, and its mass of bulky, crooked boughs reached heavenward into a dark and empty sky. Along Lennox Avenue, restaurants, bars, and cozy inns were open and busy, catering to the usual run of Friday night regulars and tourists in town for a weekend of fun in the snow, man-made and otherwise.

The parking area for Howell's guests was located along Hart Street to the rear of the building. Aware of the several cars pulling in behind him as he turned into the lot, Alex took the first empty spot he saw and climbed out of his Chevy Blazer into the sheer cold of the night. As he started down Hart Street, he heard car doors slamming shut behind him, the sound intermingled with the rise and fall of muffled voices. He stopped for a moment, listening. While throughout the day he had convinced himself that he could make it through the evening with his mind and emotions centered on the job, he was beginning to fear it might not be so easy, or perhaps even possible, after all.

He pulled up the collar of his parka and hunkered down into it.

Walking quickly, he continued along the sidewalk toward Lennox Avenue and Howell's front door. He had nearly covered the distance when the resolve he had struggled with for so long began to slip under the weight of something that refused to let go. His son's wake and funeral had been held at Howell's. Now, as he had dreaded in the hours prior, the burden of that reality took hold and grief once again knifed through him. He stopped walking, reminding himself that he would never find peace until he won the struggle over the ghosts that taunted him. He had to win, he told himself a thousand times over. But how, he had no idea.

He was all at once aware of footsteps approaching from behind him. Tugging up the collar to his parka even further, he stepped discretely to one side of the pavement, allowing anyone behind him to pass, relieved when a small group of people, chatting among themselves, stepped briskly by with barely a glance in his direction. He drew in a deep breath and closed his eyes.

Suddenly, both Carl and Rose took form in the shadows of his mind. They were as he had known them, filled with energy and laughter, with no realization of just how fragile the thread of life could be. Their deaths had bequeathed him a lesson bitterly learned. It would be forever impossible for him to take the next moment on this planet, or life itself, for granted. Not ever.

Over the next several moments, as his thoughts began to calm a bit, Alex took notice of the deepening darkness and the fresh bite of cold in the windy evening air. His steps now measured and deliberate, he moved slowly toward the old elm tree, his gaze caught by a contorted branch pointing like a crooked finger toward one of Howell's long, graceful windows where a soft light beckoned, promising shelter and warmth inside.

"There is no shame in retreat," a voice within whispered as he stared at the window's invitation. "But," another voice cautioned, "there is no victory, either." The choice he knew, was his.

He hiked up his jacket sleeve to check his watch. The service for Rose was due to begin at seven o'clock and he was already close to fifteen minutes late. Decision made, he took a last look around, squared his shoulders, climbed the steps to Howell's heavy, oak door, shoved his knitted hat into a jacket pocket, and went inside.

He had taken no more than a few steps down the long, central hallway when he was met by the heavy, floral aroma of death. Made even more heady by its contrast to the cold air outside, the repugnant odor sucked its way into his nostrils and lungs; his heart began to hammer, and icy panic moved in to claim him. He could scarcely breathe. He knew then the terrible mistake he had made. He was smothering and had to escape.

He pulled in a deep breath and then released it. He needed to clear the tumult of his emotions and somehow figure out what to do next. He glanced around. The entrance to the lounge, with its adjoining restrooms, lay to his right. To his left he noted the two sets of curtained, double French doors which opened into separate viewing rooms. From behind one of the doors, he could make out the soft hum of what sounded like voices murmuring together in prayer. At the end of the hall, several feet away, three people were huddled head to head, deep in conversation. Otherwise, he could detect no other signs of activity.

He was, however, still in the grip of an irrational panic, wondering if he was about to hit the floor. Then all at once the visions overcame him, and in that moment he knew, with cold certainty, that there was to be no escape.

There had not been a traditional wake for Carl that day at Howell's, just a short, morning vigil in a tear-filled room with a black-robed minister, holy book in hand, leading the final prayers. Eyes closed, Alex once again saw the small, white, gold-handled casket borne by solemn-eyed pallbearers, moving slowly toward him. He heard the soft shuffle of their feet as they proceeded along the deep-piled carpet of the central hallway. With racing heart, he watched them approach the open doorway to the street then continue across the veranda and down the steps to the open doors of the black hearse waiting at the curb. He saw Lisa, sobbing, dragging herself along behind the bleak cortege, her eyes red and glassy, her grief an almost tangible thing that touched everyone in a way they would never forget. And then, as now, flowers were everywhere, their cloying, perfumed scent of death saturating the air.

Then abruptly, mercifully, the scene faded, and Alex found himself standing alone, aware only of the low drone of voices emanating from behind the closed French doors where he was certain the service for Rose was being held, and where he knew he should be. Shaking and weak, he managed to extract a handkerchief from a trouser pocket and wipe away the cold sweat beading across his forehead. It was then he felt the light touch of a hand on his arm. Startled, he turned to find Jenny Wyland staring up at him, her soft, brown eyes filled with concern.

"Are you all right, Alex?" she asked, holding her voice to just above a whisper.

Alex swallowed and nodded. "I guess so. It's the heat in here, I think," he replied with a shaky grin. "I'll be okay. Just give me a minute."

Jenny's eyebrows shot up and she shook her head. "Uh-uh. You won't be okay," she stated firmly. "You can't kid a nurse, Alex. You're as white as the proverbial sheet, and if you stand there pretending heroics much longer, we're going to have a serious problem. Now, listen to me," she said, with gentle but unwavering authority. "First, take a few, slow, easy breaths. When you get your bearings, we'll head toward the door. Once we make it outside, we'll find a place to have a cup of coffee. Then, we'll see."

Too grateful for the rescue to resist, Alex let Jenny guide him out of Howell's. "Okay, breathe deeply," she ordered, watching his breath billow out and disappear, a white cloud puffed into the evening air. "Another one," she told him, and then another, until finally she was satisfied that his color had returned and he could, as she put it with a significant grin, walk a straight line.

"Now," she announced, "let's go." Then, with Jenny locked on his arm and regarding him solemnly from the corner of her eye, he was led down Hart Street to where her car was parked in the Howell lot.

"Here's my car," she said, opening the passenger door with a flourish and a sweep of her arm. "Hop in. Just remember, this is only a temporary reversal of roles, Alex. Right now you're my patient. So enjoy it. It will probably never happen again."

"Are you feeling better?" Jenny asked, when they were underway and moving smoothly along the winding road that led away from town.

"Yep, that I am," Alex said. "Thanks to you. You saved my life. I have to fess up, Jenny. My son, Carl, was buried from Howell's. I should have known better than to go back there tonight, but I thought I could handle it. I'm sorry."

"You don't have to apologize, Alex. Or explain." Jenny's voice was gentle. "I happened to leave the viewing room early and spotted you. It wasn't hard to figure out what was going on." She paused and gave him a quick, sidelong glance. "I'm glad you didn't keel over, though. You're a big fella to try and catch. I never could have done it!"

They both laughed and Alex felt the earlier tension begin to slip away. Gradually, as they sped along the highway, chatting casually in the semidarkness of the car, he was able to enjoy the ride and the company. Twenty minutes or so later, they were seated across from one another at a small wayside café, conversing over a sandwich and a glass of wine, surrounded by candle-lit tables and listening to the rhythm of soft music in the background. Inevitably Alex brought the conversation around to the subject he had planned to discuss with Jenny in the first place. He told her about his visit to the school and Ben Sayers' story of Rose's mystery woman.

"Try to think back, Jenny. Did Rose ever mention the incident to you? As Sayers told it, the confrontation wasn't a pleasant one. Not even a little bit."

Jenny frowned and tugged on an ear lobe. "Yes, I believe I do remember something," she said slowly. "Probably goes back to some time in early September. One afternoon Rose and I met going up in the High Ridge elevator. She asked me to stop by for a cup of tea, and I did. She seemed gloomy that day, which wasn't like her. We sat gabbing for awhile, and then she mentioned something about a woman and an argument of some kind that had happened earlier that day in the school parking lot. Naturally, I thought she was talking about a parent."

"But she wasn't," Alex said, remembering Sayers' similar conclusion.

Jenny nodded. "Right. When I made the remark that the parking lot was a funny place for a parent to complain to a teacher, she waved away my words with a little laugh and told me no, it was, thankfully, not a parent. Just someone, she told me, who had made an accusation that was way out of line. I can't remember all she said after that, only that the woman had really upset her. When I thought she was going to break into tears, I changed the subject. We got onto something else and had our tea. That was that."

"Apparently, it was a nasty scene," Alex commented. "According to Sayers, the woman was fighting angry. Not pretty."

"No," Jenny agreed, "not pretty at all. Just strange."

"Rose gave you no hint as to what this woman's name might be?"

"Nope. But she knew who she was. I recall some vague reference to her feeling sorry for the woman. She commented that there were a lot of sad cases in the world."

"Yeah," Alex said with the lift of an eyebrow. "I know."

"Oh, Alex," Jenny chided, a blush rising to her cheeks. "Who's the sad case, you?"

Alex's hand reached across the table and found Jenny's slender fingers. He tilted his head at an angle and grinned. "Me?" he murmured with wide-eyed mock innocence. "Never!"

Later, at home alone, Alex looked back on the evening's conversation. He was still unable to dispel his disappointment that there was no hint of the mystery woman's identity or what connection she might have had with Rose. The disgruntled parent theory was out. Irate mothers don't usually go around killing teachers they are unhappy with. But, real or imagined, there was a reason behind the woman's anger.

She apparently believed Rose guilty of some serious misdeed or misconduct. Misconduct in her role as teacher? No, that supposition puts the parent angle back into play. So, maybe she believed Rose was involved with her husband? That was another far-fetched assumption, knowing Rose. But, he contemplated with annoyance, one angle was good as another. Or, he reluctantly admitted, as worthless.

He also thought about his experience at Howell's, which he should have been able to predict. Yet whatever failing he was forced to uncover in himself over the last few hours, he could never have visualized being rescued by a beautiful woman. Because Jenny had indeed rescued him, and while the pall of his son's death still hung heavily, he now knew with even stronger certainty that he had to come to terms with the loss of Carl and get on with his life. The process was much more difficult and the pain far more overpowering than he ever could have imagined.

His thoughts shot ahead to the last few minutes he and Jenny had spent together after they arrived back at Howell's parking lot to retrieve his Blazer. They had stood facing one another in the cold, unfriendly darkness about to say goodnight when something happened. It was in that fraction of an instant when their eyes met and held that something passed between them. Something important and something real. And they both knew it.

CHAPTER FIVE
TEARS IN THE CEMETERY

The next morning, after stretching awake and then reveling in the luxury of a long, hot shower, Alex sat at his kitchen table over a cup of coffee while a boiling egg clattered pleasantly from the confines of an aluminum pan on the stove. The clock on the wall read six forty. He looked around the room with a sense of warm satisfaction as he had done so many times since buying the house, and this morning a feeling of welcome contentment was added to soften the rough edges of the past week. He drew in the zesty aroma of freshly perked coffee and took in the happy patterns of sunlight scattered across the tiled floor. He was comfortable in his new home. Very much so.

He took a sip of coffee and let his mind relax, nostalgically recalling the first time he had been given the grand tour of the place by a Clifford real estate agent. It had been an easy sale for the guy because the house suited Alex, his needs, and his income. Not spacious by any definition, still and all the first floor had the space he needed to accommodate a makeshift office, with plenty of shelf space for the books he had accumulated over the years.

Adjoining the office, or his den, as he preferred to call it, was a bath which led into a small but comfortable guest room.

Upstairs on the second floor, the master bedroom looked out over a grassy lawn that stretched back to a line of trees and brush comprising the rear perimeter. Even as a kid, he had loved the feel of dirt in his hands and the fun of watching things grow, so he had put in a vegetable garden and planted a few spindly, flowering dwarf trees in the back yard. He had also built a patio onto the rear of the house, a well-screened fortification against black flies, mosquitoes, and "no-see-em" punkies when they made their annual unwelcome, springtime appearances into the mountains.

But now the leaves on the trees were all but bare, the deep cold of winter already nibbling at autumn's edge. Flatlanders could never come to understand, Alex thought, the love of the north and the cold. But love it, he did. He loved the dramatic change of seasons, the peaks of snow on the rolling mountains, the animals and birds he fed through the food-scarce, life-threatening winter months. He loved all of it. The smell of spring, the rushing brooks filled with the trout he struggled to snare, the unpredictable weather with its sudden raucous rainstorms. All of it. Simply put, it was his kind of country.

Breakfast over, he was almost ready to roll. For Alex, Saturday had evolved into just another workday, the desk in his office piled high as ever with waiting paperwork. He reminded himself that Rose's funeral was scheduled to leave Howell's at eight thirty for Fairhaven Cemetery; he would be there in spirit only. It was just as well. Rose's murder case was in a state of stagnation. With both her apartment and the place where her body was found ruled out as the murder scene, her Honda was next on the list. The state police choppers had been working relentlessly to find it but they had come up empty. Without access to the car, the biological evidence to tell them what they needed to know could gradually deteriorate. Something had to give. And soon. He would check in later with Donahue to see what headway, if any, had been made.

It was just seven fifteen when Alex slipped behind the wheel of his Blazer and headed toward the main highway. Upon reaching the intersection, however, instead of taking the route to Weston, he found himself swinging the wheel in a different direction, heading upward into the sloping hills.

A few minutes later, he pulled into the narrow, pillared entrance of St. Mark's Cemetery, bumping slowly over the scraggly, winding, dirt road that led to the level where Carl was buried. He had just made the last curve of the hill when he saw Lisa in the distance. Stunned for the moment, Alex braked, then pulled over to the side of the road and cut the motor, his gaze locked on the woman who had once been his wife.

She was wearing a heavy, navy pea coat with the collar turned up and a blue, knit hat pulled down almost to her eyebrows. She stood with her head bent and her mittened hands clasped together in front of her, staring down at Carl's grave. Standing alone and forlorn among the gray headstones and skeletal remains of bare-boned trees, like the visions which beleaguered him, she was another apparition of grief. His thoughts turned back to the Lisa who had been his, a pretty, bright, golden-haired girl, full of fun and laughter and warmth. Once upon a time they had been deeply in love. Today, they were distant and alien strangers, their hope-filled dreams lost forever somewhere along life's fickle way.

Jolting himself awake and away from another useless plunge into the hellish throes of depression, Alex climbed out of the car and began to walk slowly across the cemetery grounds. Head down, shoulders hunched into his parka against the gusty, cold morning air sweeping over the ridge, he wondered what the next few minutes would hold. The thought made him want to retreat, but he could not. He had to try reaching into Lisa's lost, miserable world one more time.

He had almost made it to Lisa's side when the sound of his footsteps crunching over the carpet of frosted leaves caused her to start and then to look up. She stared at Alex for a long, tense moment, frowned, then turned away.

"Good morning, Lisa," Alex said quietly.

Lisa's eyes flickered toward him, then away. "What do you want?" she asked in a cold, flat voice. "What are you doing here, Alex?"

"Couldn't I be here for the same reasons you are?" he replied softly.

"Maybe," Lisa said, still not looking at him. "Maybe not. Just seems funny. I'm here every Saturday when I can make it and this is the first I've seen you." She slid her eyes upward to meet his, slyness in her glance. "I read in the papers that Rose Clifford's funeral is this morning. Why aren't you there?"

Alex frowned. "What's that supposed to mean?" he asked, surprised.

"You're in uniform." Lisa's eyes swept over him. "When we were together, you only worked on Saturday when there was a special case. Naturally, I supposed you'd be at the funeral because of the murder. Most of the town will be." She shrugged her shoulders and looked away. "Just curious why you're not, that's all."

"Well, I happen to be on the job most Saturdays these days, special case or no special case, Lisa," Alex replied in a level tone. "Times change, you know?"

"Yes," Lisa replied tartly, "I do know."

"Look," Alex tried on a gentler note, "I don't want to argue with you. But since we are here, I'd really like to know how you've been. Everything okay with you?"

Lisa reacted to the question as though Alex had struck her. "If by okay you mean am I moving and eating and going through one day after another like normal people are supposed to do? Then yes, I'm okay. Is that what you wanted to know?"

"I'm sorry I asked," Alex heaved miserably. "My mistake. It looks like I'm still the bad guy and you hate me, right?"

"Of course I hate you! I hate us both," she cried, eyes wide and wild. "We let our son die! There he is, in the ground. Our little boy is dead!"

"I'm sorry," Alex said. "I really am, Lisa. I wish I could turn back the calendar and undo all that's happened, but I can't. We lost our son and that's a tragedy we both have to face and live with. It's not easy for you or for me. I'm trying to get on with my life, Lisa. And you should, too."

"Oh!" Lisa snorted. "You mean I should find a man and get married and maybe have a few kids? Is that what you mean? Is that what you're going to do, Alex? Find yourself a woman and make a few more babies?" She pointed to Carl's grave. "There's our son, what about him?"

With that, Lisa dropped to her knees on the frost-cold ground, covered her face with her mittened hands, and began to sob. Alex felt whipped. There was no use trying to reach her, and he knew it. Lisa was lost in the miasma of grief. She was locked in it. It was the only way she could hold on to Carl. The only way left.

Head bowed, shoulders slumped, and numb to the cold, Alex trudged slowly back to the Blazer. The last thing he saw from his rearview mirror as he drove away was Lisa on her knees next to Carl's grave, her yellow hair sticking out from under the blue knit hat, arms wrapped around herself, watching him go.

CHAPTER SIX
A PICTURE OF DEATH

Alex drove to his office thoroughly shaken, not only by the encounter with Lisa but also by the reflection of himself that he had so clearly witnessed in those brief, traumatic moments at Carl's graveside. The awful realization had hit him square between the eyes that since Carl's death, he had indeed been sharing Lisa's burden, not only of loss, but of guilt. Standing in that cold, bitter morning air, he suddenly understood how deeply he had buried his own sense of responsibility for Carl's death. So deeply that only grief and pain were allowed to surface as they had the previous evening at Howell's. But guilt was there all the time, struggling to get out. And it was guilt that was killing him.

Perhaps his impulsive visit to Carl's grave had been some inner, instinctive attempt to expiate himself. To come to terms with Carl's death and his role in it. And with Carl. Well, it would take time to do that, but perhaps now he had a starting place.

As he approached the outskirts of town, Alex brought his thoughts back into the present with the stern reminder that it was time to let the past rest for now and to get on with his job. As for Lisa, he had already done all he could to fix the unfixable. There was nothing more to try, no route not taken. Now he had to face his own demons and deal with them.

Nursing a fresh cup of coffee and stopping for a brief word with one of his deputies, Alex picked up the most recent Clifford folder from forensics. Tucking it under his arm, he walked back to his office, heaved himself into his desk chair, and began to read. The first item detailed the forest area where Rose's body had been found. Most of the footprints at the scene were indistinguishable due to a thick carpet of leaves and pine needles. There was, however, a fairly obvious path where a somewhat heavy object had been dragged from the road, presumably by the killer. Last on the list were two short strands of hair found on Rose's clothing, the same as hairs found in her kitchen area. Neither matched the victim's. The hairs were very light and of natural coloration, but the strands were broken, so no hair root for DNA was possible. They could be from either a man or a woman. If they belonged to the killer, he or she had been very careful. Or very lucky.

Among the fingerprints lifted from the cups taken from Rose's apartment was one that did not belong to Rose. After running it through the system, the results were "zip" (Harry Donahue's notation). No suspects, ergo no score on the board. And the print was no match to either Fowler or Sayers, both of whom were in the system's files. As Alex reread the report, discouragement set in. The cup print proved nothing. Rose might have made coffee for an unknown neighbor or friend; the possibilities were endless. It was at this point that the phone rang. Harry Donahue was on the other end of the line.

"Hey, Banks! Just got a call. We found the Clifford Honda and it's being towed to the county garage as we speak. Get moving and meet me there in ten minutes."

Alex arrived at the garage in six minutes flat, strobes flashing all the way. As Donahue reported, the Honda had been towed in and, as expected, the interior was a sorry sight. Reminded to look and not touch, the two men made a cursory inspection of the car's interior, maintaining a careful distance, as ordered. Forensics would be going over the vehicle inch by inch before the next few hours were out, and it would tell a gruesome tale.

As he took in the sickening picture of death, Alex's jaw hardened in anger. Dried blood was everywhere, spattered over the front seats and dashboard. Next to him, Donahue cursed under his breath.

"We know she was struck from behind," Alex said, bending over for a better view of the car's interior through the driver's side window. "The killer, hiding in the back seat, evidently waited for her with a hammer and a knife. With the seat blocking victim from killer, the hammer was used for the initial strike and the knife to finish her off."

"A dirty, rotten bit of business," Donahue commented with disgust. "You can see where her body must have been dragged out of the driver's seat and shoved into the front passenger seat. Blood smears all over. Then the killer climbed in the front seat, drove to the place where he planned to leave her, got the body onto a sheet, probably plastic, and dragged her into the woods. The final touch was the leaves. Job done, he covered up his handiwork, took off, then got rid of the car."

"Yeah," Alex agreed bitterly. "First he kills her and then he disposes of her and of the murder scene, putting as much distance as he could manage between them. Pretty slick."

"Oh yeah, he's a tricky one all right," Donahue commented icily. "We were lucky that we didn't have some heavy rain, or even snow. That gully we dug the car out of is deep and messy. Anyhow, now that we have the vehicle, it would help if we also found the murder weapon. At the moment, the crime scene unit is covering the gully where the Honda was ditched. They'll crawl all over the area." He shook his head. "We're going to run a lot of hurdles if we want to catch this guy, my friend. Maybe the gully will turn up something. I'll let you know."

It was four o'clock when Alex concluded his business for the day and decided to call Jenny at home. To his pleasure, she answered right away, and when he invited her to join him for dinner anywhere she chose, she laughed and said she would like to go Italian. They did.

Sitting across the table over pasta and breadsticks dripping warm butter, Alex updated Jenny on the news, beginning with the notice he received that the Cliffords would be clearing out Rose's apartment on Monday. Then, of course, the apartment would be repainted and leased to a new tenant.

Moving on to the investigation, Alex related the facts as he knew them which included the discovery of Rose's Honda, currently being fine-combed for evidence by the crime scene techs, and a run-down on the lab reports of both the hair and the unidentified partial print yielded by the cup from Rose's apartment. "No suspects on the list," Alex commented with a helpless gesture. "At this point, nada."

Alex reached for a fresh breadstick and studied it thoughtfully. "You know, Jen, it seems strange we can't find anyone who was close to Rose. You're it, so far as we know. She lived in this neck of the woods all her life, yet no close friends?"

"Rose was Rose," Jenny replied with a wistful smile. "Very nice and very private. I believe she was the kind of woman who preferred male company to running and gossiping with the girls. Some women are like that." She paused a moment. "I've been wondering, do you really think it has to be a man you're looking for?"

Alex let out a breath. "After what I saw in that car of hers, I can't visualize a woman being able to handle the job. Or being able to drag a body from the road to where we found it. Of course," he admitted, his expression shadowing, "it's possible. Just not likely."

Jenny looked away, suddenly pale. When she returned her glance to Alex, her mouth was a tight line and there were tears crowding her eyelids. "Alex," she asked, almost choking on the words, "can we change the subject? Please?"

"Oh, boy," Alex half-groaned. "I'm sorry." He reached across the table for her fingers and massaged them gently. "Honestly, I've been so deep in this mess that I didn't stop to think what you must feel when... look, I am truly sorry."

"That's okay," Jenny assured him with a weak smile. "Please, let's not spoil our evening. I'm fine, honest."

"All right then," he said, leaning forward, still holding her fingers in his. "I've been wanting to ask you a rather personal question and now is as good a time as any to do it." He furrowed his brow and said in a low voice: "Why hasn't some guy grabbed you up, pretty lady? I'm serious. Tell me the answer, because I have to know."

Jenny snatched her fingers away, tilted her head back, and laughed, her long lashes making soft shadows on her cheeks. "Have you forgotten that we live in the North Country, Sheriff?" she said, the shine returning to her eyes. "This is mountain land where professional matchmakers are given a permanent place in the unemployment line."

"Baloney! I think you're too fussy." Alex smirked, looking straight into her eyes. "You're really a beautiful woman," he said, meaning it. "I think you'd have your pick of men."

"Well, what about Rose?" Jenny countered. "She was a happy single, right?"

"Maybe," Alex replied slowly. "But I see you differently." His eyes lit up mischievously. "I hear tell there's a heap of eligible doctors in that hospital of yours. No nibbles at your heels, at all?"

This time Jenny giggled. "I work swathed in shapeless blues, my head capped and my face covered with a mask. I stand for hours beside an entire team, doing my job, often without an exchange of a personal word, and at times not even certain who is in the room with me. We're like clones, all in identical blues, the same white masks. Dramatic, maybe, but not romantic, take my word for it. Don't believe everything you see on television."

Alex reached for one of Jenny's hands and fondled it. "Such lovely hands." Then he brought the hand up to his lips and gave the palm a light kiss. "I would like to kiss your lips, Jenny Wyland. Think you could handle that?"

Jenny bent toward him. "I think I could, Sheriff. Why don't we find out?"

SUNDAY, NOVEMBER 8

It was almost ten thirty in the morning when Jennie set a pot boiling for tea, having just returned from a nine o'clock church service, and began to dig into letters that needed writing and laundry waiting to be done. But her mind kept returning to the previous evening with Alex.

The evening had been wonderful. Not just so-so or pretty good, but wonderful. Alex had kissed her very properly, then kissed her again. He had kissed her in the car when he brought her home. Then he had kissed her at the door, this time holding close for a long, tender minute before he smiled down at her, said goodnight, and headed down the hall toward the elevator. Before he turned the corner, he looked back and their eyes locked. Then he was gone.

Was she in love? Or was she simply getting a kick from the attention of a man she once had a silly, girlhood crush on, many years ago and in another lifetime? Whatever the explanation, at the moment, she cared not. She liked the way Alex looked at her and the ways his eyes, so blue and clear, made her feel. She was glad he had asked to come over late that afternoon. It had been too long since she had felt just plain good to be around someone. There had been other men, of course, but nothing that in the end would work for a lifetime. Was Alex the guy she had waited for? Only time would tell.

Bringing herself around to the present and to the coming evening with Alex, she wrapped the good feeling around her. The gray cold outside made it a perfect time to stay home in front of a warm, romantic fire. She would surprise Alex and bake one of those things they say women are supposed to bake to please their man. With that last thought in mind, she chuckled aloud, raised her eyes to heaven, and headed for the kitchen.

It was after six o'clock that evening when Alex parked his Chevy Blazer in the lot adjacent to High Ridge Apartments. Sprinting along the paved walkway that ran the length of the building, he came to the corner and turned toward the main entrance. Once inside the outer vestibule, he ran a gloved finger along a brass panel where the tenants' names and doorbell buttons were lined up next to an intercom. He pushed the button next to apartment 610, identified himself, waited for the door buzzer to sound, and then, his step light and hurried, he entered the lobby.

Across the street someone was watching. Alex had not noticed the dark sedan that had pulled up to the curb in front of High Ridge as he turned into the lot. Only after Alex had disappeared into the building did the car cough alive, and, with a rapid shifting of gears, pull into traffic and speed away.

CHAPTER SEVEN
SURPRISES

SUNDAY AFTERNOON, NOVEMBER 8

It was moving toward noon when Ben Sayers finished grading test papers due for class the next day. Once the last paper was marked, he slipped into his overcoat, left his Grover flat, and strode down the street in the direction of Haley's Market. He would pick up a steak and pork chops plus a few things he needed for the week. Not much, only what he could carry. He could easily drive the short distance, but he needed the exercise, cold weather or no.

He was pushing the cart down Haley's grocery aisle, one eye on the list in his hand, the other scouting out the items he was looking for, when he looked up and saw a woman at the far end of the aisle, pushing her cart toward him. He paused and frowned. The woman seemed vaguely familiar. Like himself, she was concentrating on the grocery shelves, picking up an item here and there, then moving on. As they came abreast of one another she looked up and their glances met. With no note of recognition from either side, in the next instant she had passed him by. Sayers frowned again. He felt nothing close to definite recollection, only a vague nudge. He was always running into people he knew, he reminded himself, mostly the parents of kids in his class. It happened all the time. Shrugging off the incident, he returned his attention to his shopping and went on his way.

Once back in his kitchen, Sayers put potatoes and pork chops in the oven to bake and was just about to set the table for dinner when it hit him. The woman he had seen in the market was the mystery woman! It was the same person he had seen in the school parking lot with Rose.

Yes, he was certain of it. Excited, his hand reached toward the telephone to call the sheriff, but he quickly drew it back. The sheriff's office was closed. It was Sunday.

His failure to recognize the woman annoyed him. Had it come to him at the market, he could have jotted down the plate number of her car, or even followed her home if she was on foot. Well, he told himself, turning back to his dinner preparations, there was no point in letting hindsight get the best of him. He would give the sheriff a call the next day. If nothing came of it, he would find out the name of the mystery woman on his own, one way or the other.

But right now, he thought, turning toward the oven, he had other, more important matters on his mind. Some he would attend to after he had enjoyed his evening meal.

SUNDAY NIGHT

It was cold and dark outside the cabin. A light, wet snow was falling. Inside, Chuck Fowler was angry. His insides had been in a grinder since Friday and his talk with the sheriff. Pacing back and forth across the room, he mentally relived their conversation until, filled to overflowing with bilious rancor, he wanted to punch anything or anybody within reach.

Hot stuff Banks! He smoldered to himself. Him with his lousy suspicions, thinking he could push people around because he wore a badge. Acting big because his old girlfriend got herself knocked off. Banks was probably as glad to be rid of the little two-timer as he was. Yeah, little Rosie baby. Little cheating Rosie.

His racing thoughts took him back to some weeks before their date at Shepherd's Cove, and he winced, muttering to himself what a sap he was, panting at her skirts, biding his time, playing the nice guy, the gentleman. He had a good time at it, too, because he liked women with a little class. But she was the one playing with him. Just like the others, he thought with a sour grin. Well, he got in the last word, that's for sure, he snickered. He could still see the look on her face when he let her have what she had coming to her!

Now, wouldn't you know it, stinking luck? History was repeating itself. He'd found himself another babe and what happens? This one goes and gets uppity after a little tiff and he gets tossed out on his ear. Well, this little high-hat chickadee wasn't gonna get away with it, no more than Rosie did. "No way," he muttered. "No way."

Lips twisted into a self-satisfied smirk, he picked up the telephone, punched in a number, and wet his lips while he listened to it ring. "So you're home tonight," he practiced crooning into the mouthpiece. "Ya waiting for me, Cutie Pie? Well, come on out, because I'm waiting for you, too." The phone continued to ring but no one answered.

He snickered and hung up the phone. "Not home and it's after midnight. Cheating, no doubt. I'll show her," he grunted aloud as he reached for another beer. "This time I'll show her good and proper."

CHAPTER EIGHT
MURDER ON BUTLER ROAD

MONDAY, NOVEMBER 9

Marge Grant took the early morning call from the state police, transferring it immediately back to Alex's office where he was bent over a second cup of coffee and the prior week's reports, determined to catch up. When the outside phone line rang and broke into his concentration, he glanced at it with annoyance before reluctantly reaching to pick it up. Donahue's abrasive voice, so far removed from his usual smooth tenor, delivered the news that another woman had been found murdered.

"She was discovered about seven forty this morning," Donahue continued in grim monotone. "A school bus loaded with teenagers was on its way down Butler Road when one of the kids looked out a window and spotted an arm protruding from a pile of wet leaves stacked along the side of the road. From the looks of it, the body was dumped, then given a quick cover with whatever leaves were handy. There were some snow flurries last night so it was pretty messy. The victim was a twenty-five-year-old female by the name of Lonny Jerome, a waitress at Kirker's Diner. She was stabbed, just like the Clifford woman. Can't give you much more than that right now," Donahue added, disgustedly. "You might want to stop by and see Doc Morris. He can fill you in on all the morbid details."

Alex put down the phone. Another killing. Another woman dead. He went to his office door and signaled Will Burke to come in, then returned to his desk. A minute later, he was repeating Donahue's news while Will sat hunched forward in a nearby chair, his arms resting on his thighs as he heard Alex out.

"Two stabbings within a little better than a week of one another! What's going on?" Alex all but roared. "We've been trying to find out who killed Rose; now there's another woman in the morgue, and we have to rethink the entire investigation?"

"Whew," Will responded with a shake of his head. "Nothing like this ever took place in these parts as far as I've ever heard tell."

Alex looked up at the ceiling in an effort to get a grip on his thoughts, then brought his glance back to Will. He released a cynical, mirthless laugh. "All we have to do to get at the truth is to decide whether Rose was killed by someone who wanted her dead or, if by some twist of chance, she became a psychopath's murder victim of the day. While we're doing that, we tie Lonny Jerome's murder in there someplace, but who knows where? So, Will, we have to decide," he wound down, his voice rancorous. "Is there a serial killer on the loose or not?"

Will pursed his lips and frowned. "Well," he replied, taking his time to think before continuing, "first off, like you said, Sheriff, we've been going on the supposition that Rose's was a personal killing. Like it or not, we can't very well walk away from that theory. Only now there's a dent in it. We have to look at it as if maybe it was, and maybe it wasn't."

He looked across the desk at Alex and his frown deepened. "But it's odd, ya know? Whoever killed Rose took a lot of time to be mighty careful." He held up an index finger. "He kills her, hides her body and then her car. Like maybe he's playing a game and having a good laugh up his sleeve at the same time. So, let's say it's the same perp who killed Rose and the waitress, okay?" He held up another finger next to the first. "He goes on the prowl again, kills the second victim, and gets sloppy. Just dumps the body, gives it a quick cover-up with some wet leaves, then runs. Doesn't sound like the same careful killer, right? But then again, what if it is? What if he changed his MO on purpose, using the second killing to draw attention away from any personal connection to the first?"

Alex nodded in agreement. "Anything's possible, that's the problem," he grumbled disgustedly, reaching for the phone. He put in a number, spoke a minute or two, then hung up and crossed to where he had tossed his parka over a chair near the door. He picked it up and turned to the deputy.

"The Jerome woman's body is down at the medical examiner's for autopsy right now." He checked his watch and zipped into his coat. "I'll take a run over there and see what Doc Morris has to say. Cover for me here, Will. I'll get back as soon as I can."

It was almost two hours before Alex thumped his way back into county headquarters and out of the cold, gusty afternoon. After a quick hello to Marge, he hung his jacket on its hook in his office and then made a beeline for the back lunchroom with Will trailing only a few steps in his wake. He poured himself a mug of coffee from the urn on a side counter, then pulled out a chair next to one of the lunch tables and sat down. He was tired and his back ached. Worse yet, he saw only more of the same ahead.

He took a swallow of coffee, then exhaled deeply. "Looks like you might be right about us being stuck with two different directions to cover," Alex told the deputy, his voice weary. He nursed the rim of his mug, then went on. "As to the facts of this latest killing, like Rose, the Jerome woman was stabbed with a hunting knife anywhere from ten o'clock Sunday evening to around midnight or shortly thereafter. As in Rose's case, there was no evidence of sexual assault. She died very quickly. What stuck in my mind, Will, was the comment you made about the killer playing a game. That scares me more than a little bit, because if there is a crazy out there with no motive except killing women for sport, we're dealing with a real nasty psychopath who will probably strike again."

Alex rubbed a hand over his eyes, his expression drawn and anxious. "Whether it's true or not, we'll have our hands full when it gets around there's the threat of a nut on the loose. And you know as well as I do, Will, once the newshounds get wind of it, the worst will happen. The snow people will head out and others will just stay away. When profits drop, the local merchants and ski resorts dependent on the tourist dollar will break down the mayor's door."

"It'll happen," Will commented. "You can bet on it. And that's the kind of headache, Sheriff, that'll take more than an aspirin or two to cure."

Alex gave him a nod of silent agreement and strode gloomily back to his office, silently mulling through the present situation and wondering what would happen next.

By three fifteen he had come close to making his way through the stack of work on his desk when the desk buzzer jarred him alert. Marge Grant apologized for the interruption, then announced that Ben Sayers was on the line. He had some very important information.

CHAPTER NINE
HALEY'S MARKET

MONDAY, NOVEMBER 9

Hanging up the phone after Sayers called to announce he had come across the mystery woman, Alex felt a flicker of hope that one piece of the puzzle might be about to fall into place. He had agreed to meet Sayers later that day for a trip to Haley's market. If it turned out that Sayers was right, then in all probability the mystery woman would reside somewhere in Grover, probably in the general neighborhood of the market. Hopefully.

It would also mean that the woman's verbal confrontation with Rose was personal. Grover children attended Grover schools, which eliminated the parent connection. Once the woman's name was determined, they would be close to learning the whole story. The trick of the moment was to locate the woman.

He was supposed to meet Sayers at his flat in Grover at six thirty. It was now close to three o'clock and he had arranged through John Logan to interview several of the teachers at four. His curiosity banked for the moment, Alex gave Deputy Burke the high sign and the two were soon on their way to Weston Elementary.

It was six twenty-five when Alex pulled up to the address Sayers had given him. He slipped his Blazer into a parking spot at the curb, got out, and looked around. Dusk was settling in, obscuring the encircling mountains with a wintry blanket of night. With the collar of his parka pulled up against the cut of the wind, his glance took in the row of weathered, two-story dwellings caught in the streetlight's glow, then moved along to a refurbished Victorian standing regally erect amid its lesser neighbors, an ornately lighted "Bed and Breakfast" sign beckoning warm welcome to any passerby en route to the snow-covered hills. He took in a craft shop and antique store, both of which catered to – as well as depended on – the tourist trade in order to stay alive. He wondered what effect a local panic due to a psychopathic killer on the loose would have on business. No, he knew what would ensue should he be unable to do the job he had been elected to do. And soon.

Brought back to the business at hand by the sudden rise of a snappish wind, Alex rechecked the address Sayers had given him. The house was a shingled two-family with Sayers occupying the second-floor flat. The distant echoing of the doorbell as he pressed the button next to Sayers' nameplate was followed almost at once by the click of a door being opened, then closed. Then came the tap, tap of feet hurrying down the flight of stairs.

"Glad you're here, Sheriff," Ben Sayers said in greeting as he came bustling through the front door with his coat dangling over one arm. And then, with barely a pause for breath, he bounced down the steps to the sidewalk and, with Alex watching in amusement, he jostled himself into his overcoat, flung a plaid scarf haphazardly around his neck, and arranged a fur-brimmed hat atop his head. "I dare say it's getting rather nippy," he remarked, pulling a pair of leather gloves from his coat pocket. He tugged on a glove and looked at Alex questioningly as he pulled on the other. "Let's go, Sheriff. Your car or mine?"

"She wasn't at all bad looking," Sayers was saying in an animated voice, describing the mystery woman as Alex guided the Blazer through the darkening streets. "Slender, with very blonde hair. Bumping into familiar faces occurs quite often when you teach school, so I didn't give it much thought at the time. Until I got home, that is. Then, too late, I remembered."

"Well, we'll take a look around and see what we can learn," Alex remarked as they pulled into the far side of Haley's parking area adjacent to the building. A minute or so later, the two men strolled casually across the lot, turned the corner, and went in the front entrance. The market, Alex noted, was the usual run-of-the-mill convenience store. At the front of the store, grocery carts were lined up next to the entrance. A young girl at the cash register was checking through the few customers in line while a radio played country and western music to liven up the atmosphere. "She's not here," Sayers said, slapping his gloves against one hand as they finished a tour of the aisles.

Alex shrugged. "Didn't expect anything different. Just wanted to check things out and do a quick take of the neighborhood."

By the time they got back to the Blazer, a light snow had begun to fall. Fat, white flakes drifted down from the now-dark sky; already a light blanket of white covered everything in sight. Alex had just clicked open the Blazer doors when Sayers grabbed his coat sleeve and shook it.

"It's her!" He lisped excitedly. "She's just getting out of that car over there. Across the parking lot. Turn to your left a little and you'll see her."

Alex turned. Then he blinked. Several feet away a woman was closing the driver's side door of her car. He heard the lock click. Then she began to walk gingerly toward the store entrance, blonde hair sticking out from under a knit hat and bobbing against the blue of her pea coat. It was Lisa!

"That's the one!" Sayers sputtered triumphantly. "That's the woman I saw with Rose in the parking lot. You've got her, Sheriff. You've got her!"

Alex stared in disbelief. Lisa? He watched as she walked through the flutter of falling snowflakes until she came to the corner of the building and disappeared around it.

"Okay, Sheriff, what are you going to do now?" Sayers asked excitedly.

Stunned, his thought disconnected by the shock of what he had just seen and learned, Alex pulled a pad and pencil out of his jacket pocket and squinted across the distance to Lisa's car. Ignoring Sayers, he jotted something down.

Sayers threw back his shoulders. "She's in the market. I asked you what you're going to do, Sheriff," he demanded heatedly.

"Nothing," Alex told him, his voice controlled and deceptively calm.

"Not a thing, Mr. Sayers. Nothing."

Sayers gawked at him with an expression of disbelief. "Are you serious?" he stammered, clearly angry now. "What do you mean by nothing?"

"Calm down," Alex said, quietly. "I've got the license plate number. The state police will take over from here." He gestured toward the Blazer. "Now, please get in. We're leaving."

Fuming, Sayers complied, making no effort to hide his frustration on the return ride to his flat. He was seething mad. But too bad, Alex thought. He was not about to toss Lisa to the lions without knowing all the facts. Until he did, some heavy questions hung in the air. And, he thought decisively, that's the way it's going to be. Sayers could like it or not.

After dropping off the sputtering teacher at the curbside of his flat, Alex headed for home. On the drive over the mountain roads, he worked to clear the turmoil from his thoughts, concentrating on the rhythmic beat of the windshield wipers and the now-heavy swirl of fresh, plump snowflakes in their downward spiral through the glow of the headlights. He took the mountain's curved roads slowly, his peripheral vision absorbing the light traffic moving either to or from the high peaks, many with loaded rooftop ski racks, others towing snowmobiles behind them. The snow business, with its classy ski lodges, fresh powder, and challenging moguls – for the present at least, he reckoned – was making a lot of people happy as well as other people rich.

His thoughts came back to Lisa, still finding it hard to absorb the fact that she was Sayers' mystery woman. How did she know Rose? As a sense of foreboding began to take hold, he turned his thoughts to Jenny. But those reflections were instantly cooled by the guilty truth he hated to admit to himself. He was entertaining warm feelings of attraction toward a woman, while his ex-wife was digging herself into a mental hole somewhere, wallowing in her misery, hating him and hating herself. And now he learns she was in some way connected to Rose, possibly about to be implicated in a murder. He had climbed up on a soapbox trying to convince himself that it was time to move on with his life. The truth was that life was becoming a vicious treadmill. And right at the moment, he wanted to get off.

Tomorrow he would lay out the whole story to Donahue, and then he would step back and let him handle it. Alex's association with the six-foot-plus, sober-faced and smooth-tongued Irishman went back to the days when they were both at the police academy. They had met there and become easy friends. He knew Harry's wife, Janette, and their daughter, Kate. Fortunately, Harry was acquainted with most of Alex's personal history and all that went with it. Alex could trust the guy to tread easily and to be discreet.

As he reflected back on the scene with Lisa at Carl's gravesite, Alex still felt the sting of the accusations she had hurled at him. He could still hear her asking if he planned to "find yourself a woman and make a few more babies."

Could it be that her innocent question as to why he was not at Rose's funeral had not been so innocent a question, after all? As he realized where his thoughts were taking him, he sensed a cold cloud of fear closing in.

CHAPTER TEN
THE DISTRICT ATTORNEY

TUESDAY, NOVEMBER 10

Chuck Fowler's alibi for the approximate time of Rose's death, however shaky it may have appeared, proved out. His pals at the Glens Falls bar backed up his story while the bartender, although he could not swear to the exact time, stated that he recalled seeing Fowler at the bar drinking beer, shooting darts, and watching a football game with a bunch of his buddies over a time period that covered a span of several hours.

Unfortunately for Fowler, when the second murdered girl's identity was confirmed, he was back on the hot seat. Lonny Jerome, the dead girl, had been seeing Fowler for a while, and like Rose, wound up on the receiving end of his temper. According to her best friend, Lonny had run dashing into her house late one night sporting ugly welts on both arms and proceeded to pour out the story of Fowler's rage and abuse. Right after the incident, disgusted and more than a little frightened, Lonny had told Fowler to get lost. Then the nasty phone calls began. Now she was dead, and this time, Fowler had no alibi.

From the time the office door closed behind them that morning, Marge Grant and Will Burke had done little more than answer agitated telephone inquiries. As Will predicted, the story of the second murder had been blown up by the media and almost at once the phone had caught fire. Alex, however, attended to the priority item on his agenda that day, which was to shut his office door, settle down behind his desk, and contact Donahue. When he had him on the line, Alex made no attempt to mince words; he simply laid out the details as he knew them. He began with the confrontation between Lisa and Rose at the school, then went on to describe what had taken place in Haley's parking lot when Sayers' mystery woman, of all people, turned out to be Lisa.

As expected, Donahue agreed to check the matter out, adding his acknowledgment that velvet gloves were called for where Lisa was concerned. He went on to advise Alex to relax, promising to get in touch when the matter was taken care of. After hanging up the phone, Alex released a long breath of relief. Now he could get down to the business at hand.

He began by taking a good look at the impending criminal charges against Chuck Fowler for the first-degree murder of Lonny Jerome. The investigation, in his judgment, had failed to turn up enough solid evidence to result in a Grand Jury indictment against Fowler, much less conviction of murder by a jury should events proceed that far. His judgment, however, might not be one shared by an ambitious district attorney, a speculation which eventually proved out.

Alex then moved on to the forensic evidence from Rose's Honda that had been sent for analysis to the New York State Crime Lab, which had, to date, neither proved nor disproved anything. The killer had left nothing of himself behind. Both of Fowler's vehicles had been impounded and put under exacting examination by the CSU technicians. The results of their analysis would not be available for some time. Alex wondered what might eventually show up. Fowler was the proverbial dead duck if there was even a shred of evidence found to connect him to the Jerome girl's murder.

In the long run, although it seemed there was no way Fowler could be charged for Rose's murder, the irony lay in the fact that he would be tainted by it, nonetheless. Not by any legal process, certainly, but by simple implication. If the D.A. did nail Fowler for Lonny's murder, silence from the prosecutor's office regarding his status in Rose's murder could have swaying power; let the public assume what they will. Anything to take the heat off the D.A.'s office. Neat. If justice was going to be blind, she would be reaching pretty far out to do it. If it worked, the end result could mean that a murderer – the psycho who killed Rose Clifford, and yes, possibly Lonny Jerome as well – would roam the streets free.

Until the next time.

So much for speculation. Alex let out a long, tired breath. He should get a move on. District Attorney Raymond Peterson was going to make a public statement at two o'clock that afternoon. He had requested deputies be assigned to the meeting room and Alex had complied. He would be there, as well. It should be interesting.

When Alex arrived at the County Court House, he was not surprised by the number of people already gathered. Some were huddled in animated groups on the sidewalk, while others were making their way up the courthouse steps and through the ornate oak doors that graced the entrance. The townspeople had worked up a head of steam for sure, Alex reflected, as he joined those headed inside. With the news media not missing a beat when it came to speculation about the hunt for a killer, it was hardly surprising that people were hyped. They were scared and wanted answers. Many approached Alex shouting out questions, which he countered by raising up one hand and shaking his head. "No comment at this time," was his only reply.

As expected, the meeting room, when Alex came through the door, was jam-packed with people and a tumult of sound. Folding chairs, most already occupied, were set up in rows stretching from the podium to the back wall with an aisle left open down the center. News people, some with cameras perched on sloping shoulders, were forging their way toward the front, vying for the prime spots close to the podium where deputies assigned to the spectacle stood watch.

Alex had no problem locating Harry Donahue. Smiling and natty in his knife-pleated grays, the trooper was sitting half perched on the edge of a table set against the back wall.

"You look like you're poised for flight," Alex commented as he stepped aside to allow people entering the room behind him to pass by.

Donahue chuckled. "Darn right. Just waiting for the circus to begin."

Alex was about to reply when District Attorney Peterson made his entrance through a door at the front of the room near the podium. He was accompanied by Weston's mayor, Paul Russ, and two suited gentlemen Alex had never seen before. Peterson said a few words to the three men. When all three nodded agreement, Peterson, obviously satisfied that his orders were understood, left them and strode to the podium.

Raymond Peterson was a well-groomed man in his late forties. He was dressed casually in dark blue trousers, a muted plaid sport jacket, and a solid blue tie. He had a full head of brown-gray hair, a hawkish nose, and knowing, hazel eyes that missed little that went on around him. Reaching the podium, he appraised his audience. His glance took in the newspaper and television people now crowded into the space below the podium, and he smiled, conscious of the electric tension in the room. After a long, thoughtful pause, he reached for the gavel on the dais, raised it, and brought it down with a resounding crack.

In an instant, the chatter and sound of movement in the room disintegrated into a faint rustle and hum. Having gained control of his audience, Peterson folded his hands together in front of him, leaned forward, and started speaking. "First," he began, "I wish to publicly offer my heartfelt sympathies to the Clifford and Jerome families. Something very terrible and evil has brought tragedy into your lives. Now it's time," he said in solemn tones, "for justice to be served." He paused, allowing his words to linger a bit. Then he gradually reclaimed his full height, his eyes bright and alert as they moved over the room. His voice became more animated, his words saturated with confidence and promise.

"Secondly, I wish to publicly state that there is no reason for the citizens of Collier County to live in fear of a killer on the loose. In fact," he declared, staring into the camera lenses zooming in on him, "we are very close to an arrest."

At his words, there was a sudden rustle of movement throughout the room, accompanied by the agitated buzz of voices. Peterson took a step back and waited a moment, allowing his words to make their impact before he stepped back to the microphone. "I'm certain," he said in a tone placating yet forceful, "most of you understand that in the matter of any criminal investigation taking place within the jurisdiction of this, or any official office, details that could lead to a solution of a crime, or crimes, must be carefully handled. You must also understand how impossible it is to share knowledge of those details with the general public. Anything which obstructs or delays the solution of a criminal act should be, and is, considered a criminal act in itself. You must trust us, as professionals in the field of justice, to bring these cases to a speedy, satisfactory conclusion. As I have told you and will say again, we are very close to an arrest."

He then went on to offer further assurances that the killer of the two local women would soon be in custody, ending his speech with another bid for patience. After he thanked everyone for their support, ignoring the battery of questions thrown at him, he left the podium. Joined by the mayor, he slipped quickly out of the room via the same door through which he had entered. The two men who had accompanied Peterson quickly shifted to a position in front of the door, effectively barring egress to anyone bold enough to follow. The deputies joined them. The circus was over.

Alex and Donahue exchanged significant glances as they made their hurried departure from the courthouse, both eager to escape ahead of the crowds.

"Looks like our friend Fowler might just be headed for a double fall," Donahue commented once they were outside and clipping down the steps toward the street.

"Do tell," Alex replied dryly. "A new surprise every day."

"I'll call you later," Donahue shot back over his shoulder as he opened the door to the state police car parked at the curb. "Have a good one."

Alex stepped quickly along to his own vehicle parked in the official lot and went back to work. Once again in his office, he pushed all thoughts of Peterson, Fowler, and Sayers to one side and began flipping through the reports left on his desk, the duty schedules to be assigned, and the list of problems to be solved yesterday. He was grateful when Marge

Grant poked her head around the corner of his office doorway and, in her most officious tone of voice, told him it was pushing toward five o'clock and time to put away whatever he was doing and go home. She had, she informed him, already rolled incoming calls over to the state police.

Alex thanked her and wished her good night. Mentally depleted and bone weary, he locked up his office, stepped into the cold and darkening night, then headed for his Chevy Blazer and drove home. Later, settled contentedly into the warmth of his kitchen, Alex emptied a can of clam chowder into a pot, then set it to heat while he put together a couple of ham and cheese sandwiches on rye. After pouring himself a tall glass of cold milk, he dug in. Hunger appeased and the kitchen in order, he stripped down and headed for the shower. A half hour later he was clad in pajamas, robe, and slippers, almost ready to retire to the living room and his recliner, when the telephone rang. It was Donahue.

As Alex had known he would be, Donahue was as good as his word. The trooper had spoken with Lisa in the privacy of his office late that same afternoon. The discussion, he said, had scarcely begun when Lisa broke down in tears. Once she had regained control of herself and dried her eyes, she blurted out the whole story. She confessed that after learning that Alex was seeing someone, she went off the deep end for a while. And yes, she had arranged to meet Rose in the school parking lot, and yes, she had said a lot of things she had no right to say. She was wrong and she was sorry. But kill her? No, she could never do such a monstrous thing, Lisa had vehemently asserted. And Donahue believed her.

"Cross her off as a suspect, Banks," the trooper told him reassuringly. "Your ex-wife is in a bad way, no doubt about it. But she's no killer. You can relax until we have something substantial to work on. This mystery woman tidbit isn't it."

Alex hung up the phone feeling a new lightness of heart. Thanks to Donahue, Lisa was out of the fray – for the time being, anyway. Which was good enough for now.

He sat down in his recliner and put up his feet, still trying to deal with the persistent feeling that he was missing something, that there was some link in the chain attached to Rose's murder that he had over-looked. He rubbed at his eyes with the heels of his hands. His brain felt clogged, resistant to logic, to everything. He felt alone and empty and a little lost. His thoughts turned to Jenny. Should he call her? He looked down at his watch.

"Nine o'clock," he whispered under his breath. No, too late. She was due in the OR ready to scrub by six o'clock the next morning and would be on her feet for hours after that. Tomorrow, he promised himself. Tomorrow would have to do.

Eyes closed, he leaned back against the lounger's headrest. He wondered if he should let Jenny know that Lisa was Sayers' mystery woman. No, he decided almost at once, it was unfair to expose the story of Lisa's pain and problems to anyone when it was unnecessary. She had been his wife and mother to his child. Despite whatever else may have driven them apart, he still owed her a measure of loyalty and respect. If Donahue was satisfied, he would be satisfied, too.

Alex's thoughts turned to Sayers, and he wondered again if the man would be able to curb his curiosity when it came to his mystery woman's identity. He doubted it. He had been too frustrated and angry. But, maybe he has a right to be, Alex reluctantly conceded. Sayers and Rose had been coworkers and friends. Under similar circumstances, he would react the same way if unceremoniously whisked away from an important clue he had uncovered. Especially a clue which might lead to catching a killer.

He rubbed his eyes and blinked. He needed to get some sleep. His head was aching from the unanswered questions rattling around inside it. Tomorrow he would give his brain a workout, but right now he needed a good eight hours of oblivion.

Stifling a yawn, he stood up, stretched, and headed upstairs to his bedroom, switching off lights along the way. When he finally turned out his bedside lamp to let the darkness surround him, he hunched over onto his side, socked down his pillow, found just the right spot and then, with the exhale of a long, deep breath, he let himself drift off.

CHAPTER ELEVEN
SOLOMON'S GORGE HILL

WEDNESDAY, NOVEMBER 11

The snow had begun to pile up during the night. Beginning with a flurry of fat, tumbling flakes early in the evening, there was soon a straight stream of powdery white that meant business. Setting down his coffee mug, Alex looked up at the wall clock and saw that it was pushing toward six forty. He climbed into his parka, gloves, and heavy boots, pulled out the snow shovel where he had it ready to retrieve from a corner of the garage, and minutes later was tackling the job of clearing his driveway. The rumbling clatter of snow plows opening up the neighboring roadways reached him from the near distance. The world, Alex reflected, was coming to life.

Thirty minutes later he stomped into headquarters bringing a rush of cold air with him, expressing surprise to find Marge already at her post in front of a file cabinet, a sheaf of papers in her hand. Will was at his desk uploading the latest computer info; two of his deputies greeted him on their way out. Good mornings and comments on the weather exchanged, Alex hung up his jacket and headed for the back room. He filled his mug to the brim with steaming, freshly brewed coffee and went back in his office, where he sat down behind his desk, ready to face the day.

Rose's case file was in front of him. Resigned to tackle it, he very slowly and deliberately began to pick his way through the contents. He began with the coroner's report. His own firsthand inspection of the Honda, along with professional input from Jake Morris, had painted an all-too-vivid depiction of the killer's vicious attack on Rose. He stared down at the words in front of him until he felt a tightness form in his throat. Moving on, he set the coroner's report to one side and reached for the statements he and Will had taken from the teachers with whom Rose had discussed her plans for the evening she was killed. He paused here and frowned, drawing a mental picture of the faculty lunchroom.

Between the clatter of coffee cups and the rattle of lunch bags, there would have been the usual shoptalk and bits of personal news tossed back and forth, teacher to teacher. It was the time frame that caught his interest. It seemed to him that those in the faculty lunchroom comprised the majority of the isolated few aware of Rose's plans for that evening.

Whom else may she have told? More importantly, he asked himself, when would she have had the free time to tell anyone? He knew Rose had called her mother to relay her weekend plans. And she had also mentioned her plans to Jenny, but only in passing. Next in the file were the statements from Rose's college chums. When Rose failed to appear as pre-arranged, they had surmised that either she had forgotten their date, or perhaps for reasons they could not fathom, stood them up. They tried calling her apartment, but when there was no answer, they were left to their own conclusions. Lastly, he looked over her parents' statements, which did not broaden the information flow even a little bit.

Despite a strong reluctance to avoid the next step, Alex nevertheless pulled a batch of pictures out of a large envelope and laid them carefully across his desk. There were shots of the wooded area where Rose's body was found and pictures of the Honda interior. He went back to the lab reports on both and found it uncanny that the car had given up nothing. No fingerprints, no hair, no other trace evidence. Nothing.

The killer was wily and devious, no doubt about it. He had laid out the entire scenario, planned and orchestrated it down to the last detail. And, Alex concluded, feeling the old anger begin to stir, he could only have pulled it off by knowing Rose, knowing her movements, and knowing how to get into her car. Not Fowler. Aside from the fact that he had an alibi for the night in question, he had no way of knowing her movements. Nope. Not Fowler, that was a given. All else had to center on the last missing part of the puzzle: motive. Why? Why? Why?

Taunted by the list of unanswered questions nagging at his gut, Alex decided to list and document everything he knew, suspected, saw, or heard, right from day one. He could use a recorder. Perhaps something would pop up to get him moving in the right direction before the trail became completely cold and it was too late. He thought of Rose and his resolve hardened. That was something he was determined not to let happen. Not by a long shot!

MERCY HOSPITAL, GROVER

Jenny pushed the gurney through the double doors of the recovery room, turned the patient over to the RN on duty, then retraced her steps back to the OR. She was in the adjoining locker room having just changed into a fresh scrub gown when the wall phone buzzed. It was the nursing supervisor calling to inform her that help was needed in the ER, stat. Taking only a few seconds to splash a handful of cold water on her face and run a comb through her hair, she took the elevator down to the emergency room at ground level, found the nurse in charge, then quickly gave herself over to the organized turmoil. She was assigned the job of setting up triage, channeling incoming patients for medical or surgical attention according to the severity of their sickness or injury. The majority of patients were victims of the first significant snowfall of the season. People, Jenny reflected sadly, were bound to shovel heavy snow or forget to adapt to a sudden shift in driving and walking conditions after a storm. And there were always the early-season schussboomer casualties littered in via rescue squad volunteers, their brightly colored ski garb the telltale evidence that they had somehow collided with nature – or each other. And of course, Jenny thought ruefully, there were also those who sought help because they were just plain sick. The flow went on.

By three o'clock that afternoon the emergency department influx had slowed down considerably. Ambulatory patients had been treated and sent home, some on crutches; others had been either transported to special care units or assigned a bed on one of the general floors. Patient data was being carefully entered into computerized charts, and all pertinent information duly relayed to the relief staff ready to take over.

Both physically and mentally exhausted by quitting time, Jenny punched out, changed into street clothes, and a short time later was steering her car in the direction of the ramp onto I-87 toward Weston and home. The sky was dismal and gray but, she noted gratefully, it had stopped snowing. Driving conditions would soon be greatly improved, thanks to the county plows and salt trucks with their dependably superior efforts to keep the main roads clear for the heavy flow of winter traffic in and out of the mountains.

Jenny took it easy over the initial stretch of the Northway, her thoughts tracing back over the hectic day at the hospital and then, to Alex. There had been no word from him since Saturday night, and she wondered why. She missed him and the soft blue of his eyes and, yes, the way his smile said so much more than his words. Much more. Oh my, yes, she told herself, thinking back to their last few minutes together on Saturday night. The sheriff, she thought, wanting to giggle like a schoolgirl, was a dangerous man indeed.

As Jenny approached Solomon's Gorge Hill, she turned her attention to the last lap of the trek home, noting gratefully that the hill had been plowed almost down to bare asphalt. Eyes pinned to the road, she began her descent, proceeding slowly as she approached a steep, curved, two-lane section of the hill. All too familiar with this particularly treacherous, downward stretch, she shifted the car into a lower gear, braking just enough to begin a slow, easy glide.

Suddenly, her breath caught. She was not slowing down! The brake pedal was hitting the floor! Before she could react further, the car began to pick up speed and, to Jenny's horror, was now completely out of control. Reacting instinctively, Jenny reached for the emergency brake, grabbed it and with all the strength she had in her, pulled it back. Nothing happened.

The car was, in fact, slewing downward in a violent, fishtailing movement. The momentary flash of headlight beams revealed the next curve only seconds away. Fighting frantically to maneuver the vehicle and stay on the road, Jenny gripped the steering wheel, her eyes riveted on the stretch ahead. As she fought to steer into the curve of the mountain, the car went into a skid, arced wildly, jounced over the adjoining shoulders, then swung back onto the road.

Jenny froze. She had made the curve only to find two vehicles directly ahead of her on the road, and her Toyota was racing to close the gap. Without thinking, she gave one desperate pull on the wheel. The car careened erratically over the double line to the left and the next thing she knew, by some miracle, a terrible collision was avoided and the vehicles were now behind her, horns blasting a message of anger, shock, and fright.

Still barreling ahead at full speed, Jenny swung the steering wheel again. This time the car went into a half spin, half skid, weaving toward the right shoulder of the road. As another quick turn abruptly changed the car's momentum, she swung the wheel yet again to the left, thankful that the road ahead was clear. Approaching the final curve before the Gorge overlook, she banked to the opposite side of the road and once more pulled hard on the wheel. Holding it white-knuckle tightly, the car jumped another shoulder. The last thing Jenny saw was a house to the rear of a snow-covered lawn and the bulky form of the elm tree she was headed directly toward.

CHAPTER TWELVE
MERCY HOSPITAL

WEDNESDAY, NOVEMBER 11

By four thirty that afternoon, Alex had called Jenny's apartment a half-dozen times, only to reach her answering machine on each try. Disappointed, he had hung up without leaving a message. Okay, maybe she had plans, he told himself. Maybe she went shopping. People always crowded the markets when the snows hit, and heavy snow had arrived a little early this year. Or maybe she had trouble getting home over the slippery roads. It took a couple of snowstorms before drivers learned to slow down. Or she may have had to work late. Maybe, maybe.

He was just about to give up when a call came in from the state police notifying him of a vehicular mishap off Solomon's Gorge Hill. One casualty, the officer told him, a Jennifer Wyland. Alex hung up, grabbed his jacket from its hook, and tore out of the office, yelling back over his shoulder for Will to take over. He would be at Mercy Hospital in Grover.

Upon his arrival at the hospital's emergency receiving station, Alex was assured by the nurse behind the desk that yes, Jenny Wyland had been injured, but she was in no imminent danger. The doctor had set her fractured arm and was almost finished patching up a few superficial lacerations she had sustained in the accident. The young nurse smiled and promised that she would notify him as soon as the doctors were finished and admissions sent word that a room was ready for her. The patient would then be transported upstairs and he would be allowed to see her.

"Meanwhile," she suggested with a practiced smile, "why don't you make yourself comfortable in the waiting room. It's through there." She motioned toward a door a few feet away. "You can't miss it. It's right down the hall. And by the way," she added as an afterthought, "did you know there's a state trooper here? He just completed the accident report."

Alex followed her directions and found Donahue in the waiting room, leaning casually against a wall in the small, empty room talking into his cell phone. When he looked up and caught sight of Alex, he lifted a finger signaling Alex to give him a minute, then went back to whatever news was causing an already furrowed frown to grow deeper.

When he snapped the instrument shut, his voice was tight and controlled. "Jenny Wyland's car was rigged," he said bluntly, hooking the cell to his belt. "Among other things, the brake lines were cut almost completely through. She had just enough brake fluid to take her a short distance. When enough pressure was applied, her brakes were shot, period. As I understand it, she worked the day shift here at the hospital, which gave somebody easy access to her vehicle in the employee's rear lot. She was lucky. She had her seat belt hooked and for some reason, her emergency brake wasn't totally useless. Plus, she had already shifted into low gear, which gave her a flimsy edge. I don't know how many vehicles she managed to miss. She was flying down that hill before she ended up hitting a tree." He shook his head. "The collision all but destroyed the passenger side of the car. Had the impact involved the driver's side...well, flat out, my friend, she's lucky to be alive."

Alex stared at Donahue a long moment, his words storming into his consciousness. "What the blazes is going on, Harry?" he asked, his eyes flashing. "First Rose, then Lonny Jerome, and now Jenny?"

"Take it easy," Donahue replied, holding up a calming hand. "I'm told Ms. Wyland will need to stay overnight for observation, but look at the bright side. A fractured radius but no cranial damage, except a mild concussion. She's gonna have a headache but she'll be out of here, probably by tomorrow. Better than dead, ol' buddy." An eyebrow shot up and the Irish in his eyes sparked mischievously. "Special gal?"

Alex nodded. "Yeah, she is," he admitted, reason returning. "I want to find out who did this, Harry. And I want to know why!"

"As far as why, that's not too tough a question when you consider where she lived and who she was friends with," Donahue said levelly as he zipped up his jacket and opened the waiting room door. "And also consider what she might know. Could be somebody would feel safer with her out of the way?"

"Sure, it's a possibility," Alex replied, falling in with Donahue's stride down the hall to the hospital exit. "But where's the connection, Harry? Is it me? That doesn't cut it. I never knew Lonny Jerome."

"Objectively speaking, my friend," Donahue responded, softening his tone, "I believe Jenny Wyland somehow posed a threat to someone for the obvious reason that she and Rose were pals. Rose had a story to tell that the killer didn't want told. Did Rose confide the story to her friend? Could be. Now, enter the sheriff. Even eliminating any personal relationship you may have with Jennifer Wyland," Donahue finished as he reached the exit door, "the same threat holds true as far as a worried killer is concerned. And no, you're no missing link. It's the sheriff's job to ask questions. You've been asking. Think about it."

Alex nodded. "I agree with you up to a point," he conceded. "But where does Lonny Jerome fit in?"

Donahue shrugged. "Good question," he said with a grin as he pushed the door open and started outside. "Let me know what you find out."

Alex had barely resumed his place in the waiting room when the nurse gave him the news that Jenny had been officially admitted and was on her way upstairs. Furnished with her floor and room number, Alex headed for the elevator. On the way up, he willed himself to release the tension that had been building from the moment he had taken the call notifying him of the Solomon's Gorge crackup with Jenny's name as the victim involved. He let Harry's words sink in. It was true. Jenny was alive, and for the present, that was all that mattered. Working to put the pieces together would have to wait.

To his surprise, when he rapped on the door to her room and poked his head in, Jenny was sitting up in bed, smiling and alert despite blood-matted hair and taped bandage squares decorating her forehead and chin.

"Look at what my coworkers did to me," she grumbled good-naturedly, lifting her left arm to display a fresh, white cast enclosed in a sling. "Just a little fracture and they have me plastered up like a mummy."

"Oh, yeah?" Alex smirked, relieved to see that Jenny's spirit was as alive and well as her body. "You break your arm, get yourself cut up, then complain about your coworkers and their tender, loving care? Shame on you!"

Jenny shifted on the bed and tilted her nose in the air. "All right, smarty. I've only one arm to work with so you can just fluff up these pillows for me. I'm learning that pain pills don't work very fast. My back is killing me!"

Twenty minutes later, satisfied that Jenny was holding together nicely, Alex gave her a perfunctory kiss on the lips, told her to behave until he returned later on, then left the hospital. The sun was making its last westward descent beneath the mountain peaks as he took the ramp to I-87 and Weston, his mind still floundering, trying to cope with something out of his reach and control. Well, he thought wearily, thinking about the flow of evil stalking its unimpeded way through town, it just might be that Jenny's broken arm could prove a blessing. Without a doubt, it would keep her off the job and on the disability rolls for awhile. Now, if he could only tie her down someplace where she would be protected and safe, he would breathe a lot easier. Someone had tried to kill her. If he was bold enough to try once, there was a very good possibility that he would try again. But there was the question, why? Why Rose? Why Jenny, of all people?

His thoughts seemed to take off without conscious volition, returning to what Lisa had told Donahue. Her reasons for the verbal attack on Rose, she had explained, was because she knew he was dating Rose. If Lisa's reaction to Rose had set off some crazy spark, then might Jenny logically be her target now? His fist banged against the steering wheel. No! He would not let himself go there. Lisa knew nothing when it came to the mechanics of an automobile outside of fueling the gas tank and the necessity for a routine oil change. That was it! And, she was no killer. Period.

He returned to the office to find that Will and Marge were maintaining normal operations, handling calls and complaints, taking care of paperwork and the usual in-out flow of computer data. He hitched himself onto the corner of Will's desk and proceeded to fill them both in on where he had been and why, watching the shock of his story register on their faces, feeling grateful that he could, in the worst of the days ahead, count on them both.

After Will and Marge had left the office for the day, Alex locked the front door, lowered the lights, and rolled incoming calls over to the state police, always on twenty-four-hour alert. Then he went back to the locker room, pulled out the civvies he kept there for emergencies, and within fifteen minutes had changed his uniform for a pair of slacks, a green turtleneck shirt, and a tweed sport jacket. He then headed back to the hospital.

The night was clear. The snow which had covered the ground and the trees only the day before had lost all of its glistening freshness. A passing front had boosted temperatures into the fifties, helping to turn its original pristine whiteness to a dirty, mud-spattered gray. Having ignored any previous pangs of hunger, Alex stopped at McDonald's for a burger with fries and a coffee to go. He was downing the last of it when he pulled the Blazer into the hospital parking lot. He wiped his mouth, took a deep breath, and got out of the car.

This time, when Alex crossed the threshold of her room, Jenny was seated with her legs dangling over the side of the bed, attempting to eat a frothy gelatin dessert from a snack tray laid out on her over-bed table, and doing a pitiful job of manipulating the slippery cubes with her one good hand. Her hair was washed, combed, and almost presentable. She was wearing a drab, nondescript hospital robe belted about her waist, her left arm and sling confined within it. Alex thought she looked beautiful.

"Darn hospital stuff," she complained with a little laugh when she looked up and saw Alex watching her. "Good to see you. Wanna help?"

The next hour passed quickly. Jenny informed him that she was being discharged the next day. When Alex insisted he do the honors of providing transportation to her door, she went through the awkward motions of retrieving her apartment keys from her purse. She handed them to Alex, then made him write down a list of the clothes she would need to wear home and where he would find them. The clothes she was wearing at the time of the accident, she told him breezily, were now in the trash.

They talked awhile, Jenny's spirits light. Alex found himself laughing along with whatever caused her to laugh first, their conversation carefully avoiding any mention of the "accident." When it came time to leave, Alex stood next to Jenny's bed, where she was propped up on pillows, smiling at him. It came to him suddenly how much she was beginning to mean in his life, pleased that laughter passed so easily between them, realizing how much he enjoyed the comfortable sense of contentment that went with just being around her. Then he remembered the way her lips felt against his and he wanted to kiss her again. Which he did.

CHAPTER THIRTEEN
AN ANGRY D.A.

THURSDAY, NOVEMBER 12

When Alex walked through the front door of the sheriff's office after seeing Jenny safely home from Mercy Hospital, he knew he was in for a hectic day. The bright smile and greeting he had come to expect from Marge were clouded by a little tug on her lower lip, and Will, always calm and collected, bounded across the room toward him, red-faced and clutching a newspaper in his hand. Alex sensed a cloud of trouble heading in his direction and braced himself.

"Mornin' Sheriff," Will said, breathlessly. "Have you seen today's *Gazette*? If not, you better take a look at it. A reporter got hold of a copy of Jenny Wyland's accident report and, well, you best read it for yourself."

Alex took the newspaper Will was thrusting at him and read the front page article he had encircled in red. Alex froze. A reporter had indeed gotten wind of what happened on Solomon's Gorge Hill and had written a vivid account of the near fatality, embellishing it with Jennifer Wyland colorfully depicted as Rose Clifford's friend and neighbor.

"What's the connection?" the author demanded to know in melodramatic conclusion. "Was Jennifer Wyland meant to be the third victim on a killer's list?"

Stunned, as much frustrated as angry, Alex headed for his office. Two deputies were working at nearby desks, their attention half on the computer screens in front of them and half on Will and the sheriff.

After he had disposed of his parka, Alex made for the lunch room, the newspaper thrust under his arm and Will at his heels. He waited until they were both seated with a fresh mug of coffee before he let himself explode. "How the dickens did the writer know that Jenny's car was rigged?" he gritted, giving the newspaper a vigorous shake. He looked down at the circled article for a long moment before tossing the paper aside. "The leak had to come from someone at the hospital. There is no other way."

Will nodded in agreement. "I have more good news," he said. "Lt. Donahue phoned just before you got here. He wants you to get right back to him. To tell the truth, Sheriff, I think we've got a few weighty problems being heaved our way. Besides which, the phones went a little crazy after that story came out. Marge had calls on hold lined up so long, half of them got tired of waiting and hung up."

Alex gave Will a clap on the shoulder, thanked him, and went back to his office. He settled down behind his desk and called Donahue.

"It's Peterson," Donahue announced when Alex had him on the line. "He's called a meeting for one o'clock this afternoon. That story in the *Gazette* set him off like a firecracker on the Fourth of July. He's been in touch with, would you believe, the State Police Bureau of Criminal Investigation in Albany. He wants to bring in BCI to assist in nailing Fowler. A guy by the name of Phil Carroll is on his way as we speak."

"The BCI?" Alex asked, wondering if he heard right. "Is Peterson nuts?"

"Yeah, could be," Donahue laughed dryly. "This isn't going to set well with the business community, you can bet on it. But he'll pacify. Or patronize; take your pick. We'll have to see what happens."

Alex had just returned the phone to its cradle when Marge Grant tapped on his office door. He looked up to see her leaning against the door jamb, peering at him over her eyeglass rims, the tiny line of a smile on her face.

"You have the latest bulletin, I presume?" she asked dryly. Without waiting for a reply, she went on. "Regardless, I'm doing my duty by giving you a message that just arrived. You are invited to a meeting by Mr. Peterson set for one o'clock this afternoon in his office." She raised both her eyebrows. "I'm assuming, of course, that it was Donahue you were chatting with?"

"Yep, that it was, Marge." Alex replied. "And I think you've already caught on to the fact that the invitation was a command, and that things are gonna get a little rough around here?"

"So what else is new?" she quipped, unruffled. "Rough waters go with the job. That's what makes it interesting." She gave him another quick, thin hint of a smile, turned on her heel, and left the office, closing the door softly behind her.

Alex brought his arms up and rested his head back on linked fingers. The newspaper story had jolted him. And now Peterson's heavy foot was about to descend on his neck and the fun would begin. He dreaded it. All he could do at the moment was to cross his fingers and hope that Jenny would stay away from her television set, most particularly the local twelve-o'clock news. But somehow he knew the chances were slim.

It was one o'clock. Alex and Harry were sitting side by side at a long table in Raymond Peterson's conference room. Phil Carroll from the BCI was seated at the end of the table next to Peterson. Upon their arrival at the scene, a tight-lipped Peterson had performed perfunctory introductions to the small, square man from the BCI, and in the process had handed both Alex and Harry his card. Conventions concluded, he sat down and turned to Donahue, asking if he would please proceed to bring Mr. Carroll and himself up to date on the murder cases currently under investigation.

In his usual unassuming but nonetheless imposing fashion, Donahue nodded his acquiescence, picked up his notes, and rose to his feet. Tall and sharp in his official grays, he presented the facts of the cases concerning Rose Clifford and Lonny Jerome. He began with the forensic scrutiny of Rose Clifford's car that had given up little more than a definite confirmation that it was the crime scene.

"The wooded area where her body was found," he told them, "yielded unidentifiable footprints; no other evidence was collected. The weapon used in both murders was probably a buck knife or a knife very similar to it, the type of knife common to hunters and available for sale at any sporting goods store." He paused and glanced briefly at the papers in his hand.

"The report also indicated," he went on, "that the Jerome woman was standing when the fatal strike was dealt. Study of the wound suggested it was thrust by someone standing at close proximity to her, the knife entering her body at an upward angle. Judging by her height of five foot six, it was estimated that the killer's height was a maximum of two to three inches taller. Probably no more than five nine at the outside. There you have it," he concluded. With a deferential nod toward the head of the table, he laid down his notes and resumed his seat.

Peterson had listened intently to Harry's summation of the two murder cases. Phil Carroll, Alex noted, had also listened with fixed attention, somehow managing, at the same time, to maintain an air of reserved detachment. Alex had to wonder if the man was wishing himself anywhere in the wilds of New York State except in the seat he now occupied in Collier County's political bleachers. If so, he could hardly blame him.

Impatient with the whole situation, Alex stood without waiting for a formal request to speak. He opened by discussing the search for a motive for the crimes. Rose Clifford had been a well-respected member of the community with no hint of enmity anywhere in her family, professional, or social environment. Lonny Jerome was a hard-working young woman, also well known and well liked. The only interest the two had in common was Charles Fowler, better known as Chuck, whom both had been seeing socially for brief but different intervals of time. In both instances, the relationships were terminated when Fowler's display of temper erupted and he became physically abusive, and both break-ups were followed by harassing phone calls and threats. He also created a scene in the diner where Lonny Jerome was employed as a waitress, forcing the owner to physically remove him from the place. In addition, while Fowler was able to offer a fairly solid alibi for the time of the Clifford murder, at the time of the Jerome murder he said he was home alone.

"There is no solid evidence," Alex said in conclusion, meeting Peterson's stony eye, "that points to him as a viable suspect for either murder. An intense examination of his home and vehicle came up clean." He looked squarely down at the BCI man. "All reports, of course, are at your disposal."

Speech concluded, Alex sat down, crossed his arms, and waited for Peterson to take the floor. Peterson exploded. He shoved back his chair, stood up, braced both hands on the table, and leaned forward, aiming the fire in his eye at Alex, his face suffused with rage.

"What are you talking about? He killed the Jerome woman and you know it!" he fumed, slapping a hand down hard on the table. His glance shifted from Alex to Donahue, then back again. "Are you guys sitting on your rumps, or what? We've had two women murdered over the last ten days and now an attempt on another woman's life. The media is having a field day with any crumb they can dig up or make up. The mayor's on my back, and I'm not hearing anything from either of you that comes close to a solution." He made a motion toward the BCI man, now absently fingering a stone ring on his finger.

"I've asked Mr. Carroll to sit in on this meeting today because we have a state of near panic in our county. If you need help resolving these murders," he put in sarcastically, "Mr. Carroll has assured me he will gladly give you all the help at his disposal. You have his card. Do what you have to do, only get these murders solved!"

He turned to Carroll, managing to lower his tone and his temper. "Thank you, sir," he said, extending his hand ingratiatingly. "I appreciate your time."

Then, his heels hard under him, Peterson touched the BCI man's shoulder and ushered him out of the room.

"Well, that was different," Donahue cracked, his eyes on the closed door through which the two men had disappeared.

"But in a way, Peterson's right, you know," Alex commented, as they left the building, emerging into the brisk, wind-chilled afternoon.

"Yep, I know," Donahue reluctantly agreed. "We have two murders and one attempted murder, and we don't have the slightest evidence pointing to the killer. Not a print, a fiber, a hair. Nada. Is that what you're saying?"

"Yes," Alex replied, with what felt like sawdust in his mouth. "I'm afraid it is."

CHAPTER FOURTEEN
DINNER FOR TWO

THURSDAY, NOVEMBER 12

Although the events of the day had been anything but pleasant, Alex looked forward to the evening ahead with Jenny, at the same time more than a little concerned that she may now realize she is the focus of the latest media ballyhoo. He arrived at her apartment just before six o'clock armed with two steaks, fresh rolls, and the makings for a tossed salad. Jenny met him at the door, with bandages adorning her cheek and forehead and her cast in a sling. She looked great.

"You complained about the hospital food, so I'm about to fix you a meal you won't forget," he told her after he had hustled shopping bags into the kitchen, hung up his parka, and settled Jenny down on a kitchen stool where she could watch him go to work.

"I'm a pretty good cook if I do say so myself," he boasted with a playful wink. "So, I'll do the chef thing while you tell me what you've been up to since yesterday."

Jenny did just that. After she left the hospital the previous evening, she had phoned her Aunt Bea who lived in the small town of Oak Creek, not far from Weston.

"Aunt Bea took care of me after my mom died," Jenny explained. "I was practically all grown up by then. Bea, actually Beatrice, was my father's sister, but I never knew him. He and Mom broke up when I was very young. I think Aunt Bea always tried to make up for my dad moving away and starting a new life without Mom or me. When Mom died, Aunt Bea took over.

Jenny went on with her story while Alex put the salad together.

"Fortunately, Bea knew nothing about my accident. But when I called to tell her, she must have broken the sound barrier to get here. She took one look at me and dove right in. She scrubbed me up, shampooed my icky hair, and then went to work on the laundry. Before she left, she helped me get dressed so that all I had to do was wait for you. And here you are!"

The conversation continued through dinner which proved to be everything Alex had promised. The steaks were a perfect medium rare, the salad crisp, and the flaky rolls oozed with butter. Ice cream for dessert topped off the meal. Alex cut Jenny's meat, snipped her salad, buttered her rolls, and even chopped up her ice cream. And he did it all with panache. They laughed and talked, and for a little while they were able to hold the magic close and leave the world and its troubles outside.

After Alex had loaded the dishwasher, they moved to the living room. A few minutes later, snuggled down on the sofa with his arm across Jenny's shoulders and the fire in the grate spreading its warmth and contentment, Alex felt it was the right time for a talk. When he said as much to Jenny, she agreed.

"Someone tried to hurt you," Alex began, feeling the words catch in his throat. Steadying his voice, he ran through the conversation with Donahue in the emergency room.

"Those were the worst and the longest minutes of my life," Jenny whispered when he was finished. She stared into the fire for a few moments, then shifted her position in order to meet Alex's gaze. "I refuse to be intimidated, Alex. I'm too grateful to be alive. When I opened my eyes in the ER and looked around knowing I was still on planet Earth, I just took the minutes that followed one by one, breath by breath. The knowledge that someone actually tried to hurt me, no..." she corrected herself, "tried to kill me, is incredible. Was it really something to do with Rose, Alex? It must be. Why else would someone want me dead?"

Alex nodded agreement. "That's my best guess, Jen," he reluctantly admitted. "I wish I knew for certain, but I don't." He paused and took a fresh breath. "Now, to another matter. Did you happen to watch the news on television today or see the *Gazette*?"

Jenny lowered her eyes. "I didn't watch the news, Alex, no. But Aunt Bea brought the newspaper with her. The story came as a shock to us both. And there have been telephone calls, too. My aunt kept saying I was unavailable and hanging up the phone. After a bit, we let the answering machine take over. Once I knew you were on your way upstairs, I took it off the hook." She released a heavy sigh. "It's all out in the open, Alex. My questions can't be answered, of course, but I now know the miserable truth and can deal with it. It seems that the attack on me really does have something to do with Rose, but it's beyond me what it could be."

"Beyond me, too," Alex confessed. "I've been hoping you'd remember something. Anything that would give us some hint which way to turn next."

Jenny's lips compressed into a tight line. "I'm sorry," she sighed wearily, "I've tried to dig into my brain for something I might have forgotten. But there's nothing I can tell you." Her good right hand found Alex's and gripped it. "I can't begin to imagine what would drive anyone to do such a thing. Not to Rose. Not to me."

"Believe one thing," Alex whispered close to her ear. "I'm not going to let anyone hurt you, and I mean that."

Jenny rested her head against Alex's shoulder and gave a little sigh. She felt suddenly very tired. Drained. Well, she told herself, snuggling closer to Alex, whatever was happening to turn her world upside down, having this big, solid, beautiful lawman beside her was all that she needed to get through it.

Jenny tightened her grip on his hand, then relaxed it. She closed her eyes, letting the silence and the touch of her hand express what she felt. For the moment, there was no need for words.

CHAPTER FIFTEEN
A MURDER WEAPON

Alex answered his cell phone just as he was pulling into the parking area next to his office early Friday morning. It was Donahue.

"Got a call about forty minutes ago," Donahue said excitedly. "Some-body phoned in a tip that Chucky boy was in a bar last night, drinking heavily and bragging about his taking care of, ah, well, I won't use the colorful descriptive language he used to characterize Lonny Jerome, but he thought it was a great joke that: 'the cops didn't find what they were looking for when they turned my place upside down.' As soon as there was a new search warrant issued, the crime scene techs made a beeline for Fowler's place. They should be there right now, so hang in there and I'll call you as soon as I get some news. There's nothing either of us can do right now, anyway."

It was just over an hour later when Donahue burst through the front door. Slapping snow from his hat as he simultaneously stomped slush from his boots, he gave Marge a smiling good-morning and a wink, then hustled past her to Alex's office.

"Hey, you got coffee brewed?" he asked by way of announcing him-self as he came through the door and tossed his hat on a chair.

"Haven't we always?" Alex retorted, pushing himself to his feet. "Go on in the back and help yourself. I'll get hold of Will."

"The techs found the murder weapon!" Donahue announced once the three men were seated at a table in the lunchroom. Hands wrapped around a mug of coffee, he gave Alex and Will the story. "They found the hunt-ing knife in the shed behind Fowler's cabin, buried between a couple of paint cans. No prints. It was wiped clean, but the luminal test for blood was positive. That won't mean anything, of course, until forensics determines if the blood is human or not. If it's human, they'll type it. The DNA will take a little longer. They're working on it right now, if it's a match to Lonny and/or Rose's blood type, Peterson will be jumping with joy."

"You seem kind of happy yourself," Alex quietly observed.

Donahue scratched his head and chuckled. "Yeah, I tend to agree that Fowler's our man. Maybe I'm right and maybe not. Just an opinion, but I think the guy did himself in."

Alex pursued, "You said there was a tip, right? Who from?"

"Don't know," Harry admitted, then pulled a sip from his mug.

"Anonymous caller, huh? That stirs up some questions, don't you think?" Alex asked, gaining momentum. "For one thing, where did the call originate?"

"An outside public phone, but so what? The fact is we found the knife."

"All right, Harry, let me play devil's advocate for a minute. Okay, let's go back to square one when we had all the probable cause we needed for a warrant to go through Fowler's place the first time. The team came up empty. Okay? You with me?"

"Okay," the trooper replied with a patronizing grin. "I'm with you all the way."

"So how do you explain that search number two turned up something the team overlooked the first time? Fowler's not stupid. Why hide the knife at all when he could bury the thing in the woods or toss it in the Hudson River? How can anybody buy the story that he put it in a shed on his own property? Why couldn't the knife be a plant by the real killer?"

Donahue blew out a breath and laughed. "Whew! That's a lot of questions. And I've no doubt at all we'll hear them repeated a dozen times or more before the case is closed. But I think Fowler's our man. If the Jerome woman's blood shows up on that knife, Peterson will have his case. I don't care how he found the knife."

"So you really do believe the D.A. can convince a jury that Fowler killed Lonny Jerome. Okay, I'm nuts, but I don't believe it. His lawyer will tear that evidence to shreds, wait and see."

Donahue drained off the last of his coffee, stood up, stretched his shoulders and smiled. "In our job, Sheriff, we don't have to prove anything. We leave that to the State of New York. All we do is gather evidence. In my estimation, Fowler killed Lonny Jerome, and if his alibi for that Glens Falls bar starts popping holes, maybe they'll get him for Rose Clifford, too. And yes, I think that the D.A. has a good chance of convincing a jury beyond the shadow of a doubt that Fowler is guilty." He reached for his jacket then gave Will an inquiring look as he put it on. "And what's your take, Deputy? You haven't said much."

Will had been sitting with his long legs stretched out in front of him taking everything in. Now he raised his eyebrows, pulled in his feet, and stood up. "I've got doubts, too," he stated, his expression thoughtful. "But I think I'll reserve opinions for the time being. I agree, Lieutenant, that it's all up to the prosecutor's office from now on. Peterson will get his indictment if the blood on the knife nails Fowler. Then it will be up to a jury. The worst, for us at least, will be over."

Later, when Alex was alone again in his office, Will's words came back to him, loud and clear. "Oh no, it won't be over," Alex said into the empty air. "It's not going to be that easy. If Peterson leaps at the chance to nail Fowler, the worst is yet to begin."

After leaving the office, Alex drove directly to High Ridge to see Jenny. He was about to enter the building when all at once he felt an uncomfortable sense of being watched. He had felt it before and ignored it. But this time, he snapped his head around just in time to catch sight of a familiar automobile parked across the street. Holding his curiosity in check, he walked casually through the glass doors into the front vestibule, but instead of ringing Jenny's apartment, he stepped off to one side and out of the car's line of vision. Then with one quick turn he went back to the door. And there was the car, pulling away from the curb. Suddenly furious, Alex yanked the door open and rushed outside. Even through the fading light he was able to catch most of the blue Ford's retreating license plate number. It was Lisa.

CHAPTER SIXTEEN
FOWLER'S STORY

SATURDAY, NOVEMBER 14

Once the blood type on the hunting knife found in Fowler's shed proved to match that of Lonny Jerome, the district attorney moved fast. Fowler was arrested and put in a holding cell until he could be arraigned before a judge. Meanwhile, Peterson began preparing a case of first-degree murder against Fowler for the death of Lonny Jerome. He would see him arraigned without bail, he promised the media, and the case would be submitted to the grand jury before the coming week was out.

Yet Alex's doubts persisted. He finally decided that if he was to get to the heart of whatever was eating at him, he would need to have another talk with Mr. Fowler. He wanted – no, he needed – answers. And quickly. Fowler had been arrested the night before and would go before the judge for arraignment on Monday.

When the deputy let Alex into the holding cell, Fowler was sitting slumped on the edge of his bunk, arms propped on his knees, his eyes hard and angry.

"What do you want with me?" he asked contemptuously as the deputy slammed the cell door shut behind Alex and turned the key. "Whatever it is, have your say and get out of here."

Alex pulled up the only chair in the cell, turned it around, and straddled it. "Sure, I'll get out of your way soon enough, Fowler, but first there's something you should hear, so listen up. I have no idea what your personal relationship was with the Jerome girl. I don't think you like women much, and you enjoy the nasty little games you play with them. Furthermore, maybe you killed Lonny Jerome and maybe you didn't.

But, if you did, then in all probability you'll be taking the fall for killing Rose, too."

When he saw that he had Fowler's attention, Alex continued. "If your alibi is on the level, you couldn't have killed Rose. But with the right kind of pressure in the right kind of places, your alibi for the time of her death could be shot down by the D.A. without too much trouble. It depends on how well the citizens who vouch for you can stand up under the heat. You were all pretty loose with the alcohol, as I recall. But I'm also thinking that if you did kill Rose, and went to the trouble to make sure you had an alibi, why not the same with Lonny Jerome? It could be argued that it happened so suddenly you didn't have time to work out an alibi. But that's not going to happen because the D.A.'s going for the big murder one. Premeditated. That changes the picture."

"There is no picture. I didn't do anything!" Fowler snarled.

"Were you in a bar last Thursday night?"

"Yeah, you know the story. I was at Solly's Bar on Miller Road, alone. Just chugging a few. Got home about one in the morning. Next day this so-called crime unit comes charging through my door waving a search warrant in my face. Then I'm told they found a hunting knife behind some paint cans in my shed. They say they got a tip about me. The next thing I know the troopers are back at my door, I'm in handcuffs, and here I am. End of story." He studied Alex for a long minute before his handsome features curled into an expression of fury and disgust. "I didn't kill anybody! Not your Rose or Lonny Jerome. Neither of them!"

Alex's spine stiffened. "What do you mean by 'my Rose'?" he asked.

Fowler smirked. "Your Rose," I said. "You had a thing going with her. You denying it?"

Alex bit back the words on the edge of his tongue and resisted the urge to take a swing at Fowler's face. Instead, he nodded. "I liked Rose," he replied with deceptive calmness. "We were good friends. I've known her since we were teenagers in high school. So what?"

Fowler uttered a derisive chuckle. "Yeah, sure. Rose was friends with everybody. Had lots of friends and all of 'em guys!" With that he got up and spit into the small sink angled into a corner of the cell.

"I'm telling you the way it was," Alex said, fighting to stay cool. "Rose was a friend but nothing more. Now tell me the truth, how did you know I was seeing her? Somebody tell you? Did Rose tell you?"

"I don't remember. Maybe," Fowler returned grudgingly. "I met her and we hit it off. We were interested in each other; we didn't talk about you." He took a few steps until he reached the cell wall, crossed his arms over his chest, and leaned back against the slabbed concrete. "She saw other guys, I knew that for a fact. Like that teacher friend she was so buddy-buddy with. Or so she said. You know what happened. Our last date was the end of our so-called relationship. I just got back from another long run downstate, glad to see her, and well, let's just say I discovered I was one out of many."

"But the two of you weren't serious, so why should it matter what she did? Or who she saw?"

Fowler uncrossed his arms and returned to where he had been sitting on the cot. "Nah, we weren't serious. But maybe I wanted it to be. I treated her like she was special, hands off and all that. I thought maybe it would go someplace. But she played around and I got mad. End of story."

"Let me get something straight," Alex said slowly. "You were seeing Rose right around the end of August and into the first part of September. That right?"

Fowler shrugged. "I don't know. Sounds right. Yeah, I guess."

"And you think she was seeing others, too, at the time, that right?"

"Yeah." The word spilled out like a low, guttural laugh.

"And then later, after Rose died, you began seeing Lonny." This time it wasn't a question and he hurried on. "If you're telling the truth and you didn't kill Rose, then somebody else had to know about you and Lonny. Somebody who followed your love life and knew your temper, using it to set you up for Rose's murder. But suspicion on you wasn't moving fast enough so the noose had to be tightened. Then along comes the tip – a call made by somebody who knew you were in the bar. A nice, neat set up."

Fowler put up a hand to slow Alex down. "You're talking crazy,

Sheriff. Some looney killed both those women. And it wasn't me. That's all I know."

Alex stood up and called the guard. "You know more than you think you do," he said over his shoulder as the deputy closed the cell door behind him.

"And now I do, too," he repeated to himself. "And then he left.

Alex spent the evening with Jenny. He brought Chinese takeout for dinner and afterwards they opened their fortune cookies in front of the fire. They laughed, sipped hot tea, held hands, and just talked. If Jenny wondered why Alex was leaving early that night without explaining why, she showed no sign of it. When she walked him to the door, he pulled her into his arms, kissed her, and held her close, arm cast and all, for a long, warm moment. Lips touching her hair, he reminded her again to please not open the door for anyone and not to buzz anyone through she was not intimately familiar with. Then he promised to come back in the morning.

Loving the feel of his arms around her, Jenny would have promised him anything.

CHAPTER SEVENTEEN
OLD LOVE REVISITED

SATURDAY, NOVEMBER 14

As much as he dreaded entering the private world in which Lisa had imprisoned herself, Alex could find no other alternative if he wanted to learn the truth. He knew now that she had been lurking outside Jenny's apartment building, obviously watching him. Probably she had even followed him. And, he thought with a tired sigh, she had been at it for some time.

After leaving Jenny that evening, Alex had telephoned Lisa shortly after reaching home. To his surprise, the call was received far more graciously than expected, especially since their last encounter was still burning at the edge of his gut. Yes, Lisa told him, her voice clear and sweet, he could come by about five thirty on Monday evening. She would be home from work by then. Would that be convenient?

SUNDAY, NOVEMBER 15

The next day, Sunday, Alex spent with Jenny. Snow cover was everywhere. The sun had decided to come out, so when Alex suggested a drive, Jenny bubbled over.

"Let's go!" she shouted, dragging him to the door. "I'm gonna smell fresh air!"

The drive turned out to be a long one, covering the picturesque, spiraling Route 74 to Ticonderoga, then south again on Route 9 through the town of Schroon Lake. A little further along they made a stop at Pottersville and ate a hearty meal at the Black Bear Restaurant. From there it was Route 15 to the old-fashioned Adirondack General Store where Jenny ogled the homemade jelly and jams, and let Alex buy two of her favorites for her. They had then rambled along to the nearest Northway ramp and headed for home. The drive had been an escape through snow-capped, mountainous terrain made even more glorious by the clear air and the spectacular panorama spread out beneath a magnificently blue sky.

By seven o'clock that evening, they were back at Jenny's. By nine, Alex was on his way home. He had come close to confiding to Jenny about his plans for the next evening, but the words stayed hidden, held captive by both feelings of loyalty and compassion for Lisa and the pain that would not let go.

MONDAY, NOVEMBER 16

When Alex made the drive to Grover on Monday, he had no problem locating the address, noting that as he had previously conjectured, Lisa had moved into the same general neighborhood as Ben Sayers, and like Sayers, had rented a second-floor flat. When Lisa met him at the door, she was quite composed. Smiling pleasantly, she invited him inside and led him up the hall stairs and through her tidy flat to a bright and cheerful kitchen. She motioned toward a table in the center of the room and told him to make himself comfortable. She had just made fresh coffee and she would pour a mug for him, black with two sugars, the way he liked it.

Watching Lisa fuss about the kitchen, Alex was touched by the reminder of happier days. Back then the kitchen table had been a place where they shared their day and worked out their problems. The picture of Carl formed in his mind, a baby in his highchair, then a little man in his booster seat. Those were the images he wanted to preserve. So much else had turned sour that he held tight to what had been good.

Lisa surprised him. Unlike the Lisa at the cemetery, she was smiling, setting out cookies with their coffee mugs while she chattered on about nothing important. Alex responded in kind, keeping the conversation light, wondering if indeed Lisa's chameleon change of temperament would last. He also noticed that she was still a lovely woman. If there were dark circles under her eyes and she was by far too thin, and if her yellow-white hair was more like straw than the golden silk he once loved to touch, it was all due to the grief and pain that had taken its toll on her mind, as well as her body.

Aware that Alex was watching her, Lisa took a sip from her cup and very slowly set it down on the table. "I know you're here to talk about what's been happening, Alex. And that it's awkward for you. It's awkward for me, too." She ran a finger over the rim of her cup, her eyes downcast for a second or two. "When Trooper Donahue had me come to his office to answer questions, it was awful exposing such a private part of myself. Humiliating, really." She swallowed hard and wet her lips before continuing. "It sounds foolish maybe, but I did blame you for leaving me behind after we lost Carl and making a new life for yourself. I was jealous, hurt, and a lot of other emotions rolled into one. I still am. I knew you were seeing Rose Clifford and I suppose I went a little crazy." She flushed and blinked back tears. "So! Now what can I tell you today that you don't already know?"

Alex came right to the point. "You can tell me," he said, his eyes searching into hers, "why you've been parking outside Jenny Wyland's apartment building and why you've been following me."

Lisa flushed again, lowered her gaze, and stared at her hands. Finally, she raised her head and broke the silence laying like lead between them. "Yes, I have," she admitted in a sad, tight voice. "I still love you, Alex. I never stopped. Only I felt that I didn't have a right to you anymore. Not after we lost Carl. I was home with him that day. It was a bicycle we both picked out that took him to his death."

Alex felt a lump form deep in his throat. There was nothing he could say in reply, so he waited in the pain-filled moment for Lisa to continue.

"When I first found out you were seeing Rose," she said at last in a childlike voice, "I hated you for daring to be happy. I acted like a fool, I know that. Later, I even went to Rose's apartment to apologize for the scene at the school. She was killed that same night, and afterwards, I was so afraid someone would think I had something to do with it, I never told anyone that I was there."

Alan stared at Lisa in disbelief. "You were with Rose at her place the same Friday she died?"

"Yes," Lisa whispered, "in the late afternoon. She was very nice. And understanding. She also promised not to talk to anyone about what I had done. I appreciated that. I'm sorry she's gone."

"Did you know that Jenny Wyland was her neighbor?" Alex rested his coffee mug on the table, his hands encircling it so tightly that his knuckles went white.

"No, not then. I found out later when I followed you. You know all that, Alex," Lisa murmured through trembling lips. "Don't make me go through it again."

After taking a moment to collect herself, she gave Alex a long, searching look, her eyes filled with emotion. "Do you think you could love me again, Alex?" She stretched her hand across the table and laid it gently on his. "Do you?" she repeated softly.

Shaken, Alex pulled his hand away and leaned back in his chair. "I asked you something first, Lisa. I want to know why you went back to spying on me. And why you're still doing it."

Lisa shook her head and sighed. "Maybe I'm punishing myself. I'm not sure why. I wanted to know what you were doing and if maybe you had fallen in love with somebody else."

"Yes, Lisa," Alex said in a tight, strained voice, "I have."

At his words, Lisa slumped in the chair, color draining from her face. "I guess that says it all," she murmured, her eyes brimming with tears. "But I still love you and probably won't stop. I'm sorry for what I did, Alex. For messing up our marriage and for the crazy way I think. And for the way I acted at the cemetery. Losing Carl" she added with a shudder, "broke my heart."

"Yes," Alex replied with a nod, "it broke both our hearts." He took a deep breath. There was one more question he needed to ask. "Lisa, I want you to be honest with me. Did you have anything at all to do with Jenny's car accident?"

Lisa's eyes flashed with surprise. "What do you mean? What are you talking about?"

Alex shook his head. "Never mind. It was a stupid question but I had to ask." He stood up, pulled his parka from the back of the chair, and shrugged into it. "Now, I've got to be on my way, Lis. Thanks for the coffee."

Lisa stood up. "I'll walk you to the door," she said politely.

Alex had just opened the door to the front hall when Lisa touched his arm. When he turned around, she was gazing up at him, eyes filled with emotion. "Will you kiss me one last time, Alex? Just one last time, please?"

Staring down into Lisa's upturned face, Alex felt something give. For no reason he could explain either then or later, in the next instant Lisa was in his arms, the warmth of her body against his. Without thinking, his lips came down hard on hers in a deep, passionate kiss.

Suddenly, he snapped awake. Breathless and confused, he reached up and detached Lisa's arms from around his neck, took a step backward, and looked down into Lisa's searching gaze. "I apologize for that, Lisa," he told her, shame and anger flooding through him. "It's the last time, the very last time something like that will ever happen, I promise you."

Then as Lisa silently watched him go, Alex fled down the stairs to the street and in seconds was back on the sidewalk, headed for his car and home.

Driving over the dark stretch of the Northway, thoughts came hurling at him with hurricane force. What in the deuce happened back there? he asked himself, totally unnerved by what he had done. Was he nuts? The Lisa part of his life was over. Their divorce had been not a choice, but a necessity. And that was the bottom line. Okay, he reasoned, whatever happened today was done and over with. He had initiated the talk with Lisa because there were questions he had to have answered. Now he had asked his questions and he had his answers. It was time to move on. As for Lisa, she was an enigma, skipping from one emotional level to another, on a high one minute, then angry, crying, or shouting invectives at him in the next. She needed help. But then, he recalled hotly, help had been offered and summarily rejected after Carl's death. As adamantly as Lisa had refused grief counseling then, it was almost certain she would do the same today. Self-loathing twisted through him, reminding him of what a fool he had been to lose control like he did. One last kiss! It was not only unkind, it was a stupid thing to have let happen. For both of them.

Alex had parked the Blazer in the garage and was just about to hang up his parka when the telephone rang. It was Lisa.

"I want to tell you I'm sorry for what happened, Alex," she said, her voice calm and empty of emotion. "I was wrong to let you know my feelings. I've hurt you too much already. I won't bother you anymore, I promise."

Before he could reply, the phone went dead.

Alex did not sleep well that night. The past haunted him. Lisa haunted him. And there was nothing he could do about any of it. Nothing at all.

CHAPTER EIGHTEEN
SPECULATION

TUESDAY, NOVEMBER 17

It was noontime. The day had begun with news he'd expected. D.A. Paterson had forged ahead and brought Fowler before a judge for arraignment the previous day, and he would have his grand jury indictment before the week was out. Also as expected, Fowler was considered a flight risk, so there was no bail. In short, Alex concluded, Fowler was in a peck of trouble.

The mental labor Alex had expended trying to solve both murders had earned him naught. Worse yet, since his encounter with Lisa, he had found himself rapidly sinking into an emotional morass. Jumpy and tired, he needed sleep. Without it he was a blind man groping in the dark, getting nowhere. He decided to check in on Jenny before leaving for lunch and a quick burger at McDonald's.

"I have great news," Jenny told him when he reached her. "Aunt Bea got tired of nagging me to bunk down with her, so she decided to move in here with me for as long as she's needed. At the moment that makes her my star boarder. Isn't that great?"

"It sure is," Alex said, meaning it more than Jenny could ever suspect. "Can't wait to meet her."

When he hung up the telephone, to his surprise, he found himself smiling. One worry off his shoulders. Bless Aunt Bea. She would be company for Jenny as well as another pair of watchful eyes. It lay heavily on him that whoever tried to harm Jenny once could very well try again. Maybe things were starting to look up. He hoped so. He checked his watch, locked up the office, and went out into the cold, wintry day.

WEDNESDAY, NOVEMBER 18

The next day, wrapping up the final reports on his desk, Alex suddenly realized how quickly the week was moving along. Fowler's case was going before the grand jury the next day with Peterson pushing for murder one, which came as no surprise. As far as Alex was concerned, Peterson was grandstanding to public opinion and good luck to him. He would not be too quick to place any bets on what the estimable district attorney would achieve in the end.

The night before, Alex had been introduced to Beatrice Wyland, Jenny's aunt. She lived up to Jenny's description: a pleasant, somewhat plump, white-haired woman with a face that was frequently lit up by the fresh glow of a smile. The evening had been filled with stories of Jenny's earlier years, engendering howls of protest from the subject, loudly defending herself against Aunt Bea's delightful intimations of Jenny's misspent youth and the rescuing of the roguish maid by her formidable self. The evening had been a refreshing and reassuring one, Alex reflected on the drive home. Jenny was in very capable and devoted hands.

But later that same evening, despite the warm thoughts of Jenny and Aunt Bea, he couldn't stop thinking about what occurred at Lisa's flat and her subsequent phone call. Worse yet, he thought miserably, he had finally reached a place in his life where he was close to finding order and peace after many years with neither. And now here he was in the center of a maelstrom of ghosts and self-recriminations, frozen into the kind of emotional and mental inertia he was all too familiar with.

No, he resolved fiercely, he would not regress. He would not allow the pangs of past discouragement to sink their teeth into him. His old life was over. First he lost Carl and then Lisa. His family and the future they planned together were gone. For too long it had been a fight to feel anything except grief and loss and emptiness. He would not backslide now. No, it was not going to happen.

THURSDAY, NOVEMBER 19

Both Alex and Harry Donahue waited in the courthouse with bated breath to hear whether Fowler would be bound over for trial. Neither of them expressed surprise that Peterson was asking for a charge of murder one. In fact, it would have come as a surprise if he had not. Fowler's fate was the ante. The poker game was about to begin.

It had begun to snow that morning. A slate-gray sky hung low, all but obscuring the view of the surrounding mountains. Alex and Harry emerged from the court house, stopping briefly to comment on Patterson's indictment. Harry was satisfied that the mechanisms of the law were doing their job and that now it was time to close the book on Fowler and move on.

"And if Fowler isn't guilty?" Alex asked him.

"Then we start over," Harry retorted. "But until we get the word, the investigation is done."

It was nearing six o'clock and Alex was still behind his desk, the ever-present mug of hot coffee in front of him while he periodically chomped into a doughnut he had retrieved from the several he kept stashed in the lunchroom refrigerator. The day had indeed been long, his thoughts caught up in the quagmire of two murder cases without a clue to chase between them, all further complicated by the fact that he believed Fowler innocent of the crimes he was accused of committing.

Once again he laid out the facts of the case, beginning from the time of Rose's death to the present. He closed his eyes and did a mental backpedal to the summer weeks when he was dating Rose. Who knew? And what about Fowler's dig about it? Did Rose tell him? Anyone could have known, actually. They didn't try to hide and surely they were seen together. Aside from that, who would Rose be apt to tell? Some of the teachers at school? But school was closed in the summer. Still, there must have been other friends she talked with, although the interviews produced nothing of value.

Next, who knew he was seeing Jenny? Lisa knew. She had been following him and admitted it, along with her reasons why. But he knew that killing off women in his life would not be among the solutions she would opt for.

So who would want to harm Jen? Fowler? Did Fowler even know about Jenny, and if so, why would he care? Who would be upset by his relationship with Jenny Wyland? Did it have any connection to Rose? Was Donahue right, that the killer wanted to be certain that anything Rose may have told Jenny would be lost forever with her death?

Moving on, he wondered if there was sufficient motive for Fowler to kill Lonny Jerome. Fowler and she did split – and not on very good terms. Was there someone else who would be interested in the fact they were seeing one another? Could it be the same someone who planted the murder weapon in Fowler's shed and then tipped off the law?

Alex frowned. You did not have to be a Rhodes scholar to reason that if someone other than Fowler killed the Jerome woman, then the knife had to be a plant. Her murder might have been committed to cover up the real reason for killing Rose. Fowler had a lousy way of treating women, a fact which made him the perfect fall-guy, and Fowler's jury conviction for Lonny's murder would be embraced with glee by the district attorney. Heads would be nodding in all directions, agreeing that Fowler must have killed Rose, too. And of course, Peterson would affirm that belief by simply withholding a denial. Never mind how flimsy the evidence against Fowler for killing Rose might be. Never mind the questions that should be asked – so long as everybody sleeps well at night.

Back to the attack on Jenny. Again, why? Because she was Rose's neighbor and her friend? Did it really matter if Jenny was killed in that "accident"? Or was it just something rigged up to yet again throw the scent elsewhere? And if Jenny died in the process, so what? Or was the accident just another part of the game the killer was playing? Could be.

Could be a lot of things.

Alex decided he wanted to talk to Sayers again. It was important that he keep pressing the grapes if he wanted a sip of the wine, which he did, and better sooner than later. With that thought in mind, he picked up the phone and called Sayers.

"Sure," Sayers agreed when Alex asked for a few minutes to talk. "How about meeting me at Vincent's Grille? Some of us shopworn teachers retreat there once in awhile for a TGIF break. Tomorrow's Friday. Can you make it about five o'clock?"

CHAPTER NINETEEN
THE RATHSKELLER

Before leaving to meet Sayers, Alex decided to locker his uniform, reluctant to enter a crowded restaurant in full sheriff's garb with a holstered firearm on his hip. Vincent's was sure to be busy on a Friday evening. It was a popular restaurant and watering hole with a rathskeller well-known for great German beer, pickled cabbage salad, and homemade rye bread. He would not want to put a damper on anyone's idea of Utopia.

It was a little before five o'clock when he entered Vincent's by way of a small vestibule, a boxlike structure the purpose of which was to deflect the impact of cold, mountain winds intent on sweeping through the open door and across the hapless ankles of the restaurant patrons. The end-of-the-week regulars and après-ski snow people had not descended in force as yet, but the place, Alex noted, was fairly busy. Tables were slowly being occupied; waitresses wearing short, black skirts and white, puffed-sleeve blouses glided between tables carrying trays of drink and food. Somewhere in the background an accordion was pumping out the three-quarter rhythm of a German Schottische, blending in with the sweet yet pungent aromas of sauerkraut, sausages, sauerbraten, and German beer.

Alex took the stairway leading down into the rathskeller. Once on the lower level he paused for a moment to look around, the muted illumination making it difficult to immediately single anyone out of the crowd. To his right, a long bar, many of the stools occupied, ran the length of one wall; two waitresses were busy working tables set up in clusters throughout the adjoining dining area. He had almost made up his mind to take a seat at the bar and order a beer when Ben Sayers came striding toward him.

"Good evening, Sheriff, you're right on time," Sayers said. He nodded toward the bar.

"Can I buy you a drink of something before we sit down? A cold quaff of German beer, perhaps?"

Surprised by the offer as well as Sayers' congenial smile, Alex accepted, and a few minutes later found himself sitting across from the teacher, a bowl of salted pretzels and two frosted glasses of foamy beer on the table between them.

Sayers lifted his glass in toasting fashion, took a long, slow pull from the edge, and sat back in his chair. "So tell me, Sheriff, to what do I owe the honor of this visit?"

"Frankly, Mr. Sayers," Alex replied after setting his glass on the table, "I'm here trolling the same old waters, still working to get to the bottom of who killed Rose Clifford, and why. I firmly believe that if I find the 'why,' I'll find the killer. In brief, I'm looking for a motive and will keep right on looking until I find it. I'm here to cast another line, hoping to snag anything that will hint at a new direction. There you have it."

"As I've told you, Sheriff," Sayers replied in a patient, almost patronizing tone, "Rose could say a lot without telling you anything. As far as our relationship was concerned and how well I knew her, yes, I accompanied her to a concert or three, but so what? You may not be aware of it but I was more than ten years Rose's senior. Certainly not the contemporary or confidant you might have imagined me to be. Now, let me ask you a question. I wasn't the only person Rose knew particularly well. There was also Jenny Wyland who was her age and, possibly, her confidant. The *Gazette* story connected her to Rose. So what gives there? Couldn't she be as much of a source of information as I presumably seem to be?"

Alex picked up his glass and sipped at it, at the same time assessing Sayers. "There is no significant connection," Alex stated while maintaining a nonchalance he did not feel at the mention of Jenny's name. "They were neighbors who shared a cup of tea now and then. That's it. Another dry well."

"I see," Sayers said, drawing out his words. He looked down and studied the pretzel he was holding between his fingers. "Then let me move on to another matter, if I may." He paused a moment, his voice taking on a subtly chiding note as he spoke. "You never did fill me in on the mystery woman, you know," he said, holding Alex's gaze. "I can't help but wonder why."

"No," Alex responded, choosing his words carefully. "I didn't. Very frankly, I didn't want to implicate the woman in a murder investigation only to discover at a later date that her involvement was of another matter entirely. In this case, it was. The state police took over and determined that the woman's problem was not related to the murder. She didn't kill Rose, nor did she have anything to do with it. End of story."

Sayers lifted a shoulder. "Okay, Sheriff, if you say so," he remarked skeptically. "But let's get back to that article in the newspaper. From what I've read and what I've heard on television, this Fowler fellow is going on trial for killing Lonny Jerome. Might there be some truth in the premise that he's implicated in Rose's death, as well? After all, they were getting it on pretty tight."

Alex took a deep breath and expelled it slowly. The last thing he wanted was to expound on Fowler's predicament, certainly not with Sayers. "I take it you haven't dug up any recollection at all regarding Rose's personal life that she may have mentioned somewhere along the way?" Alex asked, deliberately ignoring Sayers' question to counter with one of his own.

"Oh my, no, Sheriff, I would have told you," Sayers sputtered, his face flushing with indignation. "When school started in September, we were running around like crazy getting settled in with our new classes. Whoever Rose saw over the summer, or even later on, was not something we even had time to discuss. You and I covered that ground already." He caught his breath, then rushed on, softening his tone. "And you didn't answer me a moment ago when I asked what you thought of the theory, or rumor if you will, that Fowler was responsible for her murder as well. Is it possible?"

Alex shrugged, his annoyance peaking. "It's a possibility but a highly remote one," he said shortly. "There are a lot of theories out there that make no sense, Mr. Sayers. They will all be addressed in good time. Now isn't it."

Impatient as much with himself as with Sayers, he glanced at his watch, drained the last of his beer, stood up, and reached for his parka on the back of his chair.

"Do you have to leave so soon, Sheriff?" Sayers asked, eyes narrowed behind the round rims of his eyeglasses as he watched Alex with an almost pained expression on his face.

"Yep, I sure do. I'm sorry to have wasted your time, Mr. Sayers. Thanks for the beer." Alex tipped a finger to his forehead in a parting salute. "Enjoy your evening. I'll be in touch."

Then he headed for the stairs.

He had just reached the main floor and was almost to the door when over the accordion music, he thought he heard someone call his name. When he glanced over his shoulder, he saw Lorna Kelly, ski jacket flapping open, hurrying toward him.

"Do you remember me, Sheriff?" she asked, slightly out of breath as she reached him.

Alex grinned down into a pair of green eyes below a mop of red hair. "You bet I do," he grinned. "You're Lorna Kelly. We met in Mr. Logan's office."

"Really, I'm so sorry to bother you," Lorna apologized, pushing back a loose tendril of hair from her face. "I was downstairs and saw you with Mr. Sayers. I wanted to catch you before you left because I have to talk to you a minute. Is that okay?"

"Of course it's okay," he assured her. "But let's see if we can find some corner away from the traffic and the noise." He pointed to several long, cushioned benches placed off to one side to accommodate those waiting for a table. They found an empty bench, claimed it, and sat down.

"I hate being a pest," Lorna apologized, "only I had to ask you a question."

"No problem," Alex said patiently. "Ask away."

"Well," Lorna began hesitantly, "I've been thinking about Rose Clifford a lot. All that terrible stuff in the newspapers and, well, I just wanted to know if you were any closer to, well, solving the case?"

Alex looked down into the green eyes staring into his and frowned. "Not at the moment, Lorna," he admitted, wishing there was any other answer he could come up with except the truth. "In fact, we're still in the process of trying to find a lead. Any lead at all. It's been tough."

Lorna's mouth tightened. "I wish I could help," she said. "At school Rose was always busy with groups of kids and teachers. It was all school activities. Everything was the school."

"Unfortunately, that's the rub." He gave Lorna a sheepish grin. "So beware. If anyone crowds the top of the pest list, it's going to be me. Please, if you ever think of any crumb that you may deem helpful, give me a call, okay?"

Lorna flushed and smiled. She was on the verge of a reply when at that moment, a group of energetic arrivals spilled into the restaurant with lift tickets hanging from jacket zippers and faces glowing from a day in the cold, open air. Most had just been escorted into the main dining room when Ben Sayers, topcoat over one arm, came ambling toward them.

"Well, hello again, Sheriff. Or should I say good evening?" He stood in front of the bench as he maneuvered into his coat. Then he gave his red plaid scarf a dramatic flip over one shoulder, pulled gloves from his coat pocket, and brushed off his fur-trimmed hat. He smiled at Alex benignly. "The place is filling up fast. Had time for one last beer, now home it is."

His glance swept to Lorna. "And good evening again to you, too, Miss Kelly. Most of our group has abandoned ship, it seems. Ah, well. See you Monday morning bright and early? Ta, ta." Before either Alex or Lorna could reply, as suddenly as he had materialized, Sayers sallied out of the door.

Returning his glance to Lorna, Alex caught her blank stare into the space where Sayers had disappeared. "He does give one a jolt, doesn't he?" he asked quietly.

"Yes," Lorna answered in a low, flat tone. "He sure does."

Alex drove home heavy in thought. The snowfall had let up, but the temperature had dropped into the twenties. All around him the early evening light was a drab, heavy gray. What nudged the edges of his mind was the way Lorna had reacted to Ben Sayers. Maybe it was the way most people reacted to him, Alex thought. Still, it was difficult to figure out how he and Rose had formed a friendly, working relationship. Odd duck? Oh yes, he was a strange man to say the least.

And why the honeyed reception tonight, the animated welcome, the beer, and the questions? A short while ago the man had been spitting furious at him. While tolerable civility this afternoon would have been expected, the royal welcome was close to ludicrous. And Sayers also managed a neat reversal of roles. He had taken over their conversation and deflected attention away from himself by asking questions that rolled off his tongue as though, Alex considered uneasily, they had been thought out well ahead of time.

Upon arriving home, Alex found a message waiting from Barbara Owens, Lisa's mother, asking him to call. A minute later, she was blurting out the news that Lisa was missing. "She never showed up at the bank this morning, Alex," Barbara Owens told him, panic in her voice. "I don't know who else to call. She's been in such a terrible frame of mind for so long. What should I do?"

SATURDAY, NOVEMBER 21

Alex sat at his desk wondering why the dickens he was working on another Saturday. Sleep the night before had eluded him. Lying with his eyes open and staring at the ceiling, he had wrestled first with guilt, then worry, then anger that Lisa could cause such heartache not only to him but to her parents. Barbara and Jack Owens were outstanding people. They had been almost as crushed by their only grandson's death as he had been. When he spoke to Barbara the night before, he told her truthfully that while he would call in a missing person report in the morning, it was far too early for any formal search to be put into play. Why this now? Why? Alex asked himself again. Unless, as with Rose's before her, Lisa's disappearance meant something else.

Alex gave his head a shake. No, he would not go down that road. Instead, he turned his attention to the stack of paperwork on his desk and plunged in. At eleven twelve, Marge buzzed him with a call. When Alex answered it, Jack Owens was on the other end of the line.

"Lisa's okay," Jack told him, his voice cracking with emotion. "She went off by herself and took a hotel room in Glens Falls. Said she wanted to think. I got her call a little while ago. She says she's willing now to get counseling, and she's agreed to stay with us for the time being. We've all been a little crazy, Alex. Sorry Barb brought you into this, but things will be okay now."

When he hung up the phone, Alex was all at once aware of the degree to which stored-up emotion had played havoc with him over the last twenty-four hours. His limbs felt like lead; his head ached. Moving almost mechanically, he turned back to the reports on his desk. He pushed through them until the noon hour, then closed up the office and headed home.

When he spoke with Jack on the phone, Alex had resisted the temptation to ask the name of the hotel where Lisa had taken a room. Now he asked himself if it was Alex-to-the-rescue time? He wondered if he ever knew Lisa at all. Could anyone ever be absolutely certain of what those close to them might be capable of given the right circumstances? And could he believe what Lisa told him about Rose? Had he shut his eyes to what he might not be willing to see?

Once back home, he took a long shower and threw himself on the bed. Within minutes he was asleep. It was more than two hours later when he woke up. The nap had recharged his system. His headache was gone and it was time he quit feeling sorry for himself. And for Lisa. After changing into comfortable clothes, Alex went to the phone and called Jenny. If he was going to get on with his life, he reckoned with a grin, Jenny was the most pleasurable place he could think of to start.

CHAPTER TWENTY
A Lie Revealed

SATURDAY, NOVEMBER 21

Jenny's Aunt Bea had gone home for the weekend leaving the apartment as spotless as Bea herself. Looking around, Jenny took in the freshly vacuumed carpeting, the sparkle of recently washed window panes, and the pleasant odor of furniture polish. The kitchen was in order, dishes in place in the cupboard, and the entire apartment was far more tidy and uncluttered than Jenny ever had time to keep it. Bea had even baked a luscious apple pie as a treat, mentioning when she left that there was ice cream in the freezer if Alex liked his a la mode.

Feeling content and relaxed, Jenny had just settled herself on the couch with a magazine and was about to leaf through the pages when the telephone rang. It was Alex.

"Are you hungry?" he asked without preamble.

"It's too early for dinner," Jenny replied, glancing at her watch. "It's barely three thirty."

"Well then, we'll find ourselves a cozy spot with a roaring fire where we can sip on champagne or something until we work up an appetite."

"Jenny's place has all that," she replied airily. "There's no champagne in the fridge, but there's a fire in the fireplace and some wine, if you like it light and white."

"Hmmm, sounds like it might be just the ticket. Be right over. I'll pour."

MONDAY, NOVEMBER 23

It was Thanksgiving week. Restricted from her normal routine, Jenny decided it was time to take a good look at her situation. Thanks to Bea, she had come through a period in her life which most likely would have spelled chaos without her aunt's generous help. Not only had she found herself suddenly thrown into a forced sabbatical from her job, but she was without a car, her lifeline. Of course, even if she had one, in all likelihood she would not be able to drive. Not with only one good arm. Not right now, anyway.

Thankfully, Bea had stood by her through it all, but there were other problems on her list. Most importantly, there was the fact that someone had tried to hurt, even kill her. And she didn't know why.

Now she was wondering if there could possibly be a connection to her seeing Alex? Or, more likely, did it have something to do with her friendship with Rose? And what about Lisa? While she could feel compassion toward a woman who had suffered the terrible loss of a child, she still had to wonder how far Lisa would go if another woman came into Alex's life. Rose had done just that and now, so had she.

She wanted to ask Alex these questions, but she could not. Whenever she mentioned Alex's ex-wife, he immediately became distant and edgy. So, after a few attempts that went nowhere, she backed off. Regardless, she still wanted answers, and sooner or later she would have them.

When it came to Alex, there was no doubt now that her feelings for him were deepening, and she was almost, but not quite, convinced he felt the same. There was still something she was having difficulty pinning down. While she loved being with him and the story their lips told when they kissed, there was still a vague distance and self-control Alex held onto, even at their closest moments. Strange!

Their weekend together had been great. Saturday night they went out after all, at Alex's insistence. They began with dinner at the Blue Barn where they listened to a jazz quartet and even tried a dance or two, arm in a sling and all. On Sunday they shared a lazy few hours with little talk of violence or tracking down killers. When Aunt Bea arrived just before six o'clock that evening, the three devoured thick roast beef sandwiches followed by the chunky chocolate brownies that Bea brought along for dessert.

Then all too soon, the weekend was over and Alex was saying good-night at the door, the pressure of his lips telling Jenny only a little of what she wanted to know. She clung to him for a long minute before let-ting go and stepping back. Returning to Aunt Bea's happy chatter in the kitchen, she felt a loneliness she could not quite define.

The newspapers on Monday hit hard on the upcoming trial of Charles Fowler for the murder of Lonny Jerome, as did most of the television stations in upstate New York. The double murders were big news, the fire stoked by the not-too-subtle intimation that Rose Clifford may have been his victim, as well. However, the news hawks maintained there was not yet enough evidence to charge him. Alex read the reports with grow-ing frustration. Fowler, the ready target. A quick jury conviction for the Jerome murder. Just as quick a conviction – by implication only – for vic-tim number one. Would the public buy it? He wondered.

Alex tossed the newspaper aside in disgust. There was nothing left to do now except wait for whatever was lurking around the next corner. And what it might be was anybody's guess.

TUESDAY, NOVEMBER 24

Alex was in his office on Tuesday morning when a smiling young lady with unruly tendrils of red hair was ushered in by Marge. It was Lorna Kelly, her expression as usual shy and reserved.

Lorna took a seat next to Alex's desk and primly adjusted her skirt. "Thursday is Thanksgiving," she explained. "Mr. Logan is out of town, so I'm off for the rest of the week." She looked hard at Alex, shifting in her chair before continuing.

"I remembered something," she said nervously. "I don't know why I didn't think of it sooner, but I was concentrating so hard on trying to remember who I thought might be close to Rose, that I didn't think about who wasn't."

Alex blinked. "Who wasn't?"

"Yes," Lorna said, fluttering a hand. "What I mean is, Rose was a nice lady and she got along with everybody, especially the kids in her class. She seemed to relate to them in a special way. Anyway, like I told you, Rose and Mr. Sayers were real friendly. That is until a few weeks or so before she was killed."

"Go on," Alex prompted, intrigued.

"Rose asked me to print out some lesson plans for her and to take care of some materials she needed to be copied. She knew I liked to make a little money on the side, and since she hated to spend time on the computer or the copier if she didn't have to, I'd do her typing and copying for her. I had just finished up the last job she gave me and was headed over to her classroom to deliver it. Only when I got to the door, I heard Mr. Sayers' voice and stopped in my tracks. He sounded really mad."

Alex leaned forward. "Where were her students?"

"Oh," Lorna said, gesturing. "They were all gone home. It was four o'clock, at least."

"Go on," Alex urged. "Then what happened?"

"Well, like I said, Mr. Sayers sounded mad but I couldn't make out what he was saying. Then he slammed something down on the desk. I didn't hear Miss Clifford say anything. When I got to the door and he looked up and saw me, his face was beet red and his eyes blazing. Then he kind of pulled himself together and turned around, told Miss Clifford he would see her later, and left the room. When he walked by me, he gave me a big smile. Like always. I didn't think too much of it at the time, and Miss Clifford was pleasant and nice when I gave her the lesson plans, although her face was flushed and I could tell she was embarrassed."

She wet her lips and went on. "It felt funny, though, when Mr. Sayers smiled at me. As though he'd molted from one person to another one, like magic. He reminded me of an onion. Like he peeled off one skin and, a second later, there was another one underneath. If that makes sense. It was eerie."

Alex thought carefully for a brief moment before he spoke. "Why do you feel this is important, Lorna? Lots of people have words, then it's over."

Lorna dropped her eyes, then slowly raised them. "Maybe it isn't important, Sheriff Banks. To tell the truth, I've always liked Mr. Sayers a lot. Really. But what struck me funny was after that day he and Miss Clifford hardly seemed like friends the way they had been. Honest, I didn't pay that much attention at first. But that I can tell you. They weren't good friends anymore." She paused and took a breath before she met Alex's steady gaze and went on.

"I guess I didn't know what to make of it. Like you said, friends have words now and again. But then a couple of times in the lunch room, I caught Mr. Sayers giving Rose a real cold, strange look. From then on, I admit, I wondered what was going on. I noticed that they still sat at the same lunch table as the other teachers, but they didn't sit together like they used to."

"I see," Alex said, unable to comment further.

Lorna rose from the chair, her cheeks flushing pink. "I feel really rotten coming to you and blabbing all this. It might not be fair to talk about Mr. Sayers behind his back. The more I thought about it, well," she paused, "I almost didn't come to see you, as a matter of fact."

Alex stood up, came around the desk and laid a consoling hand on Lorna's shoulder. Her expression was bleak. "You did the right thing, Lorna. Please know that what you told me will be handled carefully and with discretion. Whatever took place between Rose and Mr. Sayers may, or may not, be significant. But you weren't wrong coming here. Not at all. Everything I learn about Rose, even if it's only a piece at a time, is a step closer to the truth."

When Lorna was gone, Alex beckoned Will Burke into his office. When Will was seated, Alex leaned back in his chair, hands latched behind his head.

"I think we're finally onto something," he said slowly, watching Will's reaction as he spoke. "I think I know what wouldn't fit before. Sayers told an out-and-out lie and I never caught on to it until just now. He told me right off the bat that he knew of nobody Rose was dating. Nobody, yet the other night at Vincent's, he made the comment that Rose and

Fowler were 'getting it on pretty tight.' Rose had to have spoken to him about Fowler. Not only that, I just learned that the good friends story is bunk, too." He paused and took a deep breath.

"Sayers and Rose had a serious falling out. My little friend Lorna was the one who put her finger on it. She described Sayers as playing a part. Changing skins, like peeling an onion, as she put it." He chuckled softly. "Leave it to a young, naïve girl to see what us old, weathered professionals let get by us."

"I'll be danged," Will laughed, scratching his head.

"The man is an actor, Will. Darned if we might be on the right track at last. Sayers knew of Rose's plans for dinner that Friday night and there were ways he could have got his hands on her car keys. There's still nothing to link him to Lonny Jerome, so we have to keep digging. We know more now than we did yesterday, but there's still a heck of a lot we need to find out."

Will's serious, young eyes fastened on Alex. "Knowing is a far stretch from proving," he replied solemnly. "We've got a long way to go from here, Sheriff. And that's for sure."

CHAPTER TWENTY-ONE
JENNY GOES SHOPPING

WEDNESDAY, NOVEMBER 25

For some reason he was unable to explain, Alex was more on edge than usual. Or perhaps it was better explained as a niggling anxiety he could not quite put his finger on. The day had seen just the usual run of problems around town and the county, disturbances quickly and quietly handled, on the books and off again.

One obvious basis for concern was, of course, Lorna Kelly's story. But that was not all of it. If Sayers was their man – and Alex believed he could very well be – he would be brought down. But even that was not at the heart of whatever was eating at him.

Perhaps it was Jenny's decision to get back out into the world, as she termed it. She had cheerfully briefed him on her plans to take advantage of the wonderful pre-Thanksgiving sales. Aunt Bea had gone home to prepare for the holiday; Jenny would spend the day Christmas shopping in Glens Falls. Transportation was not a problem: she would take a bus and put her selections on layaway.

Perhaps Alex only imagined the not-too-subtle declarations of independence? *Well, why not?* he asked himself. Was he, after all, a man who preferred a fair and helpless maiden to whom he could play Sir Lancelot? Sickening thought. He put it aside.

Christmas shopping. He grunted. The holiday had been the furthest issue from his mind, yet he would have to come up with a gift for Jenny before long. And for his parents, as well. They were the kind of folks who cared more for letters and cards than things, and he had fallen behind in that department, big time. But he did call regularly. Maybe a visit come spring would keep him warmly wrapped in their good graces. Besides which, he wanted to see them. It had been awhile.

As the day wore on, Alex made and returned calls, but the edgy feeling persisted. After sending Marge home early to stuff her bird for the next day, he handled the office calls until the last deputy had signed in and it was time to close up. Certain that he was rotten company, he spent the evening alone and pensive, his solitude broken for a brief ten minutes on the phone with Jenny while she expounded on how great her shopping day had been.

Moping about the house, he stayed busy digging into a load of laundry and working on a crossword puzzle. Come eleven o'clock, he switched on the television, anxious to pick up the latest media foray into Fowler's upcoming trial. As expected, the puffing and shouting and ten-cent prophesies were still going strong. Disgusted, and glad the day was finally at an end, he turned off the set and headed for what he hoped would be a good night's sleep. Tomorrow was Thanksgiving Day.

Barbara and Jack Owens were sitting in the somber inner sanctum of Dr. Philip Zeibrich's office of psychiatry. He had telephoned them a few days before, requesting a meeting. He had, of course, secured Lisa's written permission to be as candid as needed. "I owe them," she had assured the psychiatrist, who was a stickler on client confidentiality. "I also need them to understand the way things are with me."

"I am not going into any great detail regarding your daughter's confidences to me," he told them from behind his impressive mahogany desk. He was a man in his early fifties, clean-shaven with thick brown hair streaked with gray.

"An important point you need to understand, Mr. and Mrs. Owens, is that I am treating a very unpredictable young patient. Lisa has been deeply traumatized by the death of her son and collapse of her marriage, so much so that she has taken refuge in her own world and her own emotions, totally engrossed in both. She is, in fact, attempting to make the past reconstruct itself. She wants vindication, to get back what she lost and blames herself for losing." He leaned toward them, fingertips together. "For your part in her recovery process, I advise you to be supportive in any way you can. I commend your decision to bring her into your home. But don't interfere. Lisa doesn't need a crutch; she needs to find the power to stand alone. Give her love and support and advice when she asks for it. Otherwise, she'll carry the weight of her burdens for the rest of her life. She'll continue to receive professional help from me and the therapy sessions she's already been attending. I've had fair reports from the clinic, but I'm certain you understand that only time and a lot of work can bring her into balance again."

Later, over coffee in a nearby restaurant, Barbara and Jack Owens sat across from one another looking sad and lost. "What are we going to do?" Barbara asked her husband.

"We'll do what the doctor says, I guess," Jack answered slowly. "What else can we do, hon? You heard what he told us."

"Yes, I heard," Barbara replied in a half whisper. Then she sighed. "I don't think we can help her, Jack. She's shut us out. Sometimes I look at her and I don't know who she is. It's an awful feeling."

Jack extended a hand over the table which Barbara, in turn, covered with her own. "Tomorrow is Thanksgiving and we can try to make it a special day for the three of us. Don't worry, hon. We'll stick by her and she'll come back to us," Jack told his wife with an assurance he wished he felt. "Lisa will be Lisa, again. Wait and see."

CHAPTER TWENTY-TWO
THANKSGIVING DAY

THURSDAY, NOVEMBER 26

It was a perfect day for a holiday. According to plan, Alex was at Jenny's apartment before ten in the morning for coffee and a fresh baked pastry. Laughing, their spirits light, they set out for Aunt Bea's house in Oak Creek where they would spend Thanksgiving Day. Driving along under the cold, cloudless sky through the rugged gray and green panorama of the Adirondacks, Alex glanced at Jenny and smiled admiringly.

"You look pretty good for a broken nurse," he remarked, looking her over.

"Never you mind," Jenny scolded with a crooked grin. "Keep your mind on the road."

Alex returned the grin and gave her a wink. "You'd be surprised where my mind is," he countered.

With that, Jenny laughed and sat back, content to enjoy the scenery and Alex beside her. Within a short time they were pulling into the drive of a neat, blue-shingled house, greeted by Aunt Bea standing in the doorway, a bright smile of welcome on her apple-cheeked face. She was wearing an apron with a cardigan sweater over it, her short, salt-and-pepper hair bouncing to the rhythm of her step as she hurried down the porch stairs to greet them.

"Oh, Aunt Bea, get back inside out of the cold," Jenny exclaimed as the older woman hugged them both in turn.

"Don't fret about me," Bea laughed, scurrying ahead of them toward the stairs. "Come along, the two of you. It's going to be a grand turkey day."

And that it was. Alex collected the two bottles of wine he had tucked into a cooler in the back of his Chevy Blazer and scooped up the basket of fruit and box of Bea's favorite chocolates which were Jenny's offerings toward the occasion. Once inside the house, they stopped to dramatically inhale the tantalizing aroma emanating from the kitchen. Bea glowed.

The easy mood continued through the day. Alex was treated like someone Bea had known for years; the wine was opened and poured; troubles were put aside.

By six o'clock, Bea's elegantly set dining room table had been cleared of the feast, her best dishes washed and put away. Sated and content, the three moved into the living room and collapsed before a small fire crackling in the fireplace.

"Can I talk you into staying the night, Jen?" Bea asked shyly, glancing toward Alex for support. "We can go back to your place tomorrow. To tell the truth, dear – and forgive me for asking again – I wish you would consider staying here for awhile."

Alex gave Bea a nod of agreement. "Bea is right, Jen. I'd feel a lot better if you were somewhere other than your apartment, at least until you get back to work at the hospital. This is a great spot. The mountains spread out at your back and the road to everywhere lies practically at your feet." He grinned and spread his hands. "What more could you ask for?"

Jenny gave Alex a tight-lipped smile, then looked at Bea. "I'm happy to be coerced into staying the night, Aunt Bea, but I want to go home in the morning. I appreciate your offer to let me move in for awhile, I really do. And I know you're right, Alex. But I can only promise to think about it. That good enough?"

Bea's head bobbed, pleased with her minor victory. "Oh, of course it is, dear," she said, smiling contentedly. "On the drive home we'll talk again, perhaps."

In Grover that same day, Ben Sayers was alone. For a few hours that morning he had done some reading, then he had taken a walk. Along the way he recalled the walks he and Liz used to take together. As the name slipped into his thoughts, he winced. He hadn't meant to think about Liz. No, he wanted to think about Rose. He needed to think about how Rose would love the blue skies and the crisp, cold, bright day. Of course he was thinking of Rose. The same as he always did. Only Rose.

Later, in the well-stocked kitchen set up to accommodate the cooking he so enjoyed, Sayers pulled a steak from the refrigerator and tossed it on the countertop. Turkey was not a favorite of his, Thanksgiving or no. So he had opted for a juicy steak instead. Humming as he worked, he began preparing his Thanksgiving meal, savoring the solitude and the quiet.

He had learned a long time ago to enjoy his own company. An older faculty member, a woman, had invited him to her home for the holiday. He appreciated the invitation, he told her, but he had made other plans. It never bothered him to be alone. The truth was, he preferred it.

As he moved about the kitchen, he found himself recalling another Thanksgiving Day. It was a year when Rose's parents were visiting relatives out of state. He had coaxed her into dining at his place, allowing him the opportunity to show off his culinary prowess. When she agreed, he had immediately laid out a menu: a golden-brown turkey baked to perfection with all the trimmings. The day, he recalled pleasantly, had turned out to be a memorable occasion. He imagined Rose as she looked that afternoon sitting at his dining room table, leaning toward him, politely attentive to whatever he was saying. He recalled how her eyes reflected the candlelight as she sipped wine from the rim of a long-stemmed, crystal wine glass, and the way she could send a smile across the table straight into his heart.

She looked so beautiful that day. In hindsight, he probably should have made a move on her while he had the chance. But something held him back. The stumbling block was Liz and what she had done to him. The risk of being rebuffed was too great. He was still carrying the scars of her rejection, of the miserable days and nights he suffered after she left him flat without even a final goodbye. He could never bring himself to chance that sort of rejection again. Ever!

He had honestly believed that Liz loved him. She said she did, and they talked about getting married. It was only later, after she walked out on him, that he got wind of the stories making the rounds behind his back, Liz telling people she was actually afraid of him. He could hardly believe she would say such rotten things. All lies. Rotten!

He felt the anguish beginning again, and the fiery rush of the old mortification coursing through him. He took off his glasses and rubbed his eyes. Afraid of him? Well, she was right. Maybe if she hadn't moved away he might have given her reason to be afraid. But she did leave. One day she was gone, off to another teaching job in another state. And to another man, he was sure of it. Then he moved away, too. He had seen the way people looked at him, pity in their eyes. Worse yet, he saw fear there, too. Thanks to Liz.

He was a good teacher, so it had not been that difficult to find a new place to work and to live. Which is what he had done. He had escaped.

The picture of Rose returned. It was funny how from the first minute he met Rose he was reminded of Liz. In fact, Rose looked like her. Same dark, shiny hair and bright, intelligent eyes, only younger. He released a long, shuddering sigh.

Back into the memory closet for Rose, where he had put Liz a long time ago. Right now there were other matters that needed his full attention. And his dinner was one of them. He began to hum again.

CHAPTER TWENTY-THREE
GULLIBLE WOMEN

It was mid afternoon, the day after Thanksgiving. Although the sun had been out most of the day with temperatures considerably improved from an early morning dip into the twenties, the man shuffled along the snow-encrusted Pine Road sidewalk huddled into a thick, hooded jacket, collar turned up and both hands shoved deep into the pockets. Some forty minutes earlier he had left his car parked across the street from High Ridge Apartments on Pine Road and had been pacing back and forth ever since.

Traffic along Pine Road was light, mostly sports buffs with skis secured atop their vehicles, eager to reach the powder of the upper slopes for the remainder of the long holiday weekend. As he watched them pass, he thought of Rose, and he was reminded of how much she used to enjoy skiing. For a few wayward moments, he allowed himself to think back to the days when they were, at the least, good friends. It seemed a long time ago. He was never much on skis himself, but he had joined her on a few trips to Gore and Mount Snow. He would sit in the lodge to read and relax while she tackled the slopes. Later, skis strapped onto the roof of her car, they would stop on the way home for a late dinner and talk about books or the new performances slated to open in the spring at one or the other of the many area theaters and music centers.

Well, that was all in the past, over and done with, he thought, reminding himself of where he was and what he was doing and why. There was no time to waste in futile trips into the neverland of the past. He was there to check out the enemy.

He dreaded the possibility that Rose's neighbor, the nurse, knew enough to cast a shade of suspicion in his direction. But he was stuck. She had come through the little accident he had rigged to get rid of her, so now he had to back off and bide his time. At least for awhile. What-ever Rose might have told her, she probably would have spilled by now, anyway. But that did not mean she was off the hook. He was keeping an eye on her.

Just then the sun went behind a cloud and he felt a new, cold shift in the wind. Disgusted by the discomfort of his vigil, which had thus far proven to be a waste of time, he was ready to head back to where he had parked his car when he looked up at the same moment Alex Banks drove by in his black Chevy Blazer. As he watched, Banks made the turn into High Ridge and then passed out of sight into the parking lot beyond. Seconds later, he came trotting around the corner of the building, head down against the wind, hurrying toward the High Ridge entrance.

The minute he saw Alex enter the building, the man hurried back to his car and started the motor, impatient for warmth. Lips pressed together, he speculated on what he had just seen. He did not have to be a genius to figure out who the sheriff was calling on. Jenny Wyland, of course. He smiled, crossing his arms across the rim of the steering wheel, his gaze honing in on the doors of the apartment building, keep-ing his fingers crossed that the sheriff was calling on the lady for a date and not a mere visit. His patience was rewarded not ten minutes later when Alex emerged from the building. He was not alone. He was, in fact, laughing down at the young woman at his side, the empty left sleeve of her coat flopping uselessly as they hurried through the cold toward the parking lot and Alex's car.

"Well, what do you know," he chuckled aloud, "the sheriff and the lit-tle nurse. I called it right."

He stared ahead for a moment as he deliberated on what to do next. He wanted to find out more and there was only one way to do it. As soon as he saw Alex's car merge into the Pine Road traffic, he pulled out from the curb and took the first left into High Ridge Apartments.

Inside the entrance foyer the man ran a finger down the list of tenants' names adjacent to the buzzer panel. He noted that the nurse was still in the same apartment. Good. He momentarily regretted not bringing along his key to the front entrance, one that he had made from the original way back when. Next time, he promised himself, he would remember.

Resigned to patience, he waited until an elderly woman finally appeared and entered the foyer. At the same moment, in almost dramatic pantomime, he began to fumble with the door lock, frowning as though unable to find the right key to fit. As the woman reached the door he stepped aside, allowing her to use her key to do the job. Then he held up his keys and with a sheepish smile and a shrug, took hold of the door behind her and went in. In the next minute the pair were in the elevator, and he had popped the sixth floor button.

The familiar path to Rose's apartment was quiet and empty as he followed it to apartment 608. Better not dally, he warned himself. Any of the doors along the hallway could open at any time. The last thing he wanted was to be spotted or questioned. Just then he caught the muted drift of music, voices, and canned laughter. Following the direction of the sound, he stopped in front of apartment 610. Another surprise. Somebody was in the nurse's apartment with the television on. It could be a cleaning lady, he supposed. Who else? His curiosity piqued, an idea hit him.

First, he rummaged through his pockets and pulled out a crumpled piece of paper, a shopping list he had written days earlier. After prepping himself with hat in one hand and the piece of paper in the other, he rang the doorbell of apartment 610 and took a step backward. Almost at once the television sounds faded away, replaced by the soft movement of approaching footsteps. A plump woman clad in a flowered apron over an old-fashioned, cotton housedress opened the door a crack and peered out. "Yes? Can I help you?" she asked politely.

The man smiled with all the charm he could muster, keeping his voice hesitant and apologetic. "I'm sorry to disturb you, Ma'am. My name's Lionel King. I just made the drive up here from New Jersey for my nephew's wedding and I seem to have run into a problem. Could you possibly tell me the number of John King's apartment?"

"Darned if this isn't embarrassing," the man rambled on, enjoying his role. "I should probably just go downstairs and start from square one by looking at the name slots, but," he effected a feeble laugh and rubbed his chin, "I thought I knew my brother's new apartment number. Guess I've been on the road for too long." He laughed, again. "I'm numb."

"Oh, dear. Of course," Bea heaved sympathetically. "I know how that is. Travel can be very exhausting. But I have to tell you frankly that I don't live here. I'm only visiting my niece. I'm not acquainted with any of the other tenants. I'm sorry." She released a sigh. "I wish I could help you."

The man pursed his lips, nodded, then frowned down at the paper in his hand. "Maybe you can." He fluttered the paper a little. "I have my brother's telephone number here. Would it be too much of an imposition if I asked to use your phone?"

Bea hesitated, wavering between her promise to Alex and Jenny to keep the door locked and not to let anyone in and the harmless act of helping a stranger in distress. Decision made, she released the door chain, stepped back, and held the door ajar.

"No, oh my, no! That's an excellent idea. Of course, come in. There's a phone on an end table in the living room and another in the kitchen. Please, Mr. King, help yourself."

Mr. King stepped into the entry foyer. "That's very kind of you," he said, beaming. "Here," he nodded to the end table a few feet away from where he stood. "I'll use the phone over there and we can just leave the door open. After all," he commented with a significant wink, "I'm a stranger and you're a very nice lady, and a trusting one. What is your name, by the way?"

Bea flushed. "I'm Bea Clifford and thank you for the compliment." Glowing with good will, she nodded toward the kitchen. "I'll just leave you alone now to make your call. I'm in the middle of cutting up apples for a pie, so I'll get back to work."

Crossing from the foyer to the living room, Mr. King picked up the telephone and dialed a random number. He cut off the call when he could hear his gullible hostess moving about the kitchen busy with her chores. Moving cautiously, he stood in the middle of the living room and looked around. He took in the comfortable furnishing, glanced at the framed photographs on the mantle over the fireplace, then drew a mental picture of the apartment layout: formal dining area and kitchen with a breakfast bar to the left of the foyer; living room to the right. Bedrooms and baths obviously off the narrow hallway to the right of the kitchen. Not unlike Rose's apartment, where he knew every inch by heart.

Beaming in the glow of the lark he was having, the man resumed his role. He pretended to speak to someone, then hung up the telephone and called out his thanks for its use. He was standing by the apartment's open door to the hallway just as Bea rushed in from the kitchen, wiping her hands on her apron as she inquired how he made out.

"I want the fourth floor," Mr. King laughed, fluttering the paper he still held in his hand. "The family's waiting for me. Thank you again, dear lady, for your kindness."

"My pleasure," Bea replied as her guest made his exit. She stood in the doorway for a moment, then closed the door, locked it, and walked back into the kitchen.

"Such a nice man," she said to no one in particular. "A real gentleman."

She knew both Alex and Jenny had admonished her not to open the apartment door to anyone. But she had looked him over carefully. The man was absolutely ordinary. Certainly not a murderer! And it felt good to have helped him with his problem. Things like that happen all the time.

Still and all, she decided, it was best she stay mum about it. No sense getting Jenny and Alex all riled up over nothing. She had simply helped a neighbor, that was all there was to it. Smiling happily, she began to roll out the dough for her apple pie.

Outside the building, "Mr. King" strolled back to his car humming a tune under his breath. His mind was soaring. Jenny Wyland and Sheriff Alex Banks. Together. "Well, if that doesn't beat all!" he mumbled. But if things went off the next day the way he had it planned, nursie would be looking for another playmate. He chuckled, congratulating himself on the way he had maneuvered himself into the building and then Jenny's apartment just at the moment he needed a bit of luck. All he had to do was take advantage of opportunities as they came along. And that he had done!

And Auntie Bea. What a pleasant, very stupid lady. She never even thought to ask how he managed to get into the building in the first place.

"Ahhh...gullible women," he crooned, cracking his knuckles and turning his car toward home. "They are a joy! Truly a joy. What would the world be without them?"

CHAPTER TWENTY-FOUR
THE SHOOTER

SATURDAY, NOVEMBER 28

Inside his bedroom a handgun lay on his bed. Not a fancy gun, just a small .22 caliber Jennings. Almost palm size. It was resting on a clean towel waiting for him to decide how, or when, to use it. And on whom.

He had no cause to worry; the gun would never be traced to him. He had stolen it during his college years when a drunken sophomore had shown it off at a frat party. The poor boob had no idea where it went after he passed out. It had been carefully salted away since then. He was sure it would come in handy some day. He was right.

Alongside it lay a newly cleaned Remington 30-06 deer rifle. He had bought it years back and rarely used it. But now, both weapons were loaded and ready to go. No prints left behind, either. He wore gloves to handle the ammo, then wiped both weapons clean. He laughed and cracked his knuckles, congratulating himself on how smart he was. If he was to survive, he had to be.

He stretched, wondering where to begin. He had to be careful, he reminded himself soberly. Very careful. He could not afford any more mistakes. The game was getting more deadly than ever, and he was playing to win.

Jenny had been testy all day, the cast on her arm becoming more of an itchy nuisance by the minute. Worse yet, all she seemed to think about of late was Alex. It surprised her that she could miss him so sharply, think of him so often, and at the same time be so disturbed by her feelings. She knew there was danger in sailing beyond her emotional limits. Alex

was caring and attentive, but was he in love with her? Always surefoot-
ed and careful with her passions, she had made it this far into adulthood
with her heart still intact. Now, deep in the shadows of her mind, a caution light kept blinking, warning her of what? Of Alex? Or of the mounting intensity in their kisses and the fact that she had never before felt so
passionately about any man?

But always, even during their most passionate moments, there was
that careful distance Alex maintained between them. And it was getting
to her. Without the security of the words she needed to hear, she was
left to wonder. And for the time being, to wait.

It was nearly four o'clock. Jenny was in the kitchen with Bea, determined
to do her one-handed part toward cutting up carrots for a stew, when
the phone rang. It was Alex. He was out of breath, his voice tense as he
came right to the point.

"Look, Jen, I'm okay, but if you turn on the television for the news,
you'll find out that somebody took a shot at me. I wanted to reach you
first to let you know I am all right and that I'll be over in an hour or so. Is
everything okay there?"

"Of course, everything is fine," Jenny exclaimed, shocked by what
Alex was telling her. "For heaven's sake, Alex, what happened? I want to
know. Please!"

She could hear the catch of an impatient breath on the other end of
the line. "Okay," Alex relented, "but I'll have to make it quick. I was in the
office when a call came in," he said, lowering his voice. "It was a guy
reporting that he found a dead man lying on the ground next to the
creek up along Glen Ridge, not far from where Rose was found. Told me
exactly where and said he would meet me there. I headed out and
radioed Will on the way so he would know what was up. When I got to
the place the caller specified, there was no dead man and not a soul in
sight." He paused and cleared his throat.

Jenny's heart was tripping. "Then what happened?"

"Well, I saw a shiny object on the ground. When I bent down to check it out I heard a rifle shot, then something smashed into the tree in front of me. When I straightened up, another shot grazed the side of my neck. By this time I had my own weapon out trying to determine the shooter's position. But whoever it was must have taken off. When I got back to the car, a reporter who had picked up my relay to Will on a scanner came barreling out to investigate. He got there even before the troopers pulled in. That's it, Jen. I'm not alone here and there's a lot of commotion going on. It's hard to talk. The medics took care of my neck and I'm okay. That's what I called to tell you."

Jenny let out a long breath. "I appreciate that, Alex. I'm so glad to hear your voice." Closing her eyes, she fought off the tears welling behind them. "When will this madness go away, Alex? If Fowler's in jail, who could possibly have done this?"

When she hung up the telephone, Jenny wiped her eyes and went to the front door. She wanted to be certain the double lock was in place. Then she pulled her shoulders back, lifted her head, and returned to the kitchen, Aunt Bea, and the half-chopped carrots.

Alex was angry. Someone was playing deadly games – and he was not in on the rules. The violence was escalating and becoming more complicated by the minute. The news hawks were anxious to hype the story of the shooting as a vicious and deliberate attack on the sheriff's life, while there were others just as ready to insist the shots were wayward accidents made by a hunter who realized what he had almost done, got scared, and ran. But Alex knew better.

The caller said his name was Bob Jackson. The voice, low and scratchy, was undoubtedly disguised. All incoming calls to the sheriff's office were automatically recorded, but so what? He had been neatly set up and he knew it. It galled him that the local justice system was so eager and ready to pin two murders on Fowler, so much so that any other possible scenario which might put a crimp in their case was immediately given the cold shoulder. As a result, Alex was left to fight a one-man battle to bring a killer to justice before another man took his place in a prison cell for years to come. It was up to him to find some solid evidence to prove the truth, or this maniac would run loose. Perhaps even over his own dead body.

A little later, a bandage plastered on his neck and his jaw aching like crazy, Alex filled out and signed the official incident report and headed out for Jenny's apartment.

He had expected Jenny to be upset over the shooting, and she was. Aunt Bea was, too. Given how rotten he felt, between hurting like the dickens from the neck up and contemplating all the ramifications of an attempt made on his life, he couldn't even enjoy their coddling and care. What he really needed was a good night's sleep and a clear head. He wished that the two had stayed at Bea's house over the long weekend. Someone was out there with deadly intent, and tomorrow, who might the target be? If his head needed anything to intensify the level of pain he was feeling, that question would do it.

That, plus the certainty that the savagery was far from over.

CHAPTER TWENTY-FIVE
A Secret Comes Out

After convincing Jenny the previous evening that yes, he was in one piece and basically unharmed, Alex had hugged both ladies, begged their forgiveness for a hasty departure, and gone home. But before leaving, Alex asked if Jenny would like to spend a few quiet hours at his house the next day. She had yet to see his place, he told her. And he wanted her to. Jenny said yes, she would be delighted.

She awoke later than usual on the next day, Sunday, her head still heavy from the stress of the day before. Even the prospect of getting dressed weighed on her. Still clad in pajamas, she sat at the breakfast bar chatting with Bea, who, with her usual expansive release of energy, was dashing about the kitchen sending occasional worried glances in Jenny's direction as she shuffled pancakes on the griddle.

"What time is Alex coming by for you?" Bea asked, carefully arranging a stack of the golden cakes on Jenny's plate and topping them with warm, Vermont maple syrup. She stood up straight, hands resting on ample hips. "I'm sure he's still pretty upset by the shooting hullabaloo. My, my" she fussed with a shake of her head, "such terrible people in the world."

"Yes, I'm sure Alex is as upset as we are," Jenny replied. "I'll phone him later. He could use a bit of extra sleep and I'm in no hurry."

Bea nodded, giving the griddle an extra shake.

Impeded by the cast on her arm, Jenny had to concentrate on manipulating the fork from plate upward. She made a low murmur of pleasure. "Mmmm, Aunt Bea, these are delicious," she laid down her fork, "only right now my mind is on you. It isn't fair that you've given up so much of your time and neglected your own home to wait on me. Please sit down and eat."

"Oh, tut-tut!" Bea quipped with a wave of her hand. "You're my family. And besides, I have good neighbors. The Blakley's next door keep a watchful eye on the house as well as on me. There's no need to trouble yourself about your Aunt Bea, love. It's you and Alex that need worrying about."

"We do," Jenny agreed with a wry laugh, manipulating the last of her pancakes. "This has all been a huge nightmare." Elbows on the bar, she rested her chin on one hand, her eyes distant and thoughtful. "You know, Aunt Bea," she said after a moment, "I suspect Alex knows more about what's going on than he's been telling me. Someone has been after us both, and Fowler's in jail." She leaned back in her seat and frowned. "Something is just not adding up. The next thing you know, we'll have some maniac storming the front door of the apartment with an Uzi." She grimaced in disgust. "After all that's been happening, nothing would surprise me."

All at once Bea's smile collapsed and her fingers flew to her mouth. She stared hard into Jenny's eyes for a long moment, then looked away.

"Aunt Bea, what on earth's the matter?" Jenny asked, confused and alarmed at the same time.

Bea shook her head and dropped onto a stool. "I have something to tell you, Jen," she said, clasping her hands together as they lay in front of her on the countertop. Her fingers began kneading one another nervously. "It's something I know I should have mentioned before this but, well, it seemed so innocent at the time. Of course," she added meekly, "maybe it was."

She released a long, resigned breath. "It happened Friday afternoon," she began. "You and I had already returned from my place and settled in. A little later, Alex came by and the two of you went out for the evening. I was paring apples in the kitchen and watching a show on television when I heard the door chimes..."

MONDAY, NOVEMBER 30

Alex was angry. Angry with Bea Wyland, with the entire set of circumstances he was desperate to confront and put an end to. No one wanted to believe there was a maniac running loose, as hard as he tried to convince them there was. Then yesterday, after Jenny and he had feasted on a superb dinner of sautéed shrimp and fried rice set off with a perfect white wine, she told him the story Bea had poured out to her earlier that day.

"When she finished telling me what she had done," Jenny said at the end of the tale, "I asked her what the man looked like. After she described him, I dug out my scrapbook and showed her a newspaper clipping from the *Gazette*. It showed Weston Elementary students receiving awards from the principal, Mr. Logan, with Rose and members of the faculty standing in the background. I told Aunt Bea to take a good look at it to see if she could pick out anybody who looked like it could be her visitor. She pointed to Ben Sayers right away. She was almost positive that he and her visitor were one and the same."

Alex had waited wordlessly until Jenny finished the story. She concluded with a final account of her aunt's regret over what happened. "It took me ages to calm her down, Alex. She was miserable. I had to convince her that there was no harm done."

"No harm done?" Alex stared at her, his expression incredulous. Then he got up from the sofa and exploded. "A man accessed your apartment at the invitation of your ditsy aunt whose throat he might have slit just for the heck of it! And no harm done?" He paused for breath, his eyes glazed over with anger. "She opened the door to a stranger when explicitly warned not to!" He rolled his eyes toward the ceiling and then looked hard into Jenny's gaze. "I'm taking you home," he gritted, his voice cold and remote. "I'll get your coat."

Within a few minutes Jenny was bundled into her coat and into the Blazer, sharing a stony and uncomfortable silence on the drive to High Ridge. Once back in the apartment, Alex gathered the women together in the living room and told them he had something to say. Choosing to remain standing, he began to pace the room while Jenny and Bea sat side by side on the sofa, waiting to hear him out. After a long minute, Alex turned and looked directly down at Bea.

"Bea," he said levelly, with no mistaking the undertone of anger in his voice, "I want you to know that what I'm going to say is said out of concern and fear. Fear for your safety and for Jenny's. And, I could add, for my own. Let me paint a picture for you: First and foremost, remember that your niece very narrowly escaped being murdered, quite possibly at the hands of the man you allowed to come into her home."

Bea gasped and stared up at Alex, her eyes widening with shock and pain. Then she dropped her head into her hands and began to silently weep. Jenny gave Alex a quick, disapproving glance while slipping an arm across Bea's shoulders. Alex looked on, unmoved.

"I understand that you deeply regret your mistake, Bea. But Jenny and I might have come back here to find you lying dead on the kitchen floor with your throat cut. In any case, if the person you let in was the madman, he is now laughing at us, sending the message that he can access Jenny's home at any time and do anything he wants to do. And we can't stop him."

Alex saw that Bea's shoulders were shaking, and he paused, sorely tempted to ease off a little. But he could not do it. He had trusted Bea. Her lack of common sense could have meant her life. And still could.

"To top off this mess, we have no way to prove anything. Assuming it was indeed Sayers, we could accuse him of coming here and you, Bea, could identify him. But it would be your word against his. And what did the fellow do here, anyway? What could we accuse him of? Nothing! He just used the telephone, that's all."

He finally softened his tone. "I wish I could make this easy for you, both of you. But you need to understand what we're up against here. Please, do as I ask. Jenny will have her cast off tomorrow, and Bea, I want you to go back to your own home within a day or two after that. But until the day you leave, you stay inside this apartment. I'll send my deputy over tomorrow to see Jenny to the doctor and back."

Bea was nodding as he continued. "Please leave soon. Right now that man knows who you are and what you look like. He also knows you can identify him. Which makes you a threat. The fact that he pulled the stunt he did and left you alive to talk about it is amazing in itself. He made another mistake. Only it might be a mistake he plans to rectify. And you can figure out what that means." He turned to look squarely into Jenny's eyes, his face hard and grim. "He's quite capable of killing again and we can't stop him. I'm sorry, Jen, but that's the way it has to be for Bea's sake as well as your own."

He began to rub the ache in his neck while he stared down at the two women. Bea was bent over, wiping her nose with the edge of her apron. Jenny's arm remained across her shoulders, her expression blank. Her only words were low, consoling murmurs directed at Bea. She made no move to look up or to say anything at all to Alex.

Bone tired, Alex decided to retreat. He snatched up his parka where he had tossed it on a chair, glanced from Jenny to Bea and back again, said a hurried goodbye, then turned and let himself out of the apartment.

Driving home through the wind-driven snow, the pitch of Alex's emotions began to subside. He recognized that he had been hard on both women, but he knew there was no other alternative. He was convinced that it was Sayers who had put one over on them by taking advantage of an old lady's hospitable heart. If Sayers was hunting down anyone he envisioned could harm him, as Alex believed, who would be next on his list?

Suddenly, he thought back to the Friday afternoon at Vincent's Grille, remembering that he had been talking with Lorna Kelly when Sayers approached them as he was leaving the place. If, in some warped, remote way Sayers managed to rationalize Jenny as a potential danger to him, might he not tag Lorna, as well? A cold chill shot through him.

"Nobody is safe from that madman," Alex murmured under his breath. "Nobody."

CHAPTER TWENTY-SIX
A SHIFT IN THE WIND

MONDAY, NOVEMBER 30

Alex was at his desk early, filled with fresh determination and purpose. He had mulled over the fact that up until now Sayers had enjoyed the upper hand in the game he was playing. But now it was time, he resolved with renewed fervor, for someone else to score a few points. Even if he went so far as to issue a barefaced challenge to the man, anything was better than waiting it out to see who his next victim would be. The healing scrape on his neck was a healthy reminder that it could be anybody, at any time.

After leaving Jenny's apartment so abruptly the evening before, he had crash-landed for a good ten hours straight sleep. Today he felt rested and clear minded, determined to come up with something that would hold Sayers at bay or show him up for what he was. It was time to make a move.

Alex set the reports on his desk aside, left Marge Grant a message to give Will, and headed out for Weston Elementary. The first item on his list was a quick and discreet chat with Lorna Kelly. He had not been able to dispel the nagging sense that she was in jeopardy. When you are dealing with only wisps of smoke, Alex reasoned as he drove through town, how can you point out to anyone that there is a wildfire headed in their direction? Unfortunately, that was exactly the predicament he was in. He was dealing with wisps of smoke. What he needed was a shift in the wind.

When he arrived at the school, Alex went directly to the principal's office where Lorna, seated behind the reception desk, greeted him with a welcoming smile. "Well, good morning, Sheriff," she said. "This is a surprise. Are you here to see Mr. Logan?"

"Hello, yourself," Alex said, taking a cursory glance around the room. The chairs against the wall were unoccupied, and although the door to Mr. Logan's door was closed, he could hear the hum of voices from behind it. "No, as a matter of fact, I stopped by to talk to you a minute. Are you busy?"

Lorna blushed and shook her head. "No, not too busy for you, Sheriff, of course not."

"Can we move over there?" he asked, indicating the empty chairs out of view from the open doorway into the hall.

"Sure, why not?" she laughed. "They're reserved for students facing detention but no worry about that today."

Once seated, Alex came right to the point. "I stopped by to make sure all was okay since our last conversation, Lorna. I've given it a lot of thought. Anything new since then?"

"No, not really, Sheriff. Just the usual routine, but quiet." Lorna told him. "Everyone here is still trying to get used to Rose being...well, you know. It isn't easy."

"I want to remind you to be careful," Alex warned. "And not just here at school. Understand?"

Lorna shook her head. "I'll be very careful, Sheriff Banks," she replied in a half whisper. "I think I know who we're talking about, and I promise."

As Alex left the office and Lorna went back to her desk, he sincerely hoped she would heed his warning, both for her sake and his peace of mind. He then headed directly for the wide flight of stairs leading to the second floor, mounting them two at a time. When he reached the upper landing, he strode to the sixth grade classroom and gave a sharp rap on the door. When Sayers opened it to discover the sheriff's tall, imposing figure in the doorway, his jaw fell and he took a step back, alarm alive in his eyes.

"Sheriff Banks!" he exclaimed. "What are you...." Before finishing his sentence, Sayers slipped into the hall, closing the door behind him. He faced Alex, his eyes mere slits behind the round rims of his eyeglasses.

"What, may I ask, is going on?" he demanded.

"We need to talk, Mr. Sayers," Alex stated, holding his gaze. "And now."

Sayers shot a significant glance toward his classroom and frowned. "I have a class to teach, Sheriff. I'm giving my students a quiz in five minutes. Is it necessary that this drama take place at this very moment?"

"Yep, it is," Alex shot back. "Unfortunately, this is part of a murder investigation, as you know. So yes, it is necessary."

Sayers shrugged. "All right," he returned, not bothering to hide his annoyance. "But I"ll have to ask one of my students to monitor the class while I'm gone. Wait here, please." With that, he turned his back and went into his classroom. He returned almost at once.

"My students caught a glimpse of you, Sheriff," he declared in a high, exasperated tone of voice. "Gun, holster, badge, and all. Their curiosity can be hard to contain. So if you don't mind, let's do our talking down the hall away from eager and curious ears."

Alex agreed and followed Sayers' clipping heels past closed classroom doors, keeping in step behind him. He looked around him. He was in a school. Not even while working the streets of New York City could he have imagined the search for a vicious killer taking place in such a setting. But catching a killer was the reason he was here.

When they reached the end of the hall, Alex wasted no time. "You probably know what happened last Saturday," he began, keeping his voice low and steady despite the undercurrent of rage boiling inside him. "I answered a routine call that ended up with somebody taking a couple of shots at me."

Sayers' eyes widened, then narrowed. "Oh, of course! The story was in the *Gazette* and on television. My goodness, Sheriff, you had a lucky escape."

"Lucky?" Alex chuckled. "I suppose you could say that. The fact is the guy was a lousy shot and missed. Not once, but twice." He held up a hand to deter comment and moved on. "But to more important matters. First, a new investigation into Rose's death is afoot. I thought you would want to know. Fowler's not our man."

Sayers stared at Alex in disbelief. "Wait, you're confusing me. As I understand it, all the evidence to date proves Fowler killed the Jerome woman. I recognize that there's insufficient proof that he killed Rose, too. But most people, including those in the district attorney's office, seem to believe he did. So what has changed, may I ask?"

"Frankly, Mr. Sayers," Alex smiled, beginning to enjoy the moment, "everything. First, the D.A.'s office has been doing what it can to stave off a local panic. No one, especially a politician, wants a killer on the loose. It's much more comfortable when the voters believe their elected officials have him safely contained behind bars. Think about those shots at me. Fowler was in jail. He couldn't have pulled the trigger, so who did? And why? Maybe I'm getting a little too close to Rose's killer and he wants me out of the way. Think that might be it?"

Sayers gave Alex a disgusted look, shoved his hands in his pockets, and leaned back against the wall. "So, you don't think Fowler killed Rose because somebody took a shot at you? You have undoubtedly sent people to prison, have you not? Isn't it plausible that your shooter could be somebody who is free now and wants to even the score?"

"No, sir." Alex dismissed the idea with the wave of a hand. "I don't think so. I believe the person who tampered with the brakes on Jenny Wyland's car is the same person who pulled the trigger on me, and," he took a breath and released it with a half smile, "is the same person who killed Rose Clifford and Lonny Jerome."

"Oh, really! I can't swallow all this," Sayers snapped, standing upright. "Do you mean to say that you interrupted my class to fill me in on these cockamamie theories about who killed Rose? And why come to me with all this absurd supposition in the first place?"

"Because," Alex pressed on, his attention riveted on Sayers' face, enjoying the glint of fear in his eyes, "you were one of the people closest to Rose. Jenny Wyland was another. I think she's already told all she knows. So, let's just say I need your help, to perhaps give me some inkling of who could have gained access to Rose's car. And who might have known of her plans for the evening she was killed."

The cords of Sayers' neck tightened and his voice rose a decibel. "But we've covered everything. I don't know anything about Rose's keys or schedules. And I can't have my class interrupted like this. Please try to understand my position, Sheriff."

"Oh, but I do, Mr. Sayers." Alex's grin widened, having saved the best for last. "And I do apologize for barging in on you but, as I said, this is a murder investigation. In fact, you can expect to answer more questions very soon. And they won't be mine."

"What does that mean?" Sayers gritted, his mouth forming a thin, grim line.

Alex paused and fingered his hat for a second or two, giving Sayers time to sweat a little. "For one thing, a special state investigator is being assigned to the D.A.'s office to look into Rose's death. While I understand your position, Mr. Sayers, the plain fact is, we're going to nail Rose's killer, no matter who gets inconvenienced."

"So be it then," Sayers lisped, pulling himself up to full height before he turned to face Alex with a look of cold, defiant enmity. "I thank you for the information. But now, if you will excuse me, Sheriff, I think my place is in the classroom. Whoever calls on me hereafter, tell them to make it after school hours. Good day."

Shoulders back, he nodded curtly, and then stalked down the hall, leaving Alex to watch his hasty departure and to wonder if he had managed to raise a bead or two of perspiration beneath the man's outer layer of indignity. Even now, Alex found it hard to fathom that Sayers, behind the clear rims of his glasses and cloak of academia, was a cold-blooded killer. He was a school teacher and a good one, or so he had been told. Ironic, Alex thought. And a pity.

But he believed Sayers was a killer, and he needed to be put away for good. "And if I have my way," Alex mumbled to himself as he went down the staircase, "that is exactly what's going to happen."

Alex had left Jenny's apartment in the heat of emotion the evening before, and Jenny was glad he did. He had only said what needed to be said, she understood that, but afterward, it was best she was alone with her aunt. Bea had suffered a terrible shock. And she had been hurt as well as humiliated, if only in her own eyes. Now Jenny wanted to do or say whatever she could to erase any wrinkles that might linger in their relationship.

But she need not have worried, for early Monday morning when Jenny padded into the kitchen greeted by the aroma of brewing coffee and the friendly sizzle of eggs in the skillet, Bea greeted her with a broad smile, waving the spatula in the air.

"Well, good morning, my dear Jenny. I thought you were going to sleep all day. Now come here and give your Aunt Bea a kiss. You and I are going to spend the day together and make it special. So sit down, rest your arm, and let's have a tasty bit of morning fare. I don't know about you, but I'm starving to death!"

A short time later, Alex telephoned her to let her know that Will would be by to transport her to the doctor's office. He added that he would not see her until the following evening but would call her in the morning and they could talk then. He also reminded her she would soon have two free arms to hug him with the next time they were together. There was no mention of the miserable scene the previous evening, and Jenny gave silent thanks for Alex's tact.

By noontime, thanks to Will as official escort and guardian, Jenny was seated in the doctor's examination room waiting for the results of the x-rays taken a few minutes earlier.

"Looks good." Dr. Brown smiled down at her as he entered. "We might have gotten away without a cast on that arm but I didn't want to chance it. You were very fortunate. The break was slight but the angle could have caused a wide range of problems. So now, young lady, get yourself over here where I can cut you free."

The rest of the day was spent packing. Bea fussed about, squeezing her belongings into the suitcases she had brought with her and exclaiming that the lot had multiplied threefold.

Jenny remained at the sidelines doing what she could to help and to keep the conversation going.

The day went by quickly. They had their dinner in the dining room, even breaking open a bottle of Jenny's favorite Chardonnay. With candlelight flickering off the walls and dancing shadows hiding the sadness behind their smiles, they raised their glasses and toasted to the future and better days to come.

CHAPTER TWENTY-SEVEN
THE AFTERMATH

MONDAY, NOVEMBER 30

Ben Sayers sat down to his supper, the magazine on the table which he planned to leaf through, ignored. From the time Sheriff Banks barged into his classroom that day he had tried to subdue, without success, the rising stream of his anger. He hated that man! He hated his arrogance and the very sight of him with his shiny badge and revolver on his hip. The Lone Ranger without a horse! What a mistake the man made to play Ben Sayers for a fool. And to have the gall to make a not-too-subtle declaration that he had pegged him for killing Rose. What was his half-witted challenge supposed to do? Shake him up?

And where did Banks get his information? What made him think he knew so much? Was it Lorna? No, all she could tell anybody was that she had seen him in a snit one day. For what, a second or two? If she put a more sinister spin on the occasion, she may have blabbed it already. Well, he would take care of her soon enough.

Forcing himself into a calmer state, Sayers continued with his meal. His rage would only upset his digestion, and he had invested time and care into the cuisine he had prepared for himself. He was not anxious to waste it.

It was later on that evening that he returned to thinking about his present quandary. He concluded that the wisest course of action at this point would be to move slowly. He had to watch his step. He knew full well that the sheriff was baiting him. It was not difficult to conclude that Banks had figured out he was the one who paid the old biddy a visit at the nurse's apartment. He should have taken care of auntie when he had the chance. Unfortunately, he was in too adventurous a mood that day and having too much fun. An oversight.

Still grumbling, he turned on the television, slumped into an easy chair, and waited to catch the news. As expected, all the news channels were still drooling over the Fowler case. Some big shot commentator was expounding on the fact that Fowler had hired himself a high-profile Albany attorney. Good! The prosecutor will be all the more fired up to get himself a conviction. If Fowler should get off you can bet it would make the town very unhappy. And him, too, for that matter. He wanted… no, he needed good ol' Chucky boy to take the fall. The trial would draw a lot of publicity. He would be sure to drop in and see some of the show for himself.

The news ended with no mention of any special state investigator storming the Adirondack hills. So why keep it under wraps if it was the truth? Unless, like Banks had told him, nobody, especially the politicos, wanted to cause a panic by announcing that a killer was loose on the streets. So the big boys were moving in to catch him? Sayers snickered. He was loose and he would stay loose. He had covered his tracks too well. There was no evidence that could lead to him. None!

He snapped off the television, laid his head back, and closed his eyes. As usual, his thoughts turned to Rose. He mused back to the shrewd way he had managed to get a key to Rose's car. Abracadabra! Not even Rose had an idea what happened to her spare. She blamed herself for misplacing the thing. He had been too clever. Let the gendarmes scratch their heads over that. A smug smile played over his lips. Nobody would be tapping him on the shoulder. Abruptly, the smile faded. There was one crack in his armor. That was Lorna. She was the only one who had even the slightest hint that all was not peachy between Rose and himself. Of course, had he allowed the rift between them to continue, it would only have been a matter of time before somebody caught on.

His thoughts continued to ramble, yet he still clung to the certainty that he was able to outsmart anyone. He could admit that he should not have lost his cool with Banks, but when he opened the door to his

classroom and saw him standing there looming over him, the unexpect-
edness of the so-called visit threw him for a loop. In that terrible second
he was certain Banks was going to snap on the cuffs!

Whatever the estimable sheriff thought he was doing, the ploy did
not work. Moreover, Banks was not going to get away with it. Not by a
long shot! Still and all, he would have to be especially careful when he
took care of the next problem on his list.

Out of curiosity, he had checked out the sheriff's ex-wife a few times
of late. Lisa Banks, the mystery woman; that discovery must have given
the sheriff a turn or two. He had been wondering if perhaps she had
moved out of the neighborhood since her car was not parked in its usual
space the last few times he had driven by. Well, she was of no impor-
tance now. Maybe later. Getting back at Banks would take some careful
thought. Plans were on the drawing board to do just that.

So why was he worrying? Everything was moving along as planned.
All the pieces were fitting together. As for the local authorities, they
were frantically running their tails off trying to avert a panic. A woman-
killer was loose. All it would take to regain public confidence was the law
closing the case on a couple of murders. Who gave a hoot where the
blame fell so long as it fell somewhere. Fowler suited their purposes
nicely. And his, as well. No matter what Banks implied to the contrary.

He thought back to the day he saw the mystery woman in the market. What a kick it was to give Banks the story. What the heck, it was
true, right? Another lucky break, and a convenient one, for him. Banks
thought he was talking to a blithering idiot when he refused to tell him
who the woman was. Why, Alex old boy? Were you thrown into a panic
when your ex-wife made a sudden appearance in the game? Well, there
she was, right in the middle of the limelight. Had old Alex's head spin-
ning with questions for awhile. No doubt about it.

Banks was dead wrong if he thought he was the only one who had
caught the license plate number that night. Car, color, make, and plate
number. It took him all of thirty minutes or so to walk a few blocks that
next evening and to spot the lady's vehicle parked in front of the house

she lived in. It was not even necessary to ring her doorbell. He merely climbed up the porch steps and there was her name next to the mailbox. Imagine that? Lisa Banks. The same name as Sheriff Banks. His sister? No, his ex-wife!

Most people hereabouts knew Banks had been married and divorced. It comes with living in the public eye. And how convenient that Mrs. Banks provided a darn good motive for murder by going after Rose at school. It certainly will keep those cops busy wondering just how far a jealous ex-wife would go.

Of course, Fowler was the one who provided the ideal setup. He was the perfect patsy to take the fall. Sayers chuckled to himself, remembering the bitter taste in his mouth when Rose told him about what a great guy Fowler was. Before that it was Alex Banks. He would never leave the sheriff out of the story. After all, he had his role to play.

Then came the day that changed everything. Rose had come to school wearing heavy makeup in a feeble attempt to hide a nasty bruise on her face. When she finally admitted what happened, he lost it. He had warned her about him! He hated Fowler but he also hated Rose for getting involved with the loser. It served her right.

Unfortunately, when he let her know what a lowlife Fowler was and how in his book she was no better than the trash she had gotten herself involved with, she turned on him. She got all-fired high and mighty, asking how dare he talk to her that way. The truth was too much for her, so what did she do? She wrote him off, just like that!

She had such a good time with Fowler, did she? Was getting a backhand in the face a good time? At that point, he had enough. Day and night, all he could see, like a scene played over and over, was Rose with Fowler. Not only that, the strain he was living with every day at school was unbearable. He finally reached the decision to get rid of them both. It was then he began to formulate a way to do it, and to do it without a hitch.

He had worked out what he would do, step by step. First on the list was Chucky boy. It was mid-October when he began a casual surveillance of his target. Fowler's cabin was located north of town on one or two scraggy acres along Old Mill Road. Neighbors included a few tired, rundown homesteads on adjoining acreage. Most important were the narrow side lanes he found. Loaded with potholes and rarely traveled, they became an observation post where he could spy to his heart's content without being spotted.

Next step was a close-up study of Fowler's property layout. There was a cleared spot in the back of the cabin where Fowler left his rig when he was off the road, and a freestanding garage at the end of his driveway where he parked his Ford pickup and Chevy sedan. There was also a metal shed off to one side of the house. One day when the rig was gone, Sayers was able to take a quick look into the shed, long enough to make out the junk tossed helter-skelter inside.

It took him no time at all to get a handle on Fowler's everyday habits and to learn that when he was off the road he would either roost inside his cabin staring at the television or go out romping with the boys in one of the local bars. When he hit it lucky, a woman would be conned into thinking he was the man of her dreams for the night.

Running to kind, Fowler wasted little time after the incident with Rose at Shepherd's Cove to find himself a new girlfriend. Like a patient predator, Sayers waited. September passed. It was only a matter of time before something would tick the old boy off and then bingo, bye-bye romance. The new lady in Fowler's life would be sporting bruises and Fowler would be shown the door. Again, running to kind, he would not take the brush-off lightly. That was the best part. It had to happen. Meanwhile, October was slipping by and it was time to take care of Rose. First things first.

Sayers snapped his eyes open and headed for his desk in an alcove just off the living room. He switched on the desk lamp, then sat down and pulled a thick, black journal out of a side drawer. Flipping through the pages, he came to the one he was looking for.

When he opened another drawer for a pen, his eye fell on two keys lying in one corner. He picked them up and caressed them lovingly. They were Rose's spare car key and the key to the High Ridge lobby entrance, the one he had left at home the evening he paid Auntie Bea a little visit. He laid both keys back in their place. Next time he would be sure to have the lobby key handy. He smiled, picked up his pen, leaned over his journal, and began to write.

CHAPTER TWENTY-EIGHT
AUNT BEA GOES HOME

TUESDAY, DECEMBER 1

It was shortly after ten in the morning when Lt. Donahue, whistling a tune and wearing an unusually smug grin, came through the door of the sheriff's office waving a folder over his head. It contained the lab and ballistics report on the shells fired at Alex on Saturday.

"Wait until you hear this," he began, dropping the folder on Alex's desk with a ceremonious flourish before he pulled up a chair and sat down. "The shots fired at you were from a Remington 30-06. We dug one slug out of a tree. The other one got away. Whatever, your shooter didn't bother to pick up the casings. That would, at first glance, indicate a foolish oversight. But strangely enough, both casings were as clean as a whistle. And I mean clean. Not a smudge on either of them. Darned if they didn't look like they had been polished!"

All the week prior, Alex had been debating with himself as to whether or not he should confide what he knew to Donahue. On the one hand, he knew Donahue pulled no punches concerning his attitude toward Fowler's guilt: Fowler killed Lonny Jerome, ergo, he is guilty of Rose's murder as well. Furthermore, justice was in the works. The authorities had the murder weapon and the sworn affidavits of a half-dozen folks who had witnessed his rage in the diner where Lonny worked. Besides that, they had a record of the late-night series of calls he made to her. On the other hand, Alex reasoned, he had known Donahue for a long time and had collaborated with him on some tough cases. He was fair despite wherever he believed the evidence might lead.

Even so, in order to convince Donahue, or anyone else, that Sayers was the shooter, it would take more of a persuasive argument than he was presently able to come up with. What evidence did he have? Only what Lorna had seen and felt, which was something that could be shredded to bits in ten seconds by any competent trial attorney. Ditto to Aunt Bea's finger pointed at a newspaper photo. Even Sayers' supposed ignorance of the men in Rose's life which he later slipped up and contradicted wasn't proof. Who heard the lies except himself? He had no choice. He had to let it ride.

Yet here he was again, tempted to lay out what he considered to be fact and to let Harry be the judge. Alex leaned his elbows on the desk and leveled Donahue with an inquiring eye. "Why do you think the casings were left behind?" he began, his tone level. Without waiting for a reply, he continued. "I'll tell you why. It's a part of the killer's game. He laughs behind his hand knowing we can't touch him even when he drops contrived evidence in our laps." He nodded toward the report. "We find the casing he leaves, our hopes go up, and we zip our precious evidence off to the lab. And what do we get back? Nada. Don't you get it, Donahue?" he asked, his voice rising. "We do the dance while a killer plays the tune."

Donahue leaned back in his chair, his lips pursed, allowing Alex the time to get out of his system whatever it was he had to say.

"And maybe you can tell me how Fowler broke out of confinement to snipe at me?" Alex asked, eyebrows raised. "It was not his finger on the trigger, and you know that, right?"

"You're funny," Donahue drawled, his deep voice edged with friendly sarcasm. "So what may I ask is your take on the shooter, my friend?"

Alex leaned back and folded his hands across his chest. "If you really want to know," he said with a self-satisfied grin, "I have my theories. You want to hear them? Be glad to oblige."

Donahue's eyes narrowed slightly, his gaze level. "Let's hear it all then," he said simply. "You've got my attention, Sheriff. Shoot."

It was midmorning when Bea left for Oak Creek. Chastened and subdued, regretting her foolishness, she had ultimately accepted banishment with good grace. She understood that Alex's confidence in her, or lack of it, was well deserved. She found it difficult to blame him. She was neither worldly enough nor suspicious enough to play the part expected of her. Although she sorely wanted to stay with Jenny, she had packed up, ready to return home where, as Alex reminded her again on the telephone when he called to say goodbye, she would be safe.

As the miles fell behind her, the image of Jenny's eyes as she sniffled into a hanky brought a new rise of tears to her own. She thought she had cried enough Sunday night, but, she reckoned with just the touch of a smile, she would brush away a few more tears in the days to come, to be sure.

She loved her niece. She had no children of her own, but she was sure no daughter could be closer. The short time she had spent with Jenny and the good feeling that went with caring for somebody she loved had brought a new glow into her life. And Alex had become special to her, too. She shuddered to think she might have added to the danger Jenny and Alex were already surrounded by. With one last, long sigh, she looked out into the mountains fringing the highway and continued on toward home.

After Aunt Bea had left for Oak Creek, Jenny felt as though the apartment had fallen into a state of utter gloom. Accustomed by now to the sound of her aunt's voice and hearty laugh and the clatter she made in the kitchen, Jenny realized all at once that she had always been too busy to miss anyone. Admittedly, she now sorely missed her dear Aunt Bea.

Pushing back the threat of fresh tears, she kept her mind occupied with thoughts of the evening ahead with Alex. She took a long, soapy bath, put together a simple dinner, dimmed the lights in the living room, and lit a romantic fire in the fireplace. By seven o'clock Alex was at the door, inspecting her newly-freed arm and giving her solemn permission to hug him with it. An hour or so later, when dinner was over and they were relaxing together in front of the fire, Jenny told him of her plans.

"I can't be a prisoner in my own home anymore, Alex," she announced, a determined note in her voice. "Since my car was totaled, I've decided to lease instead of buying a new one. Not only that but I need to go back to work as soon as the doctor releases me." She raised a hand to forestall the objections Alex was about to make. "Please try to understand. I can't hide here forever, and I can't put my job on hold indefinitely. Christmas is just around the corner, and I want to get out into the stores and do some more shopping. I want to have my hair done and go to church on Sunday. Simply put, I want to go back to living a normal life. Okay?"

Looking into Jenny's soft brown eyes and reading the expectant note behind her gaze, Alex conceded that he had no right to try changing her mind. Besides, he could see it would be a waste of time. Her mind was set. She knew the risks as well as he did.

"I can't stop you, Jenny," he admitted with a long sigh of resignation. "It could be a dangerous decision, but it's yours to make, after all. Just think about it, will you?"

Jenny snuggled down into the curve of Alex's arm. "I have," she said. "I've thought and I've thought. That's the trouble – there's too much empty time to think. Quite frankly, I can't let that man Sayers control my life, which he has already accomplished to a far greater degree than I appreciate."

"Yep, I know," Alex agreed softly. "I just don't like seeing you step out into his line of fire, Jen. Can you understand that?"

Jenny didn't answer, she just snuggled deeper. She wanted to tell Alex that there were many things that went beyond her understanding. And most of them concerned Alex himself.

Alex lay in bed that night thinking about Jenny. He worried about her decision to drive again and, if he guessed correctly, of talking the doctor into releasing her for hospital duty as quickly as she could convince him she was ready and able. He could understand why she wanted to go back to living her life, but he still couldn't easily accept it. Whatever personal feelings he had for Jenny, in many ways they were separated from the professional. On the professional end, as a law officer investigating the death of two women, it was not within his purview to tell her what she could or could not do. He could only point out the danger she could be heading into. No, he corrected himself, she was already in. Breezing around town on her own made her much too vulnerable a target.

On the personal end, he was still stymied. As someone who loved her, he could ask, even plead. But that avenue of commitment had yet to be explored. Their relationship was still new; still deepening. This was not the time, when they were both stressed out to the max, to decide what they wanted from each other. Or did not want. They had nothing firmly established. Not yet. And maybe they never would.

He had no problem owning up to what he felt for Jenny. He had even let it slip to Lisa that he was in love with her. But he could not bring himself to make that emotional commitment a stated fact, at least not until Sayers was caught and locked up. Then, when they were relieved of the stress they were currently immersed in, they could take a fresh look at one another and move on from there.

Hardly beside the point, Lisa was still in the picture. He felt, to some degree, responsible for her. They had been through too much together for him to simply write her off and walk away. While he might wish differently, it was almost a certainty that he would hear from her again. He would have to call Jack Owens. He and Barbara had a lot to handle. What he could do to help, he had no clue. Perhaps at least it would relieve the feeling that he was hiding in the background letting them shoulder the load. He almost wished he was the kind of person that wouldn't bother. But no, he was not.

He brought his thoughts around to Ben Sayers, wondering what the man would do next. The waiting was the worst of it, knowing that the sick and twisted mind they were dealing with was growing more depraved by the day. Regardless, he was not about to wait passively for Sayers' next move. Not anymore. He had taken his jab at the man; now it was Donahue's turn. He would leave the timing up to Harry, thankful that at last he had an ally willing to test his theory, however skeptical or reluctant that ally might be.

His brain overworked and heavy, Alex turned over and punched down his pillow, willing his mind into neutral gear. Experience had taught him that sleep was almost impossible when his worries were stacked up like sheep to count and fret over. Eventually, as he closed off the world, the shades of sleep came down, and Alex's even breathing was the only sound in the room.

CHAPTER TWENTY-NINE
A Reluctant Ally

WEDNESDAY, DECEMBER 2

The day had begun cold and blustery, the temperatures dropping down to ten above zero during the night with a wind chill of twenty below, or worse. By four fifteen that afternoon, thermometers were hovering just under twenty-four degrees as Harry Donahue came tromping through the sheriff's office door. His face was red from the wind and his lips curved into an all-too-familiar, satirical smile.

"Gotta get some coffee before we talk." He winked over his shoulder at Marge as he headed for the back room, a chill of cold air quivering in his wake. When he entered Alex's office a minute or two later, Will right behind him, he laid down the coffee mug and flung his coat on a nearby chair. Alex recognized at once that there was something he was busting to get out. Grinning, Harry sat down, allowing neither Alex nor Will any choice but to wait it out until he was ready to satisfy their curiosity. They could dangle until then. Finally, he picked up the coffee mug, sat back, and began his tale.

That afternoon, a little less than an hour ago, he told them, he had waited for Ben Sayers in the parking lot outside Weston Elementary. He had decided earlier that the best time to have his talk with Sayers alone was to catch him as he was leaving the school.

"Right on time," Donahue said, "Sayers came trotting out of the side door and made a beeline for his car. He didn't realize there was a state police vehicle parked only two spaces away. The expression on his face when he looked up and saw me standing there leaning on the fender of his car made it worth the wait in the cold."

Donahue chuckled, took a pull of his coffee, and continued. "If ever I saw a flash of pure guilt and fear cross a man's face, it was when it dawned on him that he was my target. To add more spice to the mix, there were several teachers leaving the building at the same time, and I tell you, they were taking it all in. A bit of faculty attention which I'm sure Mr. Sayers didn't appreciate one little bit."

The interview itself, Donahue informed them, was more or less a repetition of Alex's version – blah, blah, blah, as he put it. "But it threw him," Donahue added with relish. "It sure did. The man was cool on the outside but shaking in his boots. Believe me, I know the signs."

Leaning forward, elbows on his desk, Alex felt the first surge of elation he had enjoyed in a long time where Sayers was concerned. "So! Are you telling me you agree with what I've been telling you?" he asked, an eyebrow raised with the question.

"About him killing Rose? Yeah," Donahue shot back, "I believe you hit it right on that one. And I've little doubt he was your shooter and that he had a hand in Jenny's Wyland's so-called accident. But I have to add here, my friend, that I see nothing in the way of evidence that will get Fowler off the hook. He's still the one we want for the murder of the Jerome girl, and that hasn't changed one iota."

Alex gave Donahue a satisfied grin. "Half a loaf? I'll take it. For the present time, anyway," he added with forewarning in his glance. "Now, run through that interview with Sayers again." He looked at Will who was sitting with arms crossed, grinning eagerly, then back at Donahue. "Go ahead. We want to savor every word."

That evening, Alex and Jenny were having dinner together at her place, and Alex was providing the Chinese takeout. When he arrived shortly after seven o'clock, Jenny was wearing a soft, gray cashmere sweater over darker gray wool slacks with just a small pair of pearl earrings as accent. Taken by the way she looked and moved, Alex regarded her with an admiring eye. She wore her lithe slimness as elegantly as she wore her clothes. She was a beautiful woman, and he would be a fool to let her get away.

Jenny was more sparkling and lively than Alex had seen her for some time. When they finally sat down at the candlelit table, they looked first at each other and smiled and then at the steaming bowls of food on the table: savory beef with oyster sauce, Szechuan jumbo shrimp, fried rice, and General Tso's chicken. Jenny lifted her teacup in a toast. Her eyes were reflections of the candlelight, her shining brown hair lay in alluring silkiness against her cheek.

"I want to toast to better days, Alex. And to my new car, if you don't mind. It's the day I've been waiting for. I can happily announce that I'm officially back on the road." Her smile widened. "I now have a brand new Toyota Camry. It's a pretty blue, by the way. One of my favorite colors. And to add to my sense of newfound freedom, I've also returned to my Christmas shopping. It makes me very happy to finally be able to navigate under my own power." She lifted her cup higher. "Now, let's toast to you, Alex. To whatever it is that makes you happy."

Alex smiled and lifted his cup. "What makes me happy," he said softly, "is you. I'm glad we met, Jenny Wyland. I hope you feel the same."

Jenny laughed and clicked her cup against his before reaching for the general's chicken. "Of course I do," she replied a little too abruptly. "Now come on, eat up while it's hot. Can we forget the world outside tonight, please?"

"Hmmm, I don't get invitations like that very often," Alex teased. "Now pass that chicken; I'm starved."

The cold had seen no letup, and snow was melting in languid teardrops down the warm panes of his windows. It had been a rotten day, and now the early darkness was blackening out the hills and the valleys like an inky menace devouring everything in sight.

In fact, the world outside felt more dismal than Sayers could ever remember it being. His unexpected visitor in the parking lot that afternoon had only deepened the shadows in his life. When he had seen the trooper's smug smile and the self-satisfied gleam in those cold, sharp eyes, he had come as close to panic as he had ever experienced. But not for long. It took him only a foggy breath or two to catch on to what the trooper and his sheriff pal were up to. Not only did they want to scare him into a state of panic, they also wanted to give his coworkers something to snicker and whisper about. The Lone Ranger and his sidekick thought they had him all figured out.

But they were wrong.

He laughed and cracked his knuckles.

Just how wrong, they would soon find out.

CHAPTER THIRTY
A FLASHBACK TO MURDER

Sayers was beginning to feel better than he had in weeks. In fact, as the day moved on he was certain that the wavering strands of uncertainty hovering in the corners of his mind had begun to grow weaker, while the core of what he was, or better yet, what he was becoming, was like a raging river of power ready to overflow its banks. No more would he shrink away from the barbs of rejection and humiliation that could penetrate his psyche like searing coals of red-hot fire. No, he was not about to let the enemy do that to him ever again. Not and get away with it.

He was a head above those others and he knew it. Well above the educated faculty whose eyes, glued to his every move, mirrored the unspoken suspicion, even fear, behind them. He caught all their covert glances, even those of the kitchen help and the janitor. He might be many things but he was no fool. He smiled, recalling how John Logan had stopped him in the hall during recess only a few days prior. The man had given him one of his practiced, patronizing smiles.

"Everything going all right with you, Ben?" he had asked.

"Of course," he had laughed, hating the lisp that too frequently slipped out from beneath his control. "Why shouldn't it be?"

Logan's congenial pat on the shoulder and flimsy smile as he moved on had come off as stale as last week's bread. "Too bad, Mr. Principal," he said under his breath. "Been listening to tales about me, no doubt? Keeps you wondering, huh?"

But that was yesterday's news. Today he had to think ahead. The next day was Friday, and there were matters to be resolved. He would be joining the usual gathering at the Rathskeller, ready to play his part as virtuously as he knew how. He would mingle under the watchful, appraising glances of his fellow workers until he accomplished what he was there to do, which was to pass a few, friendly words with Lorna Kelly. He wondered how the young lady would react to the overture. That was what he needed to find out.

After he neatly returned the dinner dishes from the dish rack to their place in the cupboard, Sayers wanted to move. To do something. He staved off the nervous urge by picking up the evening copy of the *Gazette* and settled down in his favorite chair to browse through it. After a few mind-rambling minutes, he gave up. He put his head back and closed his eyes, giving way to a swirl of memories that beckoned him down a long, dark tunnel. He was moving back in time. "Ahh," he whispered contentedly, aware that the tunnel's darkness as well as the present were fast fading behind him, until that time so far away became the moment's reality.

It was Friday, October 30 again.

It happened the moment he overheard Rose telling another teacher about her plans to meet some college friends for dinner at six thirty that same evening. As her words registered in his consciousness, elation coursed through him. Finally, he breathed with relief, the chance he had been waiting for. Not another day would go by with Rose snubbing him as though he had ceased to exist in her world. He had been patient and ready. Everything was well worked out. Pretty soon, he thought with grim satisfaction, Rose would never snub anybody again.

Later that afternoon he had hurried home and retrieved the few things he needed from his flat, then drove back to Weston over a pre-planned route that curved upward from Solomon's Gorge Hill into the higher elevations beyond. After a twisting climb of twenty minutes or so, he came to the area he had previously scouted out. It was a small, paved parking area off the berm of the highway designed for the use of hikers about to trek up the nearby mountain trail to the peaks. Most importantly, it was a place where anyone could leave their vehicle legally parked until dusk. The state police who patrolled the road were lenient and ticketed vehicles were rare. It was a dandy spot. Asphalt paved rather than dirt. A place that would leave no traceable tire tread marks to tell tales later on.

He pulled off the road and cut the motor, taking a slow look around to be certain he was alone. As expected, the parking spaces were empty. It was, after all, late fall, a time when the days were growing shorter and, fortunately for him, most leaf-peepers and human mountain goats were disinclined to challenge the cold and the sudden blanket of darkness which, if hikers were caught at the peak, could so quickly and dangerously obscure the miles of trails leading back to safe ground below.

Once satisfied that he was alone and unobserved, he pulled out the old bike he had recently reconditioned and stashed in the trunk of his car. It was a sad-looking conveyance if one were to judge at first sight, but it was in good working order. He had made sure of that. After donning gloves, a black hooded sweatshirt, a black knit ski hat that he pulled down over his ears, and lastly, a backpack filled with vital necessities, he was ready to go.

Taking a deep breath, he hitched himself aboard the cycle and headed out. Bent low over the handlebars, he began to coast down the sloping curves of the mountain road and through the cold dusk of evening. The greatest challenge would be the steep, serpentine descent of Solomon's Gorge Hill that lay a few miles ahead. By the time he reached the Gorge's crest, general traffic had increased. It was Friday, he reminded himself, and the weekend rush had begun. Holding to the side of the road, he managed to apply just enough brake pressure to keep the bike moving at a moderate pace while still maintaining maximum safety through the final descent. Horns blared at him here and there, but eventually, his heart thumping against his ribs and sweat trickling down his brow, he made it to Pine Street. Checking to be sure no one was around, he pedaled into the High Ridge entrance and then into the parking area, not stopping until he had reached the far end of the lot. Once there, still panting, he swung himself off the cycle. Then he checked his watch. He had made it. And on schedule. It was barely six o'clock.

Despite the mental and physical effort it took to cover the ground between the mountain and his destination, and in spite of the cold wind that was biting through the sweat on his face, he felt the euphoric thrill of accomplishing his goal. He let the feeling flow for a minute before rousing himself. He had to hurry. There was work to do.

He looked over the long, dilapidated bike rack. Moving quickly, he added his own cycle to the three well-used bikes already there. Noting the paint peeling in shriveled strips to reveal ugly, rusting blotches of metal, he was sure the bikes had been abandoned by their owners some time back. There was little risk that any of them would attract attention until cleanup time in the spring.

Next, he located Rose's Honda in its usual parking spot. Having taken her extra car key, all he had to do was slip casually into the back seat of the car, crouch down, and begin his wait. The car's interior was dark, and the only sound around him was the muted rumble of traffic along Pine Street. Hunkering down into place, he did a mental run-through of the next phase of his plans, surprised by the sudden, unexpected surge of reluctance he felt.

While losing Rose would be painful, he reasoned that it was she who betrayed something special between them. She had turned on him. Rejected him. Even if he backed out now, cold logic told him there was no chance of going back to the way things had been between them. It was a bitter fact that when the faculty got wind of their falling out, he would once again be facing the misery and humiliation that he had suffered because of Liz. Was he supposed to run away again to avoid it? No. There was nothing he could do now but give himself closure. The only uncomfortable aspect of his plan was the possibility that Rose would realize he was the one killing her. He could not let that happen.

He rechecked his watch. Dusk was falling fast. To his advantage, the parking lot's lighting system was shoddy, so dressed as he was all in black, he became part of the shifting shadows around him. He rechecked the tools he had taken from his backpack. He was ready. The minutes passed by.

Rose showed up a little before six fifteen. Squinting over the dashboard, he caught sight of her as she was rounding the corner of the apartment building heading in his direction. He hunched down and held his breath. A few moments later, she was opening the car door, sliding into the driver's seat. He gave her time to insert the key into the ignition. In that instant he took a deep breath, raised his arm as high as he was able within the confines of the car interior, and brought the hammer smashing down on her head. The action executed, Rose slumped forward over the wheel with barely a gasp, the side of her head torn open and blood pouring from the wound. He stared in frozen horror at the bloody bits of hair and scalp that had spattered across the driver's side window. Then he heard a moaning sound that told him she was still alive. On the verge of panic, he hurled himself between the front seats of the car, his hunting knife ready to finish the job with a hard thrust of the point under Rose's left rib. Then it was over. And she had not known it was him.

The next step was crucial. He had to get the window cleaned off and escape before someone driving in or out of the lot stopped to see what was going on. Without stopping to think about it, he pulled the knife out of Rose's side. The release caused a rush of fresh blood to pour out, covering everything in its path. Once again, near panic took over. He began to shake, yet he was trapped into action; he had to go on. Moving almost mechanically, he somehow managed to manipulate Rose's body out from behind the wheel and to heave it into the front passenger seat. Panting for breath, he wiped up the mess on the window with tissues Rose kept handy in the glove compartment. His stomach lurched with the stench of death. His nerves were screaming and he was frantic to get away.

Still shaking uncontrollably, he forced himself to start the car and put it in motion. In the time it took to make his way back up Solomon's Gorge Hill and to locate the stretch of woods where he planned to leave Rose's body, he had regained enough control to do what had to be done.

Fortunately, he had no trouble locating the place he had mapped out as the spot where he would leave Rose. Once there, he parked on the side of the road, got out of the car, and turned on his pocket flashlight. Perhaps twenty feet into the woods he found the packaged shower curtain exactly where he had hidden it under some broken branches near an old oak tree. Hurrying back to the car with one eye on the lookout for a hint of approaching headlights, he heaved and tugged Rose's body out of the Honda and onto the plastic curtain. Then, with the flashlight stuck between his teeth, he yanked and pulled his way into the woods. On two nerve-shattering occasions, he was forced to douse the flashlight and wait while a vehicle passed. But he made it.

At that point, he began to feel sick. Rose's eyes were wide open as she lay face up on the ground, her eyes staring at him through the flashlight's glow. Blood was everywhere. It was all over the car interior and all over his clothing. There was a warm, fetid odor to it that turned his insides sour. He knew he would have to hurry before he got sick. The last thing he needed was to splatter his DNA all over the place for the cops to find.

"Sorry, Rose," he said softly before covering her over with the leaves and pine needles he scooped from the forest floor. When finished, he retrieved the plastic curtain and got out of there.

Back at the Honda, he wrapped up the knife and hammer in the curtain before dropping it into the plastic bag he had taken from his backpack. Any telltale evidence left behind could hang him. One small oversight could turn into a very large self-made trap. Once on the road again, he covered a few miles more up the mountain road until he reached the gully where he intended to dump the Honda. With the car headlights on high beam, he made a sharp turn off the road and onto a patch of dry, bumpy dirt where he navigated the car to the gully's edge. With the motor idling and the emergency break secured, he turned off the headlights, grabbed the plastic bag on the bloody seat next to him and climbed out. He then released the brake, gave the car a vigorous shove and watched as it inched slowly over the edge and then went tumbling toward the gully bottom. Fascinated, he listened to it scrape and thump down the darkened pit of trees and rock. He had considered leaving Rose in the car, but that would have been too simple. He wanted events moving in as many different directions as he could send them – all at the same time, whenever possible.

Relieved at last to have disposed of both Rose and the stench of the Honda, he strode with renewed confidence up the darkened highway. Several minutes later, he spotted his car where he had left it near the hiking trail. As he had hoped, no ticket. Feeling better with each passing second, he unlocked the trunk and pulled out the two plastic garbage bags he had stashed there. Working quickly, he doubled-bagged the hammer, knife, shower curtain, and flashlight. The second, larger, green bag served as a receptacle for his hat and gloves, which were immediately exchanged for a fresh set from the trunk. Then he removed his bloody outer clothing right down to his trousers, socks, and sneakers. These he exchanged with waiting replacements. Once had had double-bagged the second lot, including the last pair of gloves he was wearing, he zipped up his jacket, pulled on new gloves, slammed the trunk closed, and got back on the road.

Ready now for the last leg of his journey, he took the first southbound ramp onto the Northway that he came to and drove until he saw a rest stop in the distance. Once there, he pulled in and parked, pausing only long enough to make a quick appraisal of his surroundings. He noted that a couple of truckers, diesels purring, had pulled their rigs into the separate trailer parking area. Overall, however, traffic was light both in and out of the rest stop. All he had to do was stay cool and get on with the final phase of his plan.

He deposited the green plastic bag with the bloody clothing into one of the large, half-filled trash bins next to the facilities building. He knew the trash would be hauled away courtesy of New York State sometime the next morning, long before Rose's body would be found and the search begun.

At the next rest stop he parked and repeated the process. Still wearing the last pair of gloves, he disposed of the hammer, knife, and shower curtain, careful to shove the plastic bag deep into the trash until it disappeared from sight. Mission completed, he got back into his car and drove. He was back behind his own locked doors before nine o'clock that evening. It was over.

Exhilarated by his success, Sayers removed all of his clothing and tossed the lot into the washing machine with detergent and bleach. Then he stood under a hot shower and scrubbed himself clean. Planning a perfect murder took perfect planning. No mistakes allowed. He would see that everything was just as it should be before he turned in for the night.

By the time Monday rolled around, he had well rehearsed his role as the worried friend of the missing teacher, a façade that he knew he could wear with ease. Before leaving for class, he relaxed at the kitchen table with his breakfast coffee and the morning newspaper. Staring down at the paper, he smiled. It would not take long for the headlines to start screaming the story of Rose's murder. And they would keep on screaming. He was not finished yet.

CHAPTER THIRTY-ONE
ANOTHER FRIDAY

FRIDAY, DECEMBER 4

Another Friday morning back on the job. The most Alex could say for the day, given the cold north winds that had blown him and his Chevy Blazer down the dark, murky highway into town, was that he had Jenny's company to look forward to at its end. But that promise lay many hours away. Now he was seated behind his desk looking through the list of notations Will Burke had left for him, making an effort to keep his mind where it belonged.

For most of the morning, headquarters had seen the usual end-of-the-week drift of deputies meandering in to use the computers; some of the men assigned to outside duty were downloading reports, others were picking up their latest assignments. All were hitting the back room for a bolstering draft of hot coffee before heading out into the cold. Alex sat with his own steaming mug close at hand.

He had not been surprised to learn that Fowler's trial date was yet to be set; the cogs of justice were in motion, but at a snail's pace, allowing the element of suspense and drama to effectively build, courtesy of the D.A.'s office. Ray Peterson, as expected, would be handling the prosecution himself. The man was preparing for a courtroom drama in which he would be the star player. Meantime, a very unstable killer was out there at a safe distance from the law. All Alex could do was to hold fast to his determination to dig up any shred of evidence that would tie Sayers to the crimes.

It was an unwelcome but established fact that from the time a crime is committed, every day counts if the criminal is to be caught and brought to justice. The more time that is allowed to pass, the more likely a killer would be free to kill again. Alex had been hoping that with a little prodding by first himself and then Donahue, Sayers would make a move that would trip him up. But so far, nothing.

In the meantime, Jenny's romance with her new Toyota was yet another factor increasing the chance she'd be target number three. Sayers had missed the last time, but who knew what he would try next? Or when?

He heard a slight rap on the doorjamb of his office door and looked up. Marge Grant was standing framed in the doorway, her head tilted to one side, a smile lighting her face. "Busy, Sheriff?" she asked in a low voice.

"Never for you," Alex said with a grin, leaning back in his chair. "What's up?"

"Oh, I don't know," Marge sighed, sliding her small frame into the chair next to his desk. "It's probably none of my beeswax, but I'm a little worried about, well," she hesitated, "about the tension that's been building up all over town. The county, I should say." She shook her head. "There have been a lot of incoming calls lately that haven't been any too nice. Mostly from people who want to vent, I think. I've tried to field them, but some have been kinda hairy."

"Hairy? How so? Alex asked, noting the nervous edge to Marge's voice.

Marge shrugged. "I'm sure you know not everyone believes that Chuck Fowler is guilty of killing Rose Clifford, no matter what the news tells them. Rose was well known and well liked hereabouts, and a lot of loud voices are demanding to know what's being done to find her killer. It's not the press, Alex. Uh, uh. It's the residents asking questions and not liking the only answers I can give them."

"What are you telling them?" Alex asked, frowning.

"The fact that Fowler has not been charged with Rose's murder is the crux of the problem, and I don't know what to say anymore. Telling them the investigation is still going on has worn thin. The rumble is growing, Alex. I'll bet if you check with Lt. Donahue, he'll tell you the same calls are coming in to the state police."

"I shouldn't be surprised," Alex said, blowing out a breath and raking a hand through his hair. "I haven't been confronted directly, but the television news hasn't let up on Rose's case either. Peterson has been making statements, but – as expected – always highlighting Fowler and the upcoming trial while pushing any other questions aside." He rose to his feet.

"I'll have a talk with Harry and see what's happening on his end. Just do your usual best.

In fact, why don't you get the heck out of the office. Go home early and chill out for the weekend. I don't know what else to tell you, Marge. Other than to say thanks."

"You don't have to say anything," Marge replied. She stood up, her worried frown easing into a tired smile. "It's a mess, I know. I'll hang in until the end of my shift, Alex. If you need me after that," she laughed and gave a little shake of her shoulders, "brrr...you'll find me where it's warm, you can bet on that."

By three o'clock that afternoon, Donahue returned the message Alex had left for him. He confirmed Marge's guess that a good percentage of the citizens of Collier County were clamoring to know what was being done to catch Rose Clifford's killer. Few still clung to the position that it was Fowler. Now fear had set in and was spreading. A killer was loose and they knew it.

"Stay cool," Donahue advised. "I don't think anyone will storm the citadel just yet. Not today, anyway. I'll get back to you with what I hear from this end. You do the same from yours."

It was another Friday at Vincent's Rathskeller. The dinner crowds had begun to gather early. The hardier breed of ski enthusiasts were coming off the slopes, the wind chill having forced the highest ski lifts to shut down, barring the adventurous from risking frostbite for the sake of one more run. Ben Sayers stood at the far end of the crowded bar where several fellow faculty members were gathered, a few obviously planning to make an evening of it.

Lorna Kelly was seated at a table sipping hot cider with the school principal, John Logan. Sayers, watching them from his place at the bar, was patiently waiting for his chance. The moment arrived when Logan lumbered up from his chair and headed in the direction of the men's room. Snatching at the opportunity, Sayers picked up his beer, left the bar, and began to edge his way through the tables until he paused behind Lorna's chair, just outside her line of vision.

"Well, what do we have here," Sayers said cheerfully as he moved around the table to face her directly. "All by yourself, Lorna?"

Lorna's expression at the sound of his voice revealed all Sayers had come there to learn. Her head swiveled upward; her wide, startled eyes filled with alarm. Then she smiled, but the effort came too late. He knew.

"Oh, my goodness, Mr. Sayers," Lorna said, a hand on her flushed cheek. "I didn't see you. No, I'm not alone," she added quickly, "Mr. Logan will be right back."

"I did sneak up on you, didn't I?" Sayers asked benignly, then took a sip of his beer. "Sorry. Darned if I don't have a habit of doing that. Just wanted to say hello." And then, before Lorna could reply, Sayers wiggled his fingers, gave her a "ta-ta", and walked away. The next time she looked over her shoulder toward the bar, he was gone.

By the time Alex reached High Ridge that evening, his spirits had lifted enough that even the weather did little to daunt them. In one hand he carried a bottle of Jenny's favorite Chardonnay, in the other a bouquet of roses he had stopped to pick up at a florist's en route. Jenny's smile as she stood waiting for him at her door was enough to drive away the last of any lingering ghosts that had plagued him since dawn; he knew when he closed the door behind him, they would all be left outside.

It was late. Jenny was curled into the corner of the sofa with Alex's head on her lap. He had fallen asleep. Sound asleep. She smiled and managed to squirm her way off the sofa and to gently slip a pillow under his head. Next, she fetched a blanket and covered him. She had been slow to recognize how exhausted he was during dinner and even later as they were cleaning up and loading the dishwasher, laughing and making the usual idle chatter, keeping the world and its problems at bay. It was only after they were settled down in front of the fire, sipping wine and munching popcorn, that she noticed how tired he was. It had been a lovely evening. She smiled, recalling how tall and handsome he looked standing on her threshold with a bouquet of red roses, his eyes drinking her in, his crooked smile making her giddy heart leap. And she was giddy, no doubt about it.

She checked the time. It was well after eleven. She gazed down at Alex's face in repose and smiled again. The sofa was comfortable, and it was too bitter cold a night to send anyone out into. There could be no harm in letting him stay where he was. The next day was Saturday, and he was on no particular schedule that she knew of. She would just let him bunk down and get some much needed rest.

Moving about very quietly, she tiptoed around the sofa to turn off the lamps, with the exception of a small wall light in the foyer. Satisfied, she bent down and kissed him lightly on the cheek, then crept silently down the hall to her bedroom.

It was just past one o'clock in the morning. A blue Ford sedan drove into the High Ridge parking lot. It slowed down as it neared Alex's Blazer, then kept on going to the end of the lot, where it turned around, came back, then went out of the lot and away. Behind the wheel of the car, Lisa was crying softly. Alex would be so angry if he knew she was still watching him. But she couldn't help herself. Earlier tonight she had seen him go inside the building carrying flowers and a paper bag of something, looking great. He was still there. Still with Jenny Wyland when he should be with her.

She would have to go home now and get into bed. Alone. It wasn't fair. He should be with her, not somebody else. Well, she would talk about it at her next group session. Or would she? No, they would tell her she was wrong, but she knew better. Nobody was being hurt. She only wanted to know what Alex was doing and where he was going without her. She would keep her secret to herself.

A little while later, Lisa crept silently into her parents' house by way of the back door. Without turning on a light, she crept upstairs to her room. It took only minutes for her to change into pajamas and climb into bed. Her eyes were still damp with tears, but she felt better. She remembered the way Alex had kissed her that day at her flat, and she was sure that he still wanted her. It would just take time for them to get back where they were before Carl died. She knew now that she had to let Carl go. There! She could say it. The words she hated to say. She would have to tell Alex that she was getting better. Pretty soon, she would tell him. Pretty soon...

CHAPTER THIRTY-TWO
THE MORNING AFTER

Alex opened his eyes and realized he was not in his own bed. A squinty glance at his watch told him it was after seven o'clock in the morning, and he definitely was not at home. Groggy and momentarily confused, he pushed aside the blanket covering him, heaved his long legs over the side of the sofa, and sat on the edge looking around. Gradually, straining to clear his head and think straight, he managed to piece together what must have ended his evening with Jenny. He had fallen asleep. His glance strayed from the ashes in the fireplace to the two wine glasses on the coffee table and the almost-empty bottle of Chardonnay next to them.

He smiled wanly, combing his hair back with his fingers as he stifled a yawn. He had not caved like that in a long time. Bless Jenny for tucking him in and allowing him the use of her sofa for the night. She had solicitously provided a pillow and a blanket and had even removed his shoes. Pretty good service for a guy who passed out on his girl.

Across the room the draperies were closed, creating a shadowed semi-darkness broken only by the faint glimmer of the foyer wall lamp. Alex stood up and stretched, then crossed to the nearest window and pulled the draperies open, shielding his eyes against the brilliance of the morning sun. As his eyes adjusted, he saw that everything within view was covered with a fresh blanket of snow, with more lazy flakes fluttering downward.

Almost fully awake now, he stretched and left his place at the window. What to do next? The apartment was in the depth of a sleeping quiet, which meant that Jenny was still in dreamland. He felt scroungy, badly in need of soap, water, and toothpaste. He scratched his head and wondered what he should do. "What the heck," he shrugged. With that he shuffled down the hallway to the bathroom, went inside, and eased the door closed behind him.

Forty-five minutes later the aroma of freshly brewed coffee and frying bacon filtered through the apartment. All of the draperies were now wide open to reveal a rippling stream of snowflakes melting against the warmth of the panes. Alex sat at the breakfast bar, his sandy hair still damp and tousled, his mouth made fresh with mouthwash and a brand-new toothbrush filched from Jenny's bathroom cabinet.

"Pretty domestic scene, this morning, wouldn't you say, lady?" he said with a grin as his eyes followed Jenny around the kitchen. She was wrapped in a flowery bathrobe and was about to serve him up a plate of sizzling bacon and scrambled eggs. Grinning, he began to ooh and aah appreciatively, clutching his knife and fork while leering down at his plate as she filled it.

"Stop clowning around and eat!" Jenny ordered, setting down her own plate on the counter across from him. "Toast is coming up. Jam's next to you. So's the butter."

"Sorry I zonked out on you last night," Alex told her for at least the third time, digging into his food. "Still can't believe I did that. Very bad manners."

"Yes, I agree. Now let's discuss today. I have tons of work to do around here. What about you?"

Alex's thoughts sobered. He had not told Jenny what had transpired between Harry Donahue and himself, nor about Harry's conversation with Sayers on Wednesday past. Reluctant to shatter their moment, he nevertheless felt obligated to fill her in on the basics, which he did, winding the story up with a word of caution.

"While Donahue still believes in Fowler's guilt regarding Lonny Jerome, he's at least come around to admitting Sayers is the one we want for killing Rose. It's not a good time, Jen, to make yourself an easy target, and I've got to tell you, that's what bothers me. It's a lousy day to go anywhere, so I hope you really are planning to stay home. As for me, there are a few matters waiting at headquarters which I'll dispense with before I head home and get into some fresh clothes. How about we find a place to dine and dance the evening away? Sound good to you?"

Jenny stared down into her coffee cup, silent for a long moment before she looked up and nodded. "Sure it does," she said, but her voice was flat and tinged with annoyance.

Alex gave her a long, quizzical look. "Jen, what's wrong?" he asked quietly.

Jenny shrugged. "We've had this discussion before," she said, testily. "Maybe you're reliving the old days back on the football field, but the truth is, I don't want you running interference for me, Alex. I don't need to be protected to the point of being shut away from the world. I'm aware of the dangers out there and plan to be careful. But I'm not going to be cloistered. I've already tried to explain all this to you and here I am, trying again."

Alex sighed and threw both hands high in a gesture of mock defeat. "You win. I getcha!" he said, frowning across the counter at her. "And I know when to quit. I promise not to sweat out every minute you're not with me." Then he picked up Jenny's hand and grinned lasciviously. "Now, since you brought up the sport of football," he hurried on, wiggling his eyebrows, "would you mind very much if we tried a gentle tackle or two?"

Jenny picked up a slice of toast and threw it at him.

CHAPTER THIRTY-THREE
BACK IN THE GAME

SATURDAY, DECEMBER 5

It had been snowing off and on for at least six hours, and Ben Sayers was not about to see his car buried by any man-made snow bank. It was eight o'clock in the morning, and the heavy snowfall had finally tapered off to occasional flurries. The town's plow trucks would soon be on the move. There was no time for breakfast. If his car was still parked at the curb by the time the trucks reached his street, he would be plowed in. It was the weekend, and he had no intention of being inconvenienced. He had too much to attend to.

So, after bundling into his winter clothes, he headed outside into the cold white of the morning and clumped through the snow to where his car was parked at the curb. It took only a minute to get the motor turned over; once it began to hum, he turned the defroster on full blast and went to work. He swept the snow from the body of the car, the windows, and the windshield. Then he shoveled out the bulk of snow collected around the wheels on the street side, digging at them until he was satisfied that he would have the traction needed to pull out from the curb.

The icy morning chill was gone from the car interior and the windshield wipers were effectively dispensing of the fluttering snow when Sayers climbed behind the wheel. Tapping the gas pedal gently to establish his traction, he very slowly and carefully drove the car away from the curb. He was on the road.

He had a lot on his mind. In the aftermath of the trooper's visit on Wednesday, he was convinced he had to somehow overcome the forces working against him. His eyes were narrowed behind the lens of his glasses, his face sallow under the dark blue ski hat he wore. The wheels of his mind were working, thrust into the morning ahead and what he planned to do.

In truth, Ben Sayers was fast losing all sense of reality, his present state of reasoning spawned at the very instant he made the decision to commit murder. With the act now a *fait accompl i*, there was no escaping the irrevocable end result; no way to go now, but down.

It was only a matter of time.

As implausible as it may seem, it was Sayers' aberrant, animal instinct which recognized his eventual damnation. At the same time, a faulty part of his intellect fiercely denied it. He was invincible. He was the hunter in pursuit of his prey. Nor was there guilt attached to the evil he planned, for there was no longer a conscience within his soul to stem it.

Now he drove idly along the streets, slowly navigating through the scant early-morning traffic. The Jennings was in his jacket pocket and he had purchased another knife. Small, but efficient. It felt good to know both gun and knife were within easy reach. He wished he had one of them on hand when Trooper Donahue had made his call. So humiliating! He could visualize himself as he walked into the school building on Monday to be greeted by the cold, questioning glances of his fellow teachers. He knew they would be whispering behind his back. What would they be asking each other? Do you think Ben Sayers had anything to do with Rose's murder? Is that why the state police wanted to see him?

And who had been behind all of his problems? Sheriff Banks. He had hated him right from the moment Rose began tittering like a bird about how great he was and how tough it was for the poor guy. Poor guy, indeed! The same poor guy who thought he could threaten Ben Sayers? For what? Not because he had proof of anything, but because he saw himself as a very clever sheriff. Only the fool was not clever enough.

By the time Sayers reached High Ridge, he was filled with icy calm. Without blinking an eye he pulled into the recently plowed parking area, noting with some pleasure and surprise that the sheriff's car was there. Oh, he thought with a wide smirk, the romance with nurse Wyland was progressing? Bully for him.

A minute or so later, he had the front door key in his hand, glad that this time he remembered to bring it with him. Once inside the lobby, he stomped the snow off his boots and removed his hat and gloves. It gave him the chance to look around, noting with satisfaction that nobody was about. Moving along, he took the elevator to the eighth floor, intending to take the stairs back down to the sixth. He wanted to play it safe in case he was seen. But as he emerged on the eighth floor and started to make his way toward the exit at the end of the hallway, he noticed a door marked "Maintenance Only" standing slightly ajar. Curious, he poked his head inside for a quick look and saw a vacuum cleaner, broom, mop, and pail. Wall shelves held a variety of tools. Two pairs of coveralls hung on a hook and several paint cans stood piled up in one corner.

Sayers shrugged, clicked the door closed, and resumed his stride toward the exit. Before reaching it, however, a workman clad in coveralls and a painter's cap and carrying a six-foot stepladder came out of a nearby apartment and began walking toward the janitor's closet, giving Sayers a perfunctory nod in passing.

Sayers turned to watch him, an idea beginning to take form. By the time he reached the stairs, he was wearing a smug, self-satisfied grin. He was still grinning and humming happily to himself as he turned into the corridor which led to apartment 610.

Originally, he had planned to simply stroll by the nurse's apartment with a sharp ear out for what he might pick up along the way. But as he approached apartment 608, he was brought up short by the slight sounds he heard coming from the other side of the door. His breath caught and he tensed until common sense slowly took over. Of course. Rose's apartment had been leased again. He almost laughed out loud. He should have thought of that sooner.

Giving in to the momentary distraction, Sayers stood staring at the door, imagining Rose as he had seen her framed there so many times, smiling a welcome in his direction. He loved her smile. His eyes clouded over as memory sprang back to days that once belonged to him and were now gone forever.

Then suddenly, he snapped to attention. From somewhere behind him a door opened and closed, followed by the sound of heavy footsteps heading in his direction. He frowned, took a deep breath, and then, with elaborate gestures, glanced down at his watch, shook his head in pretended annoyance, and turned to reverse his direction. He was an actor, again – just a tenant who had forgotten something on his way out. With only a quick, impersonal glance at the elderly gentleman walking past him, Sayers continued on until he reached the adjoining corridor.

Without breaking stride, he turned the corner and then stopped abruptly. No point in letting his face become familiar to anyone, he reminded himself. He had done his bit of snooping for today and it was time to cut out. Until the next time.

It struck him then that he had missed breakfast, and he realized that he had worked up an appetite. He would stop at a diner before heading for home. He'd buy a newspaper and check out the latest news on Fowler while he ate. The lovebirds behind the closed doors of apartment 610 could have their time together. He cracked his knuckles and smiled. Who knew how much of it they had left?

As the elevator carried him downward to the main lobby, he rocked up and down on the balls of his feet. It felt good to be in action again. For days he had been primed for the sound of the sheriff's boots on the stairs to his flat, wondering when he would hear a knock on his classroom door. But no more.

His grin turned into a sneer of triumph as he left the building and strode to where he had parked his car. No more the scared rabbit, he promised himself. Ben Sayers was back in the game.

CHAPTER THIRTY-FOUR
OPERATION UNDERCOVER

SATURDAY, DECEMBER 5

Lt. Harry Donahue hated to admit it, but he felt more than a little guilty for leaving Alex out of his recent machinations. Convinced now that Ben Sayers was a vicious and cold-blooded killer who had, without a doubt, murdered Rose Clifford, he felt a debt was owed to his friend. Both Alex and Jenny had been added to the list of the teacher's intended victims. They had each escaped an attempt on their lives. So far. Now it was time he took part in what Alex termed as "the game" Sayers was playing, but in his judgment it was best to leave Alex out of the game and to play it alone. For now.

Actually, he was not alone. Once he had formulated what needed to be done, Donahue dug out the card of Phil Carroll, the man Peterson had contacted from the Bureau of Criminal Investigation, and called him. Putting aside any reservations he may have felt earlier, Donahue proceeded to dive in. He laid out all of the relevant details of the situation, stressing the point that until there was sufficient evidence to warrant contact with Peterson's office, discretion was vital. What he needed for now, he explained to Carroll, was elbow room and support to get surveillance underway.

A few brief questions answered, Carroll agreed to the plan and the operation was put into play. Before the next twenty-four hours had elapsed, Donahue was being introduced to two state police detectives temporarily assigned to him and to the case.

On the day he made the promised visit to fill Alex in on his confrontation with Sayers, he had felt like a heel for not telling him about his hidden agenda. But he saw no other alternative then, or now. He had to leave Banks out of the loop. There were too many complications with Jenny, Lisa, and a murderer all inexorably intertwined. So, like it or not, personal feelings were put aside and the initial groundwork begun.

He had already spoken with Sam Barker, the High Ridge manager, and learned that Rose Clifford's apartment was still vacant due to some difficulty or other with the lease. With Barker's help and cooperation, the next step was put into play. Detective Rod Jansen took up residence in apartment 608 and quickly settled in, with his partner, Detective Fred Murphy, acting as backup. By the time Friday afternoon rolled around, two telephone lines had been brought into the apartment and cameras were covertly installed in the ceiling of the sixth-floor hallway. Under the guise of ordinary smoke detectors, the devices were positioned in the corridor in such a way as to monitor anyone approaching Jenny Wyland's apartment from any direction.

On Saturday morning, the action began. As it happened, Donahue arrived at High Ridge shortly before eight o'clock, loaded down with a bag filled with breakfast fare. Coffee was already brewing when he slipped through the door. He handed the groceries to Rod Jansen, a big man with a wiry mustache adorning a wide-lipped smile. A patch of bald head surrounded by a paucity of brown, fuzzy hair made him look older than his thirty-five years.

"You know how to feed your outlanders," Jansen said, grinning appreciatively as he shuffled a Danish onto a small paper dish. "Fred's in the bathroom and I'm watching the monitors." He indicated one of the three screens that revealed the length of the sixth floor corridor. "We have a microphone hidden out there," he went on, handing Donahue a freshly poured coffee. "Keeps us on our toes. You can hear a door open or close, even a footstep. And voices, of course. It helps."

Donahue knew that whatever evidence they dug up had to be gathered within the limits of the law. Crossing the line could mean that once Sayers was caught and brought to trial, their evidence could be thrown out of court. It was fortunate then, that the BCI agents working the case knew their business. Upon their arrival at trooper headquarters, the briefing included all aspects of the case, including an intense study of the main players. Like the professionals they were, the two men drank in the information, made suggestions, and then got down to business.

"Any problem getting into the building without attracting attention?" Jansen asked Donahue between munching bites on his Danish.

"Nope," Donahue replied. "I used the rear service elevator and, as you can see, I'm dressed like a civilian. No uniform and no official car parked outside."

Jansen smiled and nodded approval. "Good. Now comes the waiting."

"What stories is he telling you?" Fred Murphy came into the room running a comb through a full head of carrot-red hair. Younger than Jansen, he was tall and lean and muscular. He shook hands with Donahue and helped himself to coffee and a doughnut.

"All's quiet here, I presume," he said, his gaze moving across the monitors.

"Yep," Rod replied. Then he turned to Donahue. "I took the night watch. Sheriff Banks is still in the Wyland apartment. No problems"

"You slept okay?" Harry inquired of Fred.

Fred laughed. "I'm used to cots. Just give me a pillow and I'm snorin' away in minutes. Hey," he exclaimed suddenly, his attention fixed on a monitor. "What's that?"

All eyes shot to the screens, instantly alert. Ben Sayers had appeared at the far end of the hallway. He was striding toward them, his winter jacket flapping open, his hat in one hand. His step was slow, but not stealthy, and there was no sign of a weapon. The muted tread of his booted footstep over the hall carpet was the only sound in the room other then the men's soft breathing.

Then suddenly, Sayers stopped and stared at the closed door of apartment 608. His stance and the intensity of his focus on the apartment door told its own tale. He was lost in thought.

The three men could only hold their breath and wait for whatever would happen next. Then abruptly, the moment was shattered.

Apparently satisfied with his musings, Sayers turned his attention away from the door. He had only gone a few steps, however, when the click of a closing door broke the silence. Then the figure of a tall, elderly gentleman proceeding down the hall in Sayers' direction appeared on the screen.

Like an animal sniffing the air for the scent of the enemy, Sayers lifted his head slightly to assess the intrusion. Then, in dramatic pantomime, he hiked up his jacket sleeve to check his watch, shook his head, and frowned. He then did an abrupt about face and retreated back down the hall. He passed the gentleman with barely a glance and in the next instant, disappeared into an adjoining hallway.

"Well, what do you make of that?" Jansen asked, his eyes still pinned on the screen.

"I'm willing to bet this was a practice run," Donahue said dryly. "More of Sayers' games. I don't think he was looking for a confrontation with Banks or Jenny Wyland this trip, although he must have seen the Blazer downstairs and put two and two together. As you know, he's pulled this kind of stunt before."

"He must have a key to the place," Murphy commented. He chewed on his lip for a second. "You know," he said slowly. "He didn't come out of the hallway from the elevator, did you notice? He popped up from the far end of the hall through the emergency exit.

Strange bugger. What do you think he was doing on another floor before we caught sight of him?"

Donahue frowned. "Good question," he mused soberly. "He has something planned, you can count on it."

CHAPTER THIRTY-FIVE
BARON THE LAB

SUNDAY, DECEMBER 6

It was past eleven o'clock on Sunday night and the teen gathering held in St. Paul's Church hall was over. Lorna Kelly, on the cleanup committee, straightened the last chair at the long rows of tables in the large, now-empty room. She then made a swift inspection of the kitchen and serving area to be sure everything was back in place. Yes, all was in perfect order. Father McDonald would have no complaints the following day. Josie Wallace and Lois Easton were already removing their coats from the wall pegs next to the side door. Flo Kotch was turning off lights, hurrying from one wall switch to the other until she finally worked her way to where Lorna stood waiting by the door.

"All ready to go?" Flo asked, pulling her coat from a wall peg and yanking a knit hat from one of its pockets.

Lorna smiled. "Yep, all set. Let's be on our way."

Bundled into their coats, the four went up the few steps leading from the basement door to the sidewalk where they were met by a cold, night wind. After wishing one another a hasty goodnight, they pulled up their coat collars, dug their hands into the warmth of their pockets, and scurried off. Heading in the opposite direction from the others, Lorna and Flo scuttled along, chatting and laughing companionably, the soles of their leather boots making dull, slapping sounds against the pavement. A light, feathery snow had begun to drift down from a dark, leaden sky, the flakes blown about like feathers in the wind.

When they came to the corner where they were to head off into separate directions, they said their goodnights. Flo turned left, hurrying down the street to where she lived a few houses away, while Lorna crossed the road and continued on. There was another short sprint before she would reach the white, shingled house with "Kelly" painted on the mailbox. Regretting her earlier decision to leave her car at home, she quickened her step. So much, she groaned inwardly, for the prospect of some healthy exercise.

The Kelly family had lived in the same house since before Lorna was born. The small, pleasant neighborhood consisted of various sizes and shapes of one-family homes, all shaded in the summer by the lush oak and maple trees lining the sidewalks. Only now it was winter, the air was mountaintop cold, and the neighborhood was blanketed with snow. The summer green of the Kelly home's adjoining yard was presently a brittle, windblown white, the cherry trees and lilac bushes were bare, the skeletal limbs of two large oak trees in front of the house were swaying with the low, haunting sounds of the night wind rushing through them.

The home itself was on a sizeable lot with a long fence and hedgerow forming the front perimeter. A gate opened onto a walkway leading to an entrance on the side of the house and further on down the walk to a two-car garage. The garage was accessed by an alleyway which ran behind it.

When Lorna came to the gate, she paused long enough to retrieve her keys from her purse before hurrying through it. Anxious to take refuge inside the warmth of her home, she took no notice of the dark shadow melting into those of the cherry trees only a few feet away. Keys now in hand, she reached the side door of the house, pleased when she saw that her mother had left a light burning in the kitchen.

She was standing in front of the door, about to insert her key into the lock, when she thought she heard a sharp, metallic click from somewhere behind her. Turning, she peered across the sweep of the shadowed yard and through the now-heavy flakes of snow tumbling helter-skelter to the ground. Straining to hear, she caught only the gusting of the wind whistling through the cherry trees and the barren lilac bushes. Shaking her head, she frowned and turned back to the door. At that moment, the door was suddenly flung open and Baron, her black Lab, came bounding through it.

"Oh, it's you, Lorna," her mother called out. "Here, take Baron's leash and let him piddle outside. Your father's asleep and I'm in my robe. Land sakes! This dog has to go out at the darndest times!"

With that there was the swishing sound of the dog's leash being tossed into the air. It made a soft, plopping sound as it landed almost at Lorna's feet, where she was now hunkered down into a crouch, scratching Baron's ears. The happy dog was slurping her face, alternately shifting his gaze into the shadowed yard to utter low, throaty growls.

"What's the matter with that animal?" Mrs. Kelly whooped. "Get going so he can get back in and settle down. It's almost midnight and I need my sleep!"

Panting with joy at being reunited with his mistress, Baron meekly allowed Lorna to clip on his leash and lead him off toward the garage and the back alley, still throwing glances over his shoulder and grumbling quietly as he trotted beside her.

"Come on, Baron," Lorna urged, lovingly patient. "Let's get this over with. I'm freezing, so behave yourself."

After Lorna and Baron disappeared into the alley behind the garage, Ben Sayers released a long breath of relief. If he had been able to take his shot a few seconds earlier, the dratted dog would have torn out of the house and found his mistress lying dead on the walkway. Fortunately, his aim was delayed by the new falling snow. He had just cocked the gun hammer and was trying to get a bead on the back of Lorna's head when out of the blue, the dog burst out the door. He might have succeeded in shooting both of them, but why risk it? He knew a Lab the size of that monster could rip a man's arm off in one quick lunge, and he was not in the least anxious to find out who was faster. He just wanted out of there.

On the drive home, uptight and aggravated at the unexpected turn of events, Sayers reviewed his predicament. First, he had taken two rifle shots at the sheriff and come away frustrated. At a range of less than sixty feet, he should have bagged him. He would have, too, if Banks had not bent over just in the nick of time.

Then tonight. It had been no easy job choosing a time and place to pick off the little redhead, but it helped that she gave a daily update of her life. Her Sunday habits were a matter of Monday lunchtime chatter. Ten o'clock Mass followed by Bible study, which she taught. Sunday evening was young people's night, held in the church hall from eight to eleven. He had it all down pat. It was a cinch. Only he had not counted on snow blowing all over the place to throw off his aim, or on that stupid dog!

A shiver ran through his entire body as he imagined bared canines going for his throat.

Okay, he had messed up. He would have to rethink his plans – and there was little time left. He would never feel safe until all threats were out of the way. He would not consider failure. His own miscalculations and neglect in preparing for possible unforeseen circumstances would have to be corrected somehow. And correct them he would. He could not be stopped. He would not be stopped. Ever!

Satisfied to take this setback as one which would soon be rectified, he drove through the quiet, snow-muted night toward home.

CHAPTER THIRTY-SIX
OCTOBER AGAIN

MONDAY, DECEMBER 7

Like the chameleon he fancied himself to be, Ben Sayers had once again slipped back into his role at Weston Elementary, determined that he would make no further mistakes. At the end of the school day on Monday, he stopped at the market, drove home, and prepared his dinner. By seven o'clock he was in his lounger with his eyes closed, sipping lazily at the edge of a coffee cup while he began to drift off into time and space. He sighed contentedly. A moment later, it was October again.

It felt good to think back to the October night he had so brilliantly executed his plan to bring closure to the Rose part of his life. But that was over with, and he must deal with the possibility that Fowler's alibi for the time of Rose's death might let him off the hook as the prime suspect in her murder. He had to find a way to tighten the rope of guilt around Fowler's neck and thus keep suspicion away from himself. He had kept a watchful eye out for his chance, certain that it was only a matter of time before the opportunity presented itself. Which, of course, it did.

It happened quite by accident. It was a sometime in mid-October on a night when he was making a late run down Old Mill Road and saw a light in Fowler's cabin. Assuming it was one of Fowler's beer guzzling stints in front of a televised fight or football game, he turned around, ready to call it a night. He was about to take off when he looked up and saw Fowler storming out of his cabin. Like somebody gone haywire, Fowler leaped into his pickup, gunned it into reverse, backed out onto the road, then charged forward, driving like a crazy man toward the main highway.

Without a moment's hesitation, Sayers had fallen in behind the speeding vehicle, hoping that no highway patrolman was cruising the route. The last thing he needed was to be tagged with a speeding ticket; the party would be over. Anyway, he reflected with a twisted smile, he already knew where the bird was going to light.

It was only a few miles later when the brake lights on the pickup flashed on, and sure enough, he had called it. Fowler was making a left turn into the parking lot of Kirker's Diner where Lonny Jerome, his current flame, worked as a waitress. Pulling into the lot behind him, Sayers parked just in time to watch Fowler making long, angry strides toward the diner's side entrance. Once satisfied his quarry was inside, Sayers entered the diner and slipped into an empty booth near the door. By that time all eyes were on Fowler who was, to Sayers' amusement, making a delicious exhibition of himself.

Fowler put on quite a performance, Sayers mused delightedly as he drove home later that night. And before a captive audience, at that. He snickered happily at the picture Lonny Jerome made cowering like a trapped fawn behind the counter while Fowler mouthed off with language that had even the customers cringing. But then, perfectly timed, the kitchen door flew open and Joe Kirker, owner of the diner, stormed onto the stage.

Kirker was a big man with a hard, craggy face and hands like bear claws. His icy-cold eyes bored into Fowler's, a low growl demanding to know what the devil was going on. Not waiting for a reply, Kirker grabbed Fowler by the shoulder of his jacket and hauled him to the diner's entrance door, opened it, and proceeded to hoist him through it as easily as disposing of a sack of unwanted garbage. Not sure of what had hit him, Fowler stumbled down the diner steps and wobbled across the parking lot to his truck. The sound of rubber squealing over blacktop served as the dramatic finale to the episode, much to the relief of everyone in the diner. Sayers chuckled aloud. Another part of his plans had fallen unexpectedly into place. Big time.

Now he had what he wanted. From the day he learned that Fowler's newest lady love worked at Kirker's Diner, he had begun stopping by in the evening. Maintaining a low and careful profile, he would take a seat at the counter, order a coffee and maybe a doughnut, then exchange a few words with Lonny as she waited on customers. Friendly and easygoing, she was a natural socializer who chatted with everyone. Playing the part of the soft-spoken gentleman, smiling his admiration without saying much, Sayers had done himself proud. Pretty quickly, Lonny was addressing him by the name she thought was his. Delighted with the progress he had made, he had only to wait for his chance to move, which Fowler, he had no doubt, would eventually provide. The scene at the diner was it.

A RETURN TO SUNDAY, NOVEMBER 8

It was back on the same Sunday the mystery lady appeared in Haley's Market. After finishing dinner that night, Sayers decided to do another random check on Fowler. It was a cold night and he was restless. When he reached Old Mill Road and drove by the cabin, the windows were lighted and Fowler's vehicles were all in view. Leaving his car tucked into a favorite spot on one of the nearby side roads, Sayers trotted up Old Mill Road through the dark, wintry night, creeping close enough to the cabin to catch a glimpse of Fowler through a window. Sayers liked what he saw. The man was sprawled across a sofa, beer bottle in hand, the pre-game football dialogue in progress on the television screen a few feet away. And, most importantly, Fowler was alone.

Almost giddy with joy for the unexpected break, Sayers hurried back to his car and drove up the highway to Kirker's. He ordered his usual coffee and a doughnut, chatted with Lonny for a little while, then casually asked if she would like to go out after closing up. He would meet her outside at the end of her shift. They could drive somewhere for a drink or two. Afterward, he added with a suggestive half smile, when she gave the word, he would bring her back to pick up her car. She was pleased as punch to accept, and Sayers knew it.

His plan was in motion. Lonny was not too bright and had fallen for his line, just like she had swallowed his phony name and life story. At eleven o'clock on the dot, she came bouncing out of the diner, chattering gaily as she hopped into his car. Settling back in the seat, she pulled a cigarette out of her purse, lit it, and blew a cloud of smoke toward the windshield, smiling, certain she had snagged herself the interest of a new and eligible man.

When Sayers pulled over to the side of Butler Road a few minutes later, pretending that something sounded off-kilter with the motor, Lonny giggled and hopped out of the car just as Sayers asked her to do, standing discretely aside while he went around to the front of the car and lifted the hood. Bundling her coat around her against the snap of the cold wind, Lonny managed to light up another cigarette and began to smoke it.

Killing her was easy. Not personal, like killing Rose. It was just another necessary part of his plan. He simply lifted the cigarette out of her mouth and tossed it away with his gloved hand, opened her coat, and took her in his arms. Then he watched the incredulous expression on her face when, instead of the expected kiss, he drove the knife blade home. The rest was simple. This time, prepared for the bloody mess to follow once he removed the knife, he let Lonny's body sink to the ground. Then he bent down, pulled the knife out, and very carefully dropped it into the plastic bag he had brought with him.

Coldly determined, he pushed the body over to the side of the road then kicked some dead leaves over it, climbed back behind the wheel of his car and drove away. The knife he would put in a safe place. It would have a very important use a little later on.

The next day was Monday, a school day. He smiled, reminding himself that he would be calling the brilliant Alex Banks about the mystery gal. He felt a giggle catch in his throat. The sheriff will be running around in circles come morning, he thought. Another body, another murder to solve. Get out of this one, Fowler, ol' boy, he thought gleefully. And he was not through yet. Next on his list was Jenny Wyland, Rose's pal. That job would have to look like an accident.

He concentrated on the route Jenny Wyland normally took home from the hospital, once more sketching a mental image of the serpentine twists and curves of Solomon's Gorge Hill.

He cracked his knuckles and smirked. Perfect. He would take care of the Wyland problem on Wednesday. The sooner the better.

A FLASHBACK TO WEDNESDAY, NOVEMBER 11

Despite the sudden snowfall, Sayers took care of the Jennifer Wyland issue on his lunch hour. Just a fabricated trip to the post office and away he went. He knew her car and where she parked it – a section at the far end of the hospital parking area set aside for Mercy Hospital employees. He had brought along the tools he needed, and the job was accomplished and he was out of there in no time.

He was taking a chance and he knew it, but he was also aware that if Rose cried on Wyland's shoulder about her run-in with Fowler, she might also have blabbed about him. Had she whined to nurse Jenny about Ben Sayers calling her awful names? And how she now despised him?

Sayers brooded. No one knew that he and Rose had a falling out. At school, he had been careful to keep things looking normal on the surface, even managing to toss across a few words to Rose at the lunch table, leaving her little alternative other than a civil reply in return. Rude was not her style. Besides, she would never intentionally give the faculty gossips something to chew on. He had played the game well. But not well enough, he corrected himself when he learned that Wyland had somehow escaped with a mere arm fracture from what should have been a fatal accident.

"Let her enjoy her luck," he snickered aloud. "It won't last forever." No sense in beating himself up. He had to keep the game moving.

He waited until one of his covert surveillances produced the opportunity he needed. One night he had followed Fowler to a bar. After Fowler went inside, he had pulled into a parking spot and sat in his car with the motor running until he was reasonably certain that Fowler was making a night of drowning his sorrows. Finally satisfied that his pigeon was not about to fly away, he drove back to Old Mill Road. With his car hidden and his path lit only by the reflection of the moon on the snow-encrusted cabin grounds, he quickly made his way along the shoveled path to Fowler's storage shed, where he deposited the knife he had used on Lonny, being careful not to leave any boot prints in the snow. Sayers smirked, pleased with himself. Now Fowler, with no alibi, would be neatly tied to the murder. His luck was riding high.

Once safely back in his car, Sayers headed for home. An anonymous tip to the state police from a pay phone the next day would bring the discovery of the Jerome murder weapon looming into the headlines.

All of a sudden, Sayers paled. Vincent's Grille! What had he said to Banks that afternoon? He swallowed hard. Right from the start he had insisted he knew nothing about Rose seeing Fowler. Then why did he make the stupid comment about Rose and Fowler getting it on pretty tight? And, to Banks? What a fool he was!

His insides trembling, he forced himself to stay calm and to think rationally. If it came to the worst scenario, it would be the sheriff's word against his. No, he was kidding himself. Realistically, he would have to settle with Banks now. He had planned to wait but he would be crazy to chance it. There was only one way out.

Sayers brought himself back to the present with a start. There had been too many mistakes. Too many. As a result, there were still people walking around who could do him harm, not only in his worldly orbit but on the witness stand, to boot. They could undo everything. Could undo his life! His mouth felt dry. The coffee on the end table next to him was cold. He had to think. He had to think!

He went back to the kitchen and ran the tap, filled a glass with cold water, then chugged it down. His luck had to straighten out. It had been running so well in the beginning, until the mistakes started to pile up. Volcanic rage and frustration rushed through every cell in his body. He hurled the empty glass into the sink, where it shattered to bits, then he strode through the flat to the den. He pulled out his journal, and shaking all over, he sat down at his desk and began to write.

CHAPTER THIRTY-SEVEN
A PHONE CALL

TUESDAY, DECEMBER 8

Fowler's trial date had been set. Alex took in the six o'clock news, subverting with practiced calm the knowledge that his efforts thus far had gotten him nowhere, and he was looking at yet another week on the fast track. Besides which, reminders of Christmas were everywhere. He had called his parents over the weekend to check out their plans for the holidays. As expected, they wanted to see him. Could he get away for Christmas?

Maybe he should do just that. Perhaps he should just let happen what was going to happen anyway and take a much-needed vacation in the Florida sun. Why not? He knew why not. He was committed to a job and somehow or other, it was a job he intended to finish. Why fight it?

He had also checked in with Jack Owens to inquire about Lisa and was assured that she was in therapy and all was well. He wanted to believe it, but doubt was a dark specter that crept out of the past and became part of the present. He wondered: could he and Lisa ever again share a life together? As though searching for an answer, he had found himself scouring the picture albums hidden away in his den, recapturing the joy Carl had brought into their lives. He saw Lisa with Carl as an infant, holding him, love glowing in her eyes. He was taken back to that first Christmas with toys under their tree. And there was Carl's first day of kindergarten. He looked at Carl blowing out the candles on his last birthday cake. He had been so thrilled with the new, shiny bike all tied with bright bows and balloons. Heart pounding, Alex slammed the book shut. No, he could never go back. Too much had crumbled under his feet. Rebuilding was impossible. It was time to go on.

At least the almost constant snowfall had let up for a time, he observed through his living room window. The roads were cleared and driving was close to normal. The cold lingered, however. Life in the North Country, he chuckled. Who knows, he might even find the time to get out on the slopes. His skis were still in the closet. Maybe...maybe.

By ten o'clock that evening he had puttered around the house, finished a load of laundry, and worked out his finances for the rest of the month. After a hot shower, he pulled a book off the shelf, dropped onto his bed, and began to read.

Donahue hung up the telephone after talking to Rod Jansen at High Ridge. Fred Murphy had told him that Jansen had swung by the school during the day to check out Sayers' car, which, as expected, was in the lot. Just to be sure the teacher was not up to something, he had driven back later that afternoon and actually followed Sayers home. There had been no suspicious activity noted either by Murphy or by the patrol cars that made casual checks over the course of the evening. So Sayers was holed up, Donahue thought, with relief. Good. Now to see how long before he decides to make another move. When he did, they were ready.

WEDNESDAY, DECEMBER 9

Jenny had spent the afternoon running errands to places around town: the market, the bank, then the cleaners, and lastly, her hairdresser for a trim. There had been no word from Alex since the weekend, and it surprised her how important the daily contact had become. She wondered if it was due to the fact that Fowler's trial was due to begin soon. Monday, January 11, the television news had reported. Alex was so certain that Fowler was getting a bum rap. He let it get him down. She sighed and busied herself preparing dinner, all the while wishing Alex was there to share it. As she sat at the counter in her kitchen munching on her salad, her thoughts strayed briefly to her new neighbor. She had seen him only once. A tall, thin fellow with bright red hair. They had crossed paths in the hall one morning. Despite his rather serious demeanor, she had given him a small, neighborly smile which he had patently ignored. Not so much as the flicker of an eyelid. She shrugged. Different strokes for different folks, she supposed. Not a friendly fellow. Oh, well.

After dinner, Jenny glanced around the kitchen, took one last, hard look at the telephone, stuck her tongue out at it, and went into the living room to watch a mystery on television.

THURSDAY, DECEMBER 10

The phone rang just as Jenny was entering her apartment shortly before noon. Rushing to answer it, she laid her bundles down on the counter and expelled a breathless "hello" into the mouthpiece.

"Well," Alex remarked at the other end, "did I catch you working out?"

Jenny slid onto a counter stool, surprised to hear Alex's voice. She had begun to wonder if the reason she had not heard from him sooner was that he'd decided to end their relationship. The thought hurt.

"Good to hear from you," she said cheerfully. "I just came back from doing a bit of Christmas shopping. What's up?"

"Not much," Alex replied nonchalantly. "Thought you might like to take in a movie or have a late dinner somewhere tomorrow night. I've missed you."

Jenny tugged on an earlobe, unwilling to share the sentiment. "Well," she said finally, "whatever you like. Take your pick."

Alex laughed. A certain note in her voice told him he had fallen a tad out of favor.

"Dinner then. Delveccio's. How's that sound? Pick you up at seven?"

"Seven sounds fine," she agreed quietly. "I'll be ready."

After hanging up the telephone, Jenny tried to revive the petty annoyance she had felt during the week when Alex's frequent calls seemed to have vanished, but it was no use. The sound of his voice and the warmth and humor that came through was too much. But she was no fool. Not hearing from him had hurt. Had he taken her words the wrong way when she told him that she needed space? But she had only told the truth. Being held prisoner was not a fun experience.

She sighed, shook her head, and picked up her packages, already thinking about Friday night, trying to decide what she should wear.

CHAPTER THIRTY-EIGHT
DELVECCIO'S

The heavy snowfall predicted on the morning's local weather report had finally begun. Alex clicked the button that sent his garage door swinging up and away, then backed the Blazer out into a flowing, curling mass of billowy snowflakes. As appealing as they appeared dancing through the air, he knew that before long they would morph to the small, heavy variety that rained straight down and meant business.

"Wouldn't ya know it," he breathed aloud. Another snowstorm in the works. By the next day there would be another foot or more of the white stuff to contend with. So what, he told himself consolingly; there was a bright spot at the end of the day — he was spending the evening with Jenny. However, he had a few misgivings. For one, there was the note in Jenny's voice when he called her. He needed no sixth sense to pick up the hint that he was in at least tepid water for letting almost a week pass by without checking in.

Ouch! He had not meant to hurt her. *But Jenny dear,* he wanted to say, tossing some mental rebuttals around in his brain, *be fair. What was I supposed to do? Sit there while you rattle off the risks you take by running all over town, then watch you back away from a response that displeases you? And only because I literally fear for your life?*

As close as it came to a fair assessment, it fell a little short as a defense. In truth, he had been bummed out most of the week and, not unlike Jenny, he had needed a little space to himself. As far as self-images go, his had been plummeting of late. Little by little, his coping mechanisms had begun to slip.

Plaguing him all week had been the undercurrent of discontent spreading rife across the county, fueled by those who felt Rose Clifford's killer was still running loose. People had been vociferously complaining that the law was not doing its job. At the same time, there were others who, despite evidence to the contrary, continued to dump the blame for the death of both women on Fowler's shoulders. But in the end, they all wanted answers. He had none...for either camp. If that didn't change, Sayers came out the winner and a killer would run free.

By the time Alex was on his way to High Ridge that evening, the snowstorm had taken a breather, which meant an easier ride without a dozen snarls and holdups. He had managed to pull his thoughts out of the depths they had been wallowing in, reminding himself that he was on his way to spend the evening with a beautiful woman. The time had come to turn off the drippy faucet of self-pity, to relax and enjoy. And that was what he intended to do.

A few minutes later, Jenny was opening her apartment door to let him in. One look and his heart took an unexpected lurch. She was wearing an ankle-length dress of soft, vermillion velveteen that clung to her figure. Her dark hair shone, revealing a small pearl clip that daintily matched the single strand of tiny pearls adorning her slender neck. She took his breath away.

"Care for a drink or something before we leave?" she asked, extending a tentative arm for his coat.

"Good idea, but no thanks," Alex replied, his eyes locked on hers. "We have dinner reservations for seven thirty and since this latest storm is in its birth throes, I think we should get started."

Jenny gave a little shrug and reached into the foyer closet for her coat, then handed it to Alex, who was fast catching on that his earlier guess was right. The note of reserve in both Jenny's voice and her manner was unmistakable. There was no bright smile nor warm worlds of welcome. No teasing. No funny comments.

Seeing no other alternative but to play his expected role, Alex held up the long cashmere coat Jenny handed him and allowed her to slip into it. While she moved to the wall mirror to arrange a soft, knitted scarf over her hair, Alex's gaze took in the picture she made. Watching her, indulging himself in the scent of her perfume, he was happy indeed that he had dressed appropriately for the occasion: dark suit and subtle tie, overcoat, and white wool scarf.

Delveccio's was that kind of restaurant. He had wanted the evening to be perfect.

As it turned out, although not the romantic success Alex would have preferred, the evening was a pleasant one. After a glass or two of wine in the genteel atmosphere of the elegant surroundings, Jenny's demeanor relaxed and she began to smile, meaning it. They talked a little of Fowler's impending trial, then pushed that topic onto a back burner and began to chat along more pleasant lines. Alex told her of his parents' invitation to spend Christmas with them in Florida.

"I just might do that," Alex said, wondering when he made the decision. "I can drive as far as Albany and leave my car at the airport. Christmas falls on a Friday this year, so overall, it would mean a long weekend with the folks. I haven't seen either of them in ages."

"Don't your parents come north in the summer?" Jenny inquired, her eyes cool, telling him nothing.

Alex nodded. "Yes, they do. Mom has a sister, my Aunt June, in New Jersey. They usually spend a couple of weeks there and another few with my dad's brother in Maryland. Their visits up this way, as a rule, aren't very lengthy. They're usually settled back in Sarasota around the beginning of September."

Jenny smiled. "You sound as though you miss them."

"Yeah," Alex grinned, "I do. My dad and I are close. When I was growing up, we did a lot together – skiing, fishing, that sort of thing." He laughed. "Now he and my mom are on one golf course or another most of the year. They love it."

"And you're an only child, right?"

"Yep, just like you. One of a kind, both of us."

Dinner was an elegant and sumptuous repast served course by

course, slowly and with panache. A small quintet provided background music. Candlelight glittered.

"Jen," Alex asked finally, "what's wrong between us tonight? You don't seem yourself. Is it anything I've done?"

Jenny twisted the stem of her wine glass. "No, not really, Alex. I'm not certain there is a problem, or if so, how to phrase it. I think I discovered, without having realized it until this week, that I've been depending on your company, on you, a little more heavily than is comfortable. When I didn't hear from you during the week, that's when it hit me. We have no commitment between us, so I can't complain. We're good friends, there's no doubt about that. But I've discovered you have some power over my life, and that realization disturbs me."

"Power?" Alex asked, totally perplexed. "I don't get it, Jen."

"Simple. I waited for you to call me. Not so simple. I wondered why you didn't call because I had come to expect it. You were in control. Not me. In other words, without any intention on your part, you unwittingly had control of my feelings. And, Alex, that did not set well with me. Not the idea that you hadn't called me, but that I didn't know why, and I was upset. That to me is what I call discretionary power," she said with a dry laugh, "and it's something that scares me."

Alex sat back in his chair and blinked. "Whew," he whispered. "I am a dope, I think. And I'm sorry, Jen. You could have called me any time. You have power, too."

Jenny stared directly into Alex's eyes. "Do I? No, I don't think so. In fact, I don't want that kind of power." She tilted her head. "But there are always problems, aren't there, Alex?"

She gave a little laugh and sipped at the edge of her wine glass. "They work out in the end."

And the evening had worked out. For the most part. By the time they were back at High Ridge, the temperatures had dropped and the snow was coming down in earnest.

"Come in for a nightcap?" Jenny asked as they reached her door.

"Not tonight," Alex grinned, his arm tightening around Jenny's waist.

"We're in for another round of snowstorms, and while your sofa is comfortable, I think it best I hightail it home." He bent over and drew her into his arms. "If that control button is at my disposal, I'm going to use it right now." With that, he gave her a deep, lingering kiss. Then he looked down at her and smiled, the old mischief in his eyes.

"I'll call you tomorrow," he told her. "Promise." Then he pressed his lips to her forehead and said goodnight.

Jenny caught her breath and went inside.

CHAPTER THIRTY-NINE
LISA

SATURDAY, DECEMBER 12

The clock on Lisa's bedside table read eight forty. She knew she should be up and helping her mother, but she felt powerless to move. Instead she lay prone on top of her bedspread, fully dressed, one arm crooked over tightly closed eyes. She lay there thinking, mostly about Alex and how things used to be before Carl left them. She wanted to accept that Carl was in heaven. But she needed Alex to help her. She needed him desperately. She needed the feel of his arms around her and his lips on hers, like the last time. Over and over she had relived that moment. She needed to believe that Alex still loved her. Of course he did, she told herself.

But after that kiss, he had left her, yet again. She knew she was in the wrong when she pushed him away after they lost Carl, but Alex should have waited. He should never have disappeared from her life. But this was now, she reckoned, with a deep sigh. What drove them apart had to be left in the past. She loved him and wanted him back.

She opened her eyes, got out of bed, and paused to glance at her image in the dresser mirror. She was wearing dark blue slacks and a white turtleneck sweater. Her short, blonde hair was unkempt, and when she scrutinized her face, she saw new lines around her mouth, and her skin looked dry and old. She scowled at the image, turned away, and hurried downstairs.

As she entered the front hallway she could see her father through the archway to the living room. He was sitting in his favorite lounge chair engrossed in the newspaper. She knew her mother, from long habit, would be starting the Saturday wash in the basement.

Moving as silently as she could across the carpeted floor, trying her best to avoid being noticed right away, Lisa opened the hall closet door and pulled out her jacket, knitted hat, and snow boots. Deliberately ignoring the mirror on the wall next to her, she put them on.

"Good morning, Dad," she ventured at last, her tone casual as she stood framed in the archway. "Did you have any trouble getting your paper?" She zipped up her jacket and pulled her car keys from one of the side pockets. "I'm gonna have to dig my car out, I suppose. Lots of snow out there."

"We were both socked in good, honey," Jack Owens replied with a smile. "But I paid the kid next door ten bucks to shovel us both clear." The smile faded as he took in Lisa's jacket and boots and the car keys in her hand. "Are you going out now, Lisa?" he asked with a questioning frown. "Could you maybe hang around and give your mom a hand with the laundry?"

Lisa shook her head. "Can't right now, Dad," she replied. She stepped closer to the front door. "Don't worry, I'll be back in a few hours. See you then."

After the door closed shut behind her, Lisa's words echoed into the empty room. Jack's frown deepened. Don't worry, she had told him. There was reason to worry. He had been awakened by the sound of Lisa creeping into the house at nearly one o'clock in the morning only a few hours before. As he knew she had done often of late, she had left the house to spend more senseless hours looking for Alex. Now she was going out again. And maybe she would come back in a few hours...and maybe not.

No matter, he reasoned with what had become a familiar sense of resignation, he would continue to reassure his wife that their daughter would be fine. Barbara was making herself sick with worry.

He laid the newspaper down, went to the bay window, pulled aside one of the curtains, and looked out to where Lisa's car was parked at the curb. She had the motor running, letting it warm up while she brushed away a fresh dusting of snow from the windshield, her breath a cloud of icy smoke billowing in the air. She had just opened the driver's side door and was about to climb in when she suddenly looked up and met her father's gaze. She held it for a long moment, her face expressionless, her eyes conveying something Jack did not quite understand. Then she looked away and got into the car. Jack watched as it pulled into the street and then disappeared into the snow-covered distance.

Lisa drove slowly, going over what she was determined to do. First, she would stop at Lou's Diner at the edge of town. Since Alex was out of bounds, she would try to reach Jenny Wyland. Why not? Her thoughts returned to the day she had visited Rose to explain why she had acted so crazy jealous and angry at the school. She also wanted to apologize.

Rose had not only listened to what she went there to say but she had understood. She had assured Lisa that she and Alex were good friends, nothing more. She even made coffee while they talked, explaining that Alex had been working through some rough times himself, dealing with losing Carl and then the breakup of his marriage. He was not, she stated emphatically, looking for a fling. "Just like you, Lisa," Rose told her, "he's hurting."

Before she left that day, she had worked up the courage to ask Rose if she thought Alex might still care for her. Rose's answer still caught at her heart. "He just might," Rose had replied, touching her hand and smiling like maybe she knew. "He just might."

So now she would talk to Jenny. She had to find out if Alex had really met someone and fallen in love, like he said. She did not want to believe it, but she had to know for sure.

After reaching the diner, Lisa took a booth and ordered a doughnut and a cup of hot cocoa. She was never hungry, but she knew she had to eat. She had avoided her parents' scrutiny that morning, so anxious to leave the house that breakfast was the last thing on her mind. When her order arrived, she ate slowly, bracing herself for the courage to once again intrude through a side door of Alex's life. She stiffened when she thought back to his reaction when he learned she had been following him. But, she reasoned, how could he understand? It was the only way she was able to find out if he was seeing Rose. And later, Jenny. What else could she have done? What other way was there?

Finally her cup of cocoa was drained and she was almost ready to leave the diner. But first, she had one more matter to take care of. She looked toward the clock over the counter. It read close to nine thirty-five. Reaching into her purse, she pulled out her cell phone. Then she took a long, deep breath and began to punch in the number written on the piece of paper she held in her hand.

CHAPTER 40
INTRIGUE

SATURDAY, DECEMBER 12

The same as on the previous Saturday morning, Lt. Harry Donahue arrived at High Crest shortly after eight o'clock laden with fresh baked goods for the men in 608. After satisfying himself that Alex's Blazer was not parked in the lot, he took the back elevator and hurried upstairs to join Jansen and Murphy. To his surprise, Murphy was alone.

"Rod wanted to stake out the building entrance from across the street," he told Henry. "He'll call on his cell if we're about to have any unexpected company. He's in a delivery truck with the heater on and he's got high-powered binoculars. You probably feel the same as we do. It's been too quiet. Another week like this past one and you can nominate Mr. Sayers for sainthood. Not a peep."

Donahue laughed and poured himself a cup of coffee from the urn on the counter. "Yeah, got the itch, myself. How's it going here?"

"Boring as mud," Fred stated matter-of-factly. Then he smiled from the corner of his mouth. "Got a good gander at our neighbor. Passed her in the hall the other day. Nice looking gal. She and your buddy Alex went out on the town last night. Dressed to kill! Whew!"

"His car wasn't downstairs," Donahue commented uneasily. "He's not still here, I hope."

Fred shook his head. "Nope. It was pretty late when he saw the lady to her door. But he said his goodnights and left. She's alone."

"Has the camera been busy?" Donahue inqired, noting the various shots of still life on the monitor screens.

"Nah." Fred bit into his apple turnover. "A few kids in ski gear.

Nothing else."

"Have a feeling it won't stay that way," Donahue predicted wryly. "Sayers made a dry run here last Saturday, and I'm willing to bet he has something up his sleeve today."

"Keep your eyes peeled, then," Murphy said on a low, serious note. "It could be a long day. And while you're waiting, there something over there for you." He flipped a thumb toward a black Kevlar vest neatly folded on the breakfast counter. "Put it on."

By eight thirty that morning, freshly showered and dressed, Jenny looked over her apartment and decided that it was not a good day to go out, but a perfect day to clean house. She dug the upright vacuum cleaner out of the kitchen closet and set aside the dust rags and furniture polish she would need to get the job started. As she moved about the apartment, her thoughts went back to her date with Alex the night before, and she felt herself flush. Whatever possessed her to say what she did to him? Alex had gone to such lengths to show her a wonderful evening and she had acted like a brat. She shook her head, sighed, and dug into her work.

She was stacking the dishwasher when the telephone rang. The young woman on the other end of the line, her voice low and hesitant, identified herself.

"I'm sorry," Jenny replied, not sure she was hearing correctly. "Who did you say this was?"

"Lisa Banks," the woman repeated. "Alex's wife."

Jenny was stunned. "Lisa?" she echoed. "Are you calling for Alex? If you are, he's not here."

"Oh, no. That's not why I'm calling. I...I'd like to talk to you for a few minutes if you don't mind," Lisa managed unsteadily. "It's important."

Jenny paused, confused but curious. "I don't know what to say," she replied cautiously. "But, if it's important, I guess I have a few minutes. Go ahead, then. I'm listening."

"No, no, I'm sorry," Lisa stammered. "You don't understand. I need to see you. I can't talk from here. I'm in a diner. Please, it's very important."

Wearing pajamas and robe, Ben Sayers looked out at the snow piled up below his bedroom window and felt his temper flare. Not again. Another passing storm was predicted but he hoped the thing would end up somewhere else. Certainly not here and certainly not today. He checked his watch and frowned. It was close to eight fifteen. It would take a good twenty minutes to shovel himself out. Drat. Another glance through the window evidenced no sign of the town plows, which was something in his favor, at least. If he got himself moving quickly enough, he could beat them out and avoid the risk of being plowed in. By eight forty, he was fully dressed, heading for the hall closet, ready to go.

Minutes later, Sayers began the task of extricating his car from its snowy confinement. When at last the job was done and he was seated behind the wheel, he let out a long breath, relieved to be on his way. He took his time driving, both eyes on the road. Traffic through Grover was light but driving was still tricky. Once on the Northway, however, he found that the plows had been busy and the highway was well cleared, which meant he was able to make good time covering the distance to Weston.

Having felt sorely deprived of enough time for his morning repast, Sayers opted for a stop at the Weston Mall to grab a quick breakfast. Once he was out of the cold with a cup of hot coffee under his belt, maybe he would be less out of joint. Emotions had a way of raising havoc with him lately, and it was vital he keep a level head. And no more mistakes, a small, inner voice whispered ominously. He swallowed hard. No. Absolutely no more mistakes. He would take the time to clear his thoughts and to move ahead cautiously. His mind was set on what he felt compelled to do, if only to protect himself. But he was far from stupid, he mumbled through gritted teeth. He knew the enemy would trap him if they could. He had to be careful.

First, though, he would drive by High Ridge on his way to the mall. It would be interesting to see if Sheriff Banks was sharing another cozy Saturday morning *tête-à-tête* with the little nurse. He wanted to giggle. Both of them were due for a few surprises before the sun went down.

After reaching High Ridge, he drove slowly through the parking lot, then directly back onto Pine Street in the direction of Weston Mall. He had looked around carefully but had seen no sign of the Chevy Blazer. No Sheriff Alex Banks this morning? Sayers could not decide if he was disappointed or glad. Time would tell.

The telephone in High Ridge apartment 608 range twice before Fred Murphy picked it up. With the phone at his ear, he gave a grunt of surprise and looked up at Harry. "Stay with it," Murphy said into the receiver. "He will probably be back." He hung up the phone and turned his gaze to Harry. "That was Rod. Ben Sayers is on the move. He just drove into the parking lot, turned around, and drove out. We'd better keep our eyes open. Something is up."

CHAPTER FORTY-ONE
THE VISIT

Weston stores, all competing for the Christmas shopping dollar, were now opening their doors to the public at nine o'clock each morning, seven days a week. As a result, despite recent episodes of heavy snowfall, the mall parking area was more than half filled when Ben Sayers pulled into it. Reluctant to trudge through the windy bite of the cold morning air, Sayers found a spot close to the main entrance, parked, and hurried inside.

Weston Mall was not as large a shopping plaza as might be found in more populated areas, but it offered its customers a considerable choice of retail shops, boutiques, a clothing outlet, jewelry store, fast food court, and the like. Entering the main atrium, Sayers paused to look around. He took in the early morning menagerie of shoppers deterred by neither the weather nor the early hour. They hurried along the wide, store-lined walkways carrying their purchases, the mall's audio system sending a stream of Christmas music flowing in every direction. Sayers snickered to himself.

"All rot," he grunted, unzipping his jacket as the surrounding warmth settled in. The spectacle made him ill. It always had. But at least, he consoled himself, the place afforded him temporary respite from the miserable weather outside. Now, if he could just locate the McDonald's, he would get himself some sort of breakfast and then be on his way.

A short time later, he was settled into a booth with a paper cup of steaming coffee and the remains of a breakfast sandwich on the tray in front of him. His hunger finally sated and content settling into his bones for the moment, Sayers sipped on his cup and let his thoughts run ahead to his plans for the day. When he felt his heart quicken and a fresh surge of excitement begin to stir, he brought himself up short as he had done a dozen times over the past few days. He must stay calm, he reminded himself. That was the key, staying calm.

He finished off the last of his coffee and reached for his jacket on the seat next to him. His intellect was in charge now. Not his emotions. It was vital he remain in control. Glancing down at his watch, he saw that it was already after ten o'clock. It was time to get back on the road.

The snowstorm had passed but the sun was still hidden behind heavy, gray clouds when Sayers climbed back behind the wheel of his car and headed out toward High Ridge. The weather, however, was of no further interest to him. His thinking was centered on the hours ahead. The challenges of the game were now his to enjoy, as was the final laugh on those who would hurt and humiliate him if he allowed it. Anger, like an old, festering abscess, began to infuse its way into his soul. It simmered there briefly as faces from the past materialized, then faded. First Liz, then Rose and Lonny Jerome, and finally, Lorna Kelly, Alex Banks, and Jenny Wyland. How he hated them all.

Breathing hard, working to regain the control fast slipping insidiously away, Sayers reminded himself that the day was his. All his. It was what he had waited for. His moment of redemption and revenge. His lips twisted into an exultant smile as finally, up ahead of him, High Ridge came into view.

Jenny looked down at the phone in her hand, asking herself why in heaven's name she had agreed to Lisa's visit. Perhaps she gave in out of sympathy or curiosity or plain madness. In any case, Alex Banks' ex-wife was only minutes away. In a heartbeat or two she would be at her door. Recalling the few details Alex had supplied regarding his marriage, and aware of the pain the mother must have suffered at the loss of her child, Jenny was uncertain as to what to expect; she wished she knew more.

With a resigned sigh, she put the cleaning paraphernalia away and had just finished starting up a fresh pot of coffee when the entry buzzer sounded. Before she would allow herself to think further, Jenny buzzed Lisa through and waited for her by the apartment door.

"Thank you for seeing me," Lisa said shyly, as Jenny ushered her into the apartment and led the way to the living room. "I really do appreciate it."

Jenny smiled and laid Lisa's jacket and hat on a chair. "No problem," she replied, keeping her voice casual. "The only item on my agenda this morning is house cleaning. You gave me a break." She nodded toward the kitchen. "I just made some coffee and it's almost ready to pour, so why don't you get comfortable in the living room, Lisa, and I'll be right back. Coffee is okay, I hope?'

"Coffee would be fine," Lisa replied with a tentative smile. "Thank you."

By the time Jenny returned to the living room, her guest was seated in an armchair, hands folded in her lap, taking quiet stock of her surroundings. Jenny set a tray with coffee pot, cups, and saucers onto the cocktail table.

"This should help both of us," Jenny said with a cheerful smile while she poured coffee into the waiting cups. "Do you take cream and sugar?"

Curled into the corner of the sofa a few minutes later, Jenny tried to avoid being obvious as she studied Lisa, surprised that the woman was so thin and pale. She wondered if she had been more seriously ill than Alex had implied. Even her cheekbones, which were high and structurally lovely, had deep, hollow shadows where the bloom of her age ought to be.

"Tell me," Jenny asked after a few moments of silence, "what did you want to talk to me about, Lisa?"

Lisa met her gaze and flushed. Then she set her cup down, refolded her hands, and leaned forward. "I can only say this straight out, so I will. I'm still in love with my husband, Jenny," she declared, chin held high. "And I believe he's still in love with me."

Jolted by the words, Jenny stared blankly into Lisa's eyes, wondering if she was hearing correctly. Lisa's expression, however, vanquished any doubt.

"Lisa," Jenny said finally, choosing her words with care, "before you go on, I'd like to sort a few things out. Please clarify one point. First of all, when you refer to Alex as your husband, you do mean your ex-husband, don't you?"

Lisa made a dismissing motion and shrugged. "Of course, I suppose if you look at it from a legal standpoint, that's correct. But not when you talk about love, Jenny." She paused, her eyes misting. "Alex and I made a mistake when we broke up. I know what a terrible frame of mind I was in after we lost our son, but what mother wouldn't be? And don't forget, Alex and I shared a lot together." She shook her head and her shoulders slumped. "He never should have left me."

"Lisa, will you explain why you came to me?" Jenny asked patiently. "I find this to be a very uncomfortable conversation. Isn't this something you should be talking to Alex about, not me?"

Lisa straightened. "I've tried," she admitted, her eyes shifting from Jenny to the hands entwined in her lap. "Then I remembered how nice Rose was to me when I went to apologize for the terrible way I acted that day at her school." She returned her gaze to meet Jenny's. "It seemed maybe I should talk to you, too. That maybe you'd listen."

"You were the woman in the parking lot?" Jenny exclaimed, unable to contain her astonishment. "And the person who came to Rose's apartment – that was you, too?"

Lisa nodded. "Yes, it was. I had to tell Rose how sorry I was, and to explain."

"You take my breath away," Jenny heaved, sinking back into the sofa and shaking her head. "Do you realize that you were probably the last person to see Rose alive?"

Lisa's expression clouded. "I know. I explained everything to Harry Donahue, Alex's trooper friend. He had a lot of questions, and I told him the whole story. But now, Jenny," she stated, obviously anxious to dispense with the subject, "we should talk about Alex. That's why I'm here."

Jenny finally began to grasp what a disturbed young woman she was dealing with. At the same time, she wondered why Alex never saw fit to discuss the problem with her, or why he had kept to himself the fact that

Lisa had visited Rose the day she was killed. Lisa was Rose's mysterious visitor. Jenny thought back to the coffee pot and cups, so unusual in Rose's apartment, that she herself had pointed out the day Alex walked her through. Of course. Just as she had done herself, Rose had prepared coffee for her guest.

Looking back, surely Alex came to know her well enough to realize he could trust her to maintain confidentiality regarding details such as those. And on a personal basis, he had shut her out, as well. For some reason, Alex had contained everything within himself. He had kept their relationship at a safe arm's length without the burden of close, personal commitment. Or trust.

Realistically, she had to admit that the events surrounding Rose's murder could have been a plausible deterrent to a serious love affair. Add to that the hovering threat of a killer who had made an attempt on both their lives. Still, she was unable to shake the hurt she felt. Alex should have trusted her with the whole story. Now what was she supposed to do? She suddenly realized that Lisa was staring at her with hope-filled eyes, waiting for an answer.

"Are you telling me that if I step out of Alex's life, he'll go back to you?" Jenny asked, working to keep her voice steady through a whirl of thoughts and emotions.

Lisa's eyes filled with tears. It was evident to Jenny that the woman was exhausted, burned out by grief and fear and what she saw as undeserved desertion by Alex. Worse yet, she believed he still loved her and everything could return to the way it once was between them.

"Don't you think so?" Lisa asked uncertainly.

"Why don't we do this," Jenny said, uncurling herself from the sofa. "First let me pour us both some fresh coffee, then you can start from the beginning and tell me whatever you want me to know. Then, we'll see what we can work out together."

As Lisa's words poured out, Jenny listened in rapt attention. Lisa spoke in detail of the day in the cemetery when Alex had found her next to

Carl's grave and how she had screamed at him. She also admitted to the reasons she had been keeping watch on him since the summer before when he was seeing Rose. It was her jealously of Rose and fear that Alex would find someone else that caused her to act so terribly at the school. Finally, she came to the story of Alex's passionate kiss the day he had come to see her.

While Lisa's description of the kiss stung, Jenny recognized that she was facing a delicate and serious problem. Lisa was deeply obsessed with the man who had once been her husband, convinced that should the "other woman" step aside, they would reunite and live happily ever after. Unfortunately, in Lisa's mind, Jenny was the other woman.

With Lisa's words ringing in her ears, Jenny was now aware of another reason Alex had shied away from a commitment to her and why he had been so unwilling to tell her what he felt. It was Lisa. Whatever hold the past had on him or however Lisa fit into his emotions, only Alex could say.

Jenny gazed at Lisa, feeling helpless and sad. "Lisa," she began slowly, "I don't know what Alex would or wouldn't do. We have no commitment to one another. Has Alex said anything to give you that idea? Or are you making assumptions?"

Lisa lowered her eyes, then raised them, her lips trembling. "I know Alex slept here last week, for one thing. And he's with you a lot."

Unable to help herself, Jenny began to laugh. "Good gracious," she exclaimed, "Alex fell asleep on my sofa. I covered him with a blanket and went to bed. Despite whatever you may imagine, Alex and I are not lovers." Then she sobered. "You're still checking up on him, aren't you Lisa?"

Lisa shrugged, embarrassed. "I know it's wrong," she admitted, her voice low and strained. "Alex will be so angry with me when he finds out I was here. Please, just tell him how I feel and that I'm getting help. I'm in a group and I'm seeing a doctor. But I need Alex, too. I can't make it alone, Jenny. We need to be back together. Is that so hard to understand?"

Unfortunately, to Jenny, it was not. "Look," she said, leaning toward Lisa, her voice firm and her words direct. "What I understand doesn't count. I can't speak for Alex; he has to speak for himself. But when I see him, I'll urge him to sit down with you and talk things through, perhaps with your doctor or a counselor. That's the best I can do, Lisa. You and Alex are adults. I won't lie to you, he means a lot to me, too. But that's beside the point right now. One thing, however, is very, very important. You must believe and accept whatever Alex tells you. He's the only one who can make a decision for his life and what he wants in it. Can you do that?"

Lisa's response was a vague shake of her head. "I'll have to, I suppose," she said uncertainly, brushing a tear from her cheek.

"Yes." Jenny's tone was adamant. "You will have to. No matter what he tells you, you have to believe him. I know Alex wouldn't lie to you about his feelings, and I also don't believe you would want him to."

Lisa sighed, then slowly stood up. Jenny did the same. When Lisa extended a hand toward her, Jenny took it. "Yes, I want the truth," Lisa said sadly. "At least I think I do. Thank you, Jenny. I had a feeling you'd understand. Like Rose did."

Releasing Jenny's hand, Lisa glanced at her watch as she reached for her pea jacket and slipped into it. "I'll be going now," she said. "I told my dad I'd be home shortly. He worries a lot." She took a step, then hesitated. "Do you think you'll talk to Alex today?'

"Yes," Jenny answered as they walked to the front door. "I will. So please, go home to your parents and be a little patient. He'll call you there by tomorrow, I promise."

Jenny's hand reached for the knob to open the door for her guest, looking ahead toward the moment when she could close it again and wrap herself in the quiet and solitude of her home. She needed to unmuddle her thoughts and work out what must be settled with Alex that very day.

She had no way of knowing that her plans were to be rudely altered. Ben Sayers, patient and predatory, was on the opposite side of her apartment door, eagerly waiting for it to open.

CHAPTER FORTY-TWO
MALICE IN ACTION

SATURDAY, DECEMBER 12

Ben Sayers pulled into the parking lot at High Ridge, taking quick note that the sheriff's car was still nowhere in sight. Then suddenly, he slowed down as a vehicle caught his attention.

"Well, what do you know," he mumbled aloud. "Banks isn't here but look who is. Lisa Banks. Now I wonder where she might be at the moment." He threw his head back and gave a little hoot of laughter. "Yeah," he tittered gleefully, "I just wonder."

After parking his car close to the rear of the building, Sayers hurried toward the sidewalk that led to the High Ridge front entrance. Holding tight to the key which would give him access to the front lobby and maintaining the outward façade of a tenant who belonged there, he let himself in. Except for a couple who passed him as they were leaving, the lobby was empty. His watch read ten twenty-five. Determined to avoid unnecessary risks, he stood stock still for a few moments, his senses alert to any sound that would tell him he was not alone. All was quiet.

Satisfied that nobody was about, he left the lobby and turned down a connecting hallway. He passed the closed office door belonging to the manager, then a large room with a piano, table and chairs, and a television set in one corner. Continuing on to the far end of the hallway, Sayers came to a door marked "Maintenance," the room he was looking for. As in the case of the janitor's closet on his previous visit, he found the door slightly ajar. After a thoughtful pause, he gave it a tentative knock, a prepared speech ready should anyone reply.

He waited. Nothing. He then slowly eased the door open and slipped quickly inside. The room was set up as a small office with a computer, desk, and credenza on one side of the room, filing cabinets on the other. There was also a big-block duty calendar hanging on the wall, and beside it, a strip of wood inset with hooks, each hook accommodating a ring of keys.

He glanced over his shoulder, straining to pick up any hint of approaching footsteps. All remained quiet. Confidence growing, he reached up to finger his way through each key ring until he came to one he was looking for, tagged "Master." Quickly detaching it from the others, he slipped the key into his pocket, replaced the ring on its hook, and nonchalantly retraced his steps out the door and down the hallway to the lobby and the elevators.

He felt good. Now, he was sure, his good luck was on a roll. He cracked his knuckles, gave a gleeful snicker, and pushed the elevator button for the eighth floor. Yes, indeed, he thought, his spirits soaring. Luck definitely was his lady today.

At nine forty, the telephone in apartment 608 rang. Fred Murphy snatched it up. It was Rod Jansen calling from the van and he had news.

"Rod told me that a sedan with Lisa Bank's plate number just pulled into the parking lot," he relayed to Donahue upon concluding the call. "Says the lady in question is on her way into the building and in one heck of a hurry."

Donahue's eyebrows shot up. "Lisa Banks? You're kidding! What the dickens is she doing here?"

A few minutes later, the monitor screens revealed Lisa striding down the hallway in their direction. They watched in amazement as she went by, reached the door to Jenny's apartment, and seconds later disappeared inside.

Donahue let out a long breath. "Unbelievable," he whispered to himself. What could the woman possibly want with Jenny? At the moment, he was not at all sure he wanted to find out. Perhaps he had been wrong to leave Alex out of his plans with the B.C.I. The situation could easily be escalating with Bank's ex-wife calling on his current girlfriend. To add to the note of hysteria, if he could call it that, a team was standing by just next door to the Wyland apartment, primed and ready to catch a killer who would love to waste them both. He groaned inwardly. Maybe it was time to fill Alex in, after all.

Jansen called again at ten twenty-five to report that Sayers had returned to the building.

"Wait five minutes, then come on back," Murphy rumbled red-faced into the telephone.

"Something's gonna pop and we need you here." He hung up, then turned to Harry. "I'd better bring the sheriff into the game. It's probably gonna get a little messy."

Moments later, the three men were assembled in the apartment staring at the monitors with no sign of Sayers in any of them. Tensed for the trouble they knew was on the way, they had no other choice but to wait.

Ben Sayers was delighted that he would not have to force the lock on the janitor's closet.

Instead, one turn of the pilfered key and he was inside looking over the stock, hoping he wouldn't be caught, knowing the chance he would be was slight. He was certain that on a Saturday only one maintenance man would be on duty to cover any emergency that might come up. And, Sayers chuckled to himself, the guy was probably in one of the apartments right now, either goofing off, shuffling a deck of cards, or maybe even fixing a leaky faucet.

Still chuckling, he pulled a pair of paint-spattered coveralls off one wall hook and a painter's cap off another. A tool belt slung over the rung of a ladder provided him with a screwdriver and a pair of pliers, plus a place for his Jennings and his knife. In one corner stood a bag filled with rags. He extracted one and tucked it into the back pocket of the coveralls, allowing it to dangle free. Then he took the Jennings out of his jacket pocket and placed it carefully into the leather pocket of the tool belt. He chuckled again. Two of the sheriff's women together with no Lone

Ranger around to protect them. How lucky could he get! Pretty soon, he gloated, pleased with himself, he would have himself a party.

In apartment 608, the three men, black-vested and with guns holstered, waited for Sayers to appear. Ten minutes passed. Still no sign of the man. There was, in fact, no one in view on the monitor screens until a maintenance man in coveralls came around a corner. He was wearing a visored painter's cap and a tool belt, walking slowly down the hallway toward them. The three men staring at the screen turned to each other and exchanged glances. Their quarry had appeared.

Certain that he wouldn't stand out to anyone he might encounter along the way, Sayers emerged from the fire door and lumbered casually down the sixth floor hallway toward apartment 610. Eyeing it covertly from beneath the peak of the cap he wore, he made first one pass by it and then another, stopping at the end of the hall before turning back to retrace his steps. He was certain that Lisa Banks was inside with the nurse. But as close as he stood to the door, he could make out no sound that would give him a clue to what was going on inside.

In apartment 608, the men were ready. What they did not know was that Lisa Banks was preparing to leave Jenny's apartment. With Sayers now positioned a mere foot or two away from Jenny's door, the team, revolvers drawn and eyes alert, lined up, ready to break into action the second Sayers made a move they could nail him for.

Then the unexpected happened. Lisa Banks was exchanging a few last words with Jenny as she opened the door to apartment 610. Alone and vulnerable in the doorway, she gave Sayers the chance he was looking for. He pulled the pistol from his belt and lunged forward. He gave Jenny a vicious shove out of the way, slamming her backwards against the foyer wall as he dragged Lisa back into the apartment, the barrel of the pistol pressed into her neck, just under her chin.

Sayers ordered Jenny to get up and to close and lock the door. Too frightened to do otherwise, she was about to obey when three men in black burst into the apartment past her, weapons drawn, all aimed directly at Ben Sayers.

Still maintaining his hold on Lisa, Sayers took a backward step as he stared at the men. He was incredulous. "You were waiting for me!" he screamed, teeth bared. "You were waiting for me," he repeated, red-faced with fury.

"You got that right, Mr. Sayers," Fred Murphy replied in a low and menacing tone. "We were waiting for you. Now let the young lady go."

Sayers stared at Murphy, letting his eyes drift first to Jansen and finally to Donahue. Then he shook his head, staring straight at Donahue. "Why don't you just take your friends here, turn around and leave," he said, smiling malignantly. His glance swept over the weapons aimed at him. "Go," he sneered, the barrel of the Jennings dug even harder into Lisa's neck. Her head fell back at an ungainly angle and her hands flailed in the air. She gave a little moan.

"Need I say please?" Sayers snarled, enjoying the alarm written on Donahue's face.

"Don't be a fool," Donahue barked. "Put the gun down, Sayers. You're finished. Where can you go from here, man? Give yourself a break. Let the lady go."

Sayers' grin widened. "I have no intention of letting her go," he declared, with a new and deadly calm. He released the gun's safety, continuing the pressure under Lisa's chin.

"Now, all of you, get out! Or, simply put, the lady dies, right here, right now. I'll see both of these ladies dead before you take me." He looked straight at Donahue. "Want me to prove it? Do you really want to see her brains splattered all over the place? Your pal Banks wouldn't like that even a little bit, would he?"

Defeated, but only for the moment, Donahue took a step backward. Reluctantly, he lowered his weapon, his eyes locked on Sayers. Jansen and Murphy, standing to one side, lowered their weapons, as well.

Jenny, positioned in a half slouch against the foyer wall where she had fallen when Sayers shoved her, took in the dramatic crisis taking place a few feet away. Fear and desperation mounting, she knew her options were few. Taking advantage of the tense, unguarded moments while Sayers' full attention was absorbed in confronting and defending his own position against the three men, she slowly shifted her weight just enough to regain the balance she needed to pull herself to her feet. Moving a fraction of an inch at one time, she finally was able to feel the floor flat under her feet. Saying a quick prayer, she gritted her teeth, then flung herself away from the wall, throwing her entire weight, shoulders first, hard against Sayers' legs.

As the impact of her body struck him, Sayers' knees buckled, and as he was thrown off balance, his glasses flying into the air, he lost his grip on Lisa. She slipped away into a crumpled heap on the floor. Next to her, where he had gone down with the gun still clutched in his hand, Sayers managed to hoist himself up on one elbow. Snarling like an animal, he took aim at Lisa's head.

But Donahue was too fast for him. Before Sayers could get off a shot, Donahue kicked the gun out of his hand with a brutal swing of his boot. Then, as Sayers scrambled to retrieve the knife that he had planned to use as a last resort, Jensen and Murphy grabbed him. Within seconds, they had him handcuffed. By the time they dragged him to his feet, he was screaming with fury and frustration.

"No, no, no!" he screeched. "This can't happen! Let me go!"

Jensen and Murphy were reading him his rights and hauling him through the apartment door when, at that moment, as if on cue, Alex Banks appeared. Paling visibly, he stood frozen in the doorway, taking in the aftermath of the room's recent chaos. Jenny, in the foyer, was rubbing her shoulder and wincing, attempting to stand upright. Lisa lay dazed and sobbing on the floor next to her. Astonished, he suddenly found himself face to face with Donahue.

"I guess you got my message, huh?" Donahue said, with one of his best cockeyed grins. "It sure took you long enough to get here, Sheriff."

"What the heck is going on here, Harry?" Alex demanded, taking in

Donahue's holstered gun and vest and conscious of Sayers' screams fading into the distance.

"I'll fill you in on the whole story," Donahue replied, "but right now Lisa is in bad shape. She had a close shave with our friend Sayers."

Once on her feet and able to navigate, Jenny had managed to assure Lisa that the nightmare was over and Sayers was gone. Now they both stood together, Lisa obviously still in shock, Jenny with a protective arm across her shoulders. It was then Jenny looked up and straight into Alex's eyes. Still holding on to Lisa, she started toward him.

"Take Lisa home to her parents, Alex," she said when she reached him. Very gently, she transferred Lisa from her shoulder to Alex's. "She'll be fine in a little while. When the time comes, she'll want to talk to you. I suggest you listen."

Donahue tapped her on the shoulder. "You okay yourself, lady? You saved the day, you know. That was quite a tackle."

"She saved my life," Lisa whispered, barely audible, her head now resting on Alex's chest. "He was going to kill me. I know he was. Jenny saved me."

"That she did," Donahue agreed. "And as much as I hate to ask it, Miss Wyland, we'll need your statement. Think you can handle it?"

Jenny shook her head. "No, I'll need a little time," she told him soberly, brushing loose strands of hair back from her face with trembling fingers. "I'm still shaky. If you don't mind, I'll take care of it later."

"Fine with me," Donahue assured her. "Take your time. Just stop by state police headquarters, okay? Won't take long, I promise." He turned to Alex.

"It's over, fella. You were right. The Clifford case is closed, thanks to Jenny here. We'll cover all the ground later, okay?" He gave Alex a meaningful grin. "I owe you some answers. You deserve them, and you'll get them." He gestured toward the door. "Come on, let's leave the lady in peace. She's been through enough for one day."

Still confused, and with Lisa holding his arm in a viselike grip, Alex stared at Jenny uncertainly, surprised when she gave him one final, dispassionate glance, turned her back, and walked down the hall into her bedroom.

A little later, when the apartment was finally empty and she was absolutely alone, Jenny picked up the telephone and put in a call to Aunt Bea. After a brief conversation, she hurriedly packed a suitcase and closed up the apartment. Within a half hour she was in her car and headed for state police headquarters where, as promised, she gave her statement to Donahue. When they were finished, he escorted her to her car, and with a little salute, watched as she drove away. As she covered the stretch of highway that would take her to Oak Creek, Jenny looked back on the nightmare she was leaving behind, and she was sure in her heart that she had never needed her Aunt Bea at any time in her life more than she did at that moment.

CHAPTER FORTY-THREE
HIDING AWAY

Jenny pulled into Aunt Bea's driveway and sat quietly behind the wheel for a moment, looking out beyond the small, blue house toward the clear expanse of mountains spread in winter white and forest green across her line of vision. Despite the horror of what she had experienced that day, a sense of peace and finality settled over her. As expected, Bea's smiling face was a beacon of welcome behind the curtained window of the door.

Within the next few minutes, Bea had settled Jenny's belongings into the guestroom and coaxed her into the warmth of the living room, where a log crackled in the fireplace. To Jenny's amazement, instead of the usual teapot waiting in its cosy on the coffee table, unpredictable Bea had laid out a tray of sandwiches, with a bottle of Chardonnay cooling in an ice bucket beside it.

After several repeated assurances that she was comfortable indeed, Jenny sat back, and with one of her aunt's best crystal wine glasses in her hand, slowly described what had transpired earlier that day. Jenny started the story from the onset, beginning with Lisa's call and subsequent visit. She then moved on to Sayers' forced entry into her apartment and his determination to kill both Lisa and herself. She described the hold he had on Lisa, defying the troopers who had stormed into the room behind him, their weapons ready to bring him down. As Jenny's words painted the shocking scene, Aunt Bea turned ghostly white.

"Dear heaven!" she gasped, clapping a hand against her cheek. "That man wanted to kill you? I can't imagine such an evil thing. And to think I was so nice to him. Oh, Jenny, I'm such an old and foolish woman! It's no wonder Alex was upset with me!"

Curled up in a chair next to the fire, Jenny leaned back, closed her eyes, and continued. "I don't want to see or even talk to Alex until my thoughts are clear, Aunt Bea. I keep hearing Lisa's words over and over in my mind. The way she described how Alex kissed her and the way she still feels about him. Whatever my perspective on Alex and our relationship may be, those other problems belong to the two of them to settle. I want to stay out of it. Far out."

Bea nodded her agreement. "Yes, dear, you're being very wise. That poor young woman. I can't imagine what it must be like for her. And for Alex, too. But let's be grateful that Mr. Sayers is in a jail cell. So full of hate, that man. What a cruel, twisted mind!" She leaned over and gave Jenny's hand a pat. "Drink up your little treat, Jenny, love. Tonight you'll get yourself a good night's sleep and we'll talk more in the morning. We'll put aside our troubles until then. Now, let's touch the rims of our glasses together and toast to better days ahead."

SUNDAY, DECEMBER 13

Still not fully recovered from the stress of the previous day, on Sunday morning Jenny lounged about the house in pajamas, robe, and scruffy slippers, savoring the solicitous pampering by Aunt Bea, grateful to be safely away from the fray Sayers' arrest was creating. She was also grateful for a good night's rest, suspicious that the Chardonnay had something to do with it.

She smiled. Aunt Bea was a blessing. After their talk, she had all but tumbled into bed, not to be roused out of her solid slumber until the aroma of perking coffee reached her from the kitchen, where Bea had breakfast waiting when she padded in.

THE WEEK OF MONDAY, DECEMBER 14

Alex went back to work on Monday. The fuss and furor created by the news media was at its peak. Newspaper and television reporters were broadcasting the story of Sayers' capture and Fowler's release up and down the length of New York State. Sayers, the educator, was in jail, excerpts from his journal released to the press. The shocking accounts of cold-blooded murder, culminating with the details of his final capture, horrified both students and faculty alike at Weston Elementary, along with the rest of the world.

On Saturday night, when Alex had tried, unsuccessfully, to reach Jenny by phone at her apartment, he had presumed initially that she was avoiding the press, and he did not blame her in the least. But by late Monday, when he still had no word from her, Alex took a chance that she had run to her aunt and called her there. After a brief conversation with Bea, he had hung up wondering what was going on in Jenny's mind. Bea, in her sweet, placating manner, had explained that Jenny was worn out but doing fine. At the moment, Bea told him graciously, Jenny was not up to talking to anyone and was requesting that her calls wait until she arrived home. She promised that Jenny would call him from there.

While typical of Bea's soft-pedaling touch, the explanation just did not cut it. It was not like Jenny to shut him out that way. Not only that, but the furor which had played central focus in their relationship because of Sayers was done with. It was over. So why would she want to run away from him?

Confused and admittedly annoyed, Alex dug into the routine that would see him through the rest of the week, thoughts of Jenny always on the periphery. Donahue had explained his reasons for going after Sayers without including Alex, postscripting the story with an apology for his stubborn assertion of Fowler's guilt in the Lonny Jerome murder. He had been proven wrong and was glad to admit it. Peterson was not as gracious.

Still, Donahue's decision to keep Alex in blinders during the operation had evolved into the test of a longstanding friendship. It would take awhile for Alex to recoup from the stunning realization that his friend's decision could have cost both Jenny and Lisa their lives.

It was Thursday afternoon when Lorna stopped by the sheriff's office to give Alex an update on events at the school. "They've found a new teacher," she told him with a wide smile. Then she brought up her own inclusion in Sayers' journal.

"I was almost one of his victims," Lorna exclaimed, her eyes widening at the enormity of her words. "He wanted to kill me, too. My dog, Baron, scared him away!"

Alex smiled wryly at that twist of fate. Baron had protected his young mistress, yet there was the chilling reality of how close Lorna came to joining Rose and Lonny as part of the headline news.

It was early Friday morning when Alex took a call from Jack Owens. Lisa, her father reported, was now settled into a private hospital where she would receive treatment and help.

"She wanted me to tell you that she'll be fine," Jack added. "Apparently, she promised Jenny Wyland something. Whatever it was, it helped. You've done all you can do, Alex," he added, "and we appreciate it. Now get on with your own life. We'll stay in touch."

Although concerned about her obligations at home, Jenny remained with Aunt Bea for the remainder of the week. By Friday, however, she felt it was time to get back to Weston, her apartment, and her work at the hospital. Having been the center of so much publicity, she was not at all certain what the reaction of the hospital administrators would be. After bracing herself for a telephone discussion with the Mercy Hospital nursing director, however, she hung up relieved to know that she would be welcomed back whenever the orthopedist gave her a written release allowing her to return to duty.

On Friday evening, Alex called again. This time, she came to the phone.

"Are you okay?" Alex asked. "I've been worried, not hearing from you."

Jenny assured him she was fine. She had wanted to stay out of sight and avoid more unwanted publicity, which so far, she told him, she had managed to do.

"I don't blame you for that, Jen," Alex agreed. "It's been crazy here. There were reporters camped on your doorstep for days before they finally gave up. Donahue didn't give out the details of the tackle that brought Sayers down, but they knew you were part of the story and wanted an interview."

Jenny then asked about Lisa.

Alex paused a moment. "Well, it's been a rough week all around," he told her. "She was severely traumatized after the incident in your apartment. She's now in a private hospital and will be there for awhile. By the way, she told me about your talk and her promise. We got things straight and I thank you for that. Both Jack and Barbara had been more than a little nuts with worry, so you can imagine their relief that Lisa is finally going to get the treatment she needs. That's about it. So what about you, Jen?" He let out a long breath. "When can I see you?"

Jenny paused, reluctant to say words she might not be able to retract. "Why don't we take a little breather, Alex. I'll be home tomorrow, but I need to have some clear and uncomplicated time to myself for awhile. I'm anxious to get back to work but that's as far as I can plan ahead just now."

"I can take a hint," Alex returned quietly. "If space is what you want, I won't twist your arm. I don't know why the brush off, but it's your decision, not mine. So take care of yourself. Talk to you another time." Then he said goodbye, and hung up.

At the sound of the click in her ear, Jenny stood motionless for a long moment before she replaced the telephone to its cradle.

"Bad news?" Bea asked from where she was standing at the kitchen sink.

Jenny shook her head. "Not really. I don't know my problem, Aunt Bea. Just that there is one."

A little later, sitting across the kitchen table from Bea, Jenny tried to find the words to describe her dilemma. "I think at some point I knew that I was beginning to care deeply for Alex," she began. "We hadn't known each other very long, and naturally, I had to ask myself where Lisa fit into his life. Then, during our earlier visit on Saturday, Lisa told me about Alex kissing her on the day he went to see her. Passionately, by the way. She was convinced he still cared, and she wanted him back."

Jenny shook her head and her expression clouded. "But that's not all of it, Aunt Bea. Alex has not only kept things from me, but at no time has he affirmed his feelings for me. Instead, he's shown himself an expert at skirting around any hint or mention of commitment. So how could I expose my own feelings? I don't know what's going on in his mind, Aunt Bea. I only know that present circumstances don't bode well for a serious relationship between us."

Bea smiled. "Men can be like that, honey. Carrying their own burdens, I mean. What Lisa and Alex went through after their son's accident must have been a terrible weight. Lisa may never get past the grief, you know that. And didn't you mention to me that Lisa turned away from him at a time they both needed one another for comfort as well as strength? And am I correct in recalling you telling me Alex never wanted a divorce, that it wasn't a choice but something he had to do? I think that says something, don't you?"

Then Bea's face seemed to light up, and she gave Jenny a soft, secret smile. "I might never have been married but don't think for a minute that romance was never a part of my life, my dear. Only my fella was taken away one day, and another like him never came along again. I didn't mind being an old maid. It was him or nobody. So, it was nobody." Her eyes twinkled mischievously. "I'll bet you never knew that story, did you, dear? Hmmm, we all have our secrets, I suspect. I thought it might warm your heart if I shared mine."

Jenny laughed softly. "I always suspected you had many a romantic bone in your body. Maybe you'll tell me more one of these days?"

Then Jenny got up, came around the table, and landed a kiss on Bea's cheek. "Now, since this is my last evening here, I want to treat you to dinner at the best restaurant around these parts. Then I'll finish my packing. I've loved being here this past week, my dear aunt, but it's time I get back to that mad, mad world I live in."

CHAPTER FORTY-FOUR
HOME AGAIN

SUNDAY, DECEMBER 20

Jenny arrived home late Sunday afternoon. Braced to encounter a reporter or two hanging around High Ridge, she was pleased to be greeted by nothing more than a few fresh-fallen snowflakes on the sidewalk leading to the building's front door. Once back in her apartment, however, she was met by the ghostly shadows still lurking there. Determined to get rid of whatever nightmarish remnants Sayers might have left in his wake, Jenny first lit a fire in the fireplace, then ran through the rooms with dust cloth and vacuum cleaner, sweeping and polishing until satisfied that she had disemboweled each and every demon who had taken up residence. One project completed, she checked out her refrigerator and cabinets, made out a shopping list, and sorted through her mail.

By ten o'clock that night, she was propped up in bed, a book in her hands which she found impossible to read. She realized suddenly that Christmas was but a few days away, and she had never thought to remind Aunt Bea that she would be back at her door come Christmas Eve, camping in her guestroom for the holiday weekend.

Now, thankfully, she could live without looking over her shoulder. There was so much she wanted to do. Her first step was to obtain the necessary medical clearance from the orthopedist, after which she could return to her job. The arm had never given her any serious trouble; an ache or pain here and there was to be expected. There was also shopping to be done, an appointment to be made with the hairdresser, and on and on. Any diversion was welcome that would drive out recurring thoughts of Alex and dispel the urge to pick up the phone and call him.

Finally, overcome by drowsiness despite herself, she laid the book aside, turned off her bedside lamp, and in minutes, she was asleep.

TUESDAY, DECEMBER 22

Jenny saw Dr. Brooks that morning, expecting a clean bill of health. But a surprise was waiting for her. While certain her arm was healing well, Dr. Brooks, after examining a fresh x-ray, pointed out a small stress fracture developing on the distal portion of the radius, which, he explained, could mean trouble for her later on. She could return to work at the hospital, but even light lifting was out for a period of time he was unable to predict at present.

Later that same morning, after checking in with the nursing director at the hospital, Jenny was given the news that there was a staff vacancy as admissions director beginning in mid-January. Was she interested?

Thinking and weighing everything, Jenny finally decided that even though she would be leaving the surgical unit where she had worked for so long, she would be filling an interesting position, and, she admitted to herself with a smile, she would be working with people who were part of the conscious world. Quite a change.

WEDNESDAY, DECEMBER 23

At the sheriff's office in town, Marge Grant was stringing another row of popcorn on the small Christmas tree set up on a table in the corner of the room. The tiny, colored lights and tinsel threw a cheerful sparkle over the brightly wrapped packages stacked beneath it; an angel smiled at them from above it all.

"Looks pretty good, Marge," Will Burke commented when she was done. He motioned his head towards Alex's office and frowned. "Christmas this year is kinda gloomy around here, though. Know what I mean?"

"Yes, I do, Will," Marge agreed with a sigh. "Alex has been down in the dumps, true. But look at all that's happened." She tsk, tsk'd, sat down, and pushed her eye glasses into place on her nose. "Christmas is a tough time for people with personal loss, Will. And Alex has had his share."

Will compressed his lips in solemn agreement, gave a sympathetic glance toward Alex's office, then turned back to his computer.

Sitting behind his desk, Alex hung up the telephone and carefully stacked the reports he had been working on for Marge to file. Then he called the airline and realized, too late, that all holiday flights to Sarasota or anywhere else were booked for most of the weekend. His only recourse was standby. He should have realized this from the start and made earlier plans.

Thoughts of Jenny managed to distract him from everything, more so since he hung up after their talk the previous Saturday night. He hated facing the truth.

The fact was, where Jenny was concerned, he had made some major blunders in the romance department. For starters, for what seemed at the time to be very sensible, even compassionate reasons, he had chosen not to tell Jenny of Lisa's role as the mystery woman. He had held back in other areas, as well. When he learned that Jenny had been told about the kiss at Lisa's door, he wanted to shrink down into a shell and disappear. He was still cringing.

He had been a fool to hold back what he felt for Jenny. He had never expressed any serious feelings. None, at all. Just bits and pieces that contained little to nothing of himself or his heart. He had held her at arm's length. And worse yet, he had not seen it that way.

So, what could he have expected? Jenny had handed Lisa over to him that awful Saturday, and with a new air of finality, she had walked away. Why was he so surprised? Even when he phoned her, he held back. He should have been man enough to blurt out his feelings, to let her know how much it hurt that she refused to see him. But, no, he had just let it pass. So, what could he do now?

A few minutes later, Alex pulled his jacket off the hook by the door and turned to Marge and Will.

"It's quiet today," he remarked, unusually cheerful, "so if you guys don't mind, I'm turning the fort over to you and heading out. I won't be back. Any big problems you can't handle, turn them over to Donahue. He deserves them. And by the way, Marge, that tree looks pretty nice. Good job."

It was almost three o'clock that same afternoon when Jenny's telephone rang. Alex was at the other end, asking to see her. Surprised, yet pleased to hear his voice, Jenny paused a moment. "Sure," she was finally able to say. "I'll be here."

When Alex arrived at her door less than an hour later, Jenny's heart began to trip. He was dressed in jeans with a light blue pullover that matched the blue of his eyes, and he was carrying a bottle of wine, gift wrapped and tied with a huge, red bow.

"Could I talk you into a toast and then maybe dinner if I let you pick the place?" he asked, as he handed Jenny the wine.

"Sure," she replied, flippantly. "As long as I can pick the place, why not?"

"Swell, name it and I'll call in our reservations. Then I'll break open the wine and we'll have a toast. Okay with you?"

When Jenny returned from having fetched wine glasses, Alex was hanging up the telephone, the wine bottle open and waiting.

Jenny took her usual place in the corner of the sofa. As Alex proceeded to pour the wine, she asked about Lisa.

"From what Jack last reported, she's making progress," Alex told her. "They aren't expecting miracles all at once. It'll take time." He set the bottle down and leaned toward her. "It was tough going through it again," he admitted. "I didn't know what to think there for awhile. First it was finding out about Lisa's jealousy of Rose and her following me that had me running in circles. Lisa and I had a good share of kinks in our marriage. If we had managed to get past losing Carl, there were still matters between us that needed to be straightened out. But we did lose Carl and that pushed Lisa over the edge. I don't know if she'll ever be the same. She went from grief to blame to hate and then suddenly, she wanted me back." He rubbed the palms of his hands together, his head bowed in thought. When he looked up, he gazed straight into Jenny's eyes. "I could never go back, Jenny. I wouldn't. It has nothing to do with anyone else but myself. With or without having met you, I needed to reconcile myself to the guilt I felt over Carl's death and to get back a self image I could accept. That is, if I planned to have any future at all. That about sizes things up. I wanted you to know this, and I'm hoping that maybe you can understand."

Alex picked up Jenny's wine glass and handed it to her. Then he picked up his own. "Can we toast to something that means more to me than anything else in the world?" Alex asked, his eyes probing into hers.

Jenny gave him a tight smile and shrugged. "If we can toast to my car, I guess we can toast to whatever you choose."

"I'm going to toast to you, Jen. To us. I'm going to toast to a lifetime of toasts. You and me? Come on, sip on that glass."

After they had toasted and set their glasses down, Alex pulled a small box out of his pocket, opened it, and took out a ring.

"I'm asking you to marry me, Jenny Wyland. I'm telling you I love you and want you with me, always. What do you say?"

Jenny found she could say nothing. Then Alex picked up her hand and slipped the ring on her finger. It was a beautiful diamond solitaire. "If you keep the ring, you have to keep me, too."

Then he reached over and pulled her to him. "I love you. Are you going to make me wait with bated breath until you give me your answer?"

"Yes, I think I would enjoy that," Jenny said, poker faced. "I certainly would. But, since I'm too nice to really enjoy being mean, I'll tell you the truth. Yes, I do love you, Alex. And yes, I will marry you."

"By New Year's?" Alex stipulated, pulling her closer in his arms. "Could we combine a honeymoon drive to Sarasota with meeting my mom and dad? And I'm not leaving Aunt Bea out, either. She can stand up for you and I'll be nice and let Donahue act as best man."

Jenny started laughing. "You take my breath away, Alex."

Alex pulled her even closer. "I haven't even begun. You and I are going to start the new year out right. And that's a promise."

A NOTE FROM THE AUTHOR

A native New Yorker, I look back to those early years when I would sit pen in hand in my place in our Old Town Canoe writing stories or poems at my leisure while my husband juggled his fishing line in one of the lush, mountain lakes we both loved so well. Time passed, and the mountains, moods, and invitations to adventure were challenged with expectation and promise. The years moved along to a quieter aspect of mountain life: a Schroon River camp at Lake Wakonda with the nightly crackle of a campfire blending in with shared reminiscent junkets to those rugged days of tenting on the Saranac Islands or our first bear encounter at Forked Lake. Whatever the memories, they are as alive today as they were in the days we lived them.